MW00396023

THE AMERICAN WAR IN
CONTEMPORARY VIETNAM

Tracking Globalization

ROBERT J. FOSTER, EDITOR

EDITORIAL ADVISORY BOARD:

Mohammed Bamyeh

Lisa Cartwright

Randall Halle

THE AMERICAN WAR IN CONTEMPORARY VIETNAM

Transnational Remembrance and Representation

Christina Schwenkel

INDIANA UNIVERSITY PRESS
BLOOMINGTON & INDIANAPOLIS

Published with the generous support of the
Association for Asian Studies, Inc.

This book is a publication of

Indiana University Press
601 North Morton Street
Bloomington, IN 47404-3797 USA

http://iupress.indiana.edu

Telephone orders   800-842-6796
Fax orders   812-855-7931
Orders by e-mail   iuporder@indiana.edu

© 2009 by Christina L. Schwenkel
All rights reserved

No part of this book may be reproduced or
utilized in any form or by any means, electronic
or mechanical, including photocopying and
recording, or by any information storage and
retrieval system, without permission in writing
from the publisher. The Association of American University Presses' Resolution on Permis-
sions constitutes the only exception to this pro-
hibition.

The paper used in this publication meets the
minimum requirements of American National
Standard for Information Sciences—Permanence of Paper for Printed Library Materials,
ANSI Z39.48-1984.

Manufactured in the United States of America

Schwenkel, Christina.
    The American war in contemporary Vietnam :
transnational remembrance and representation /
Christina Schwenkel.
        p. cm.
    Includes bibliographical references and index.
    ISBN 978-0-253-35306-1 (cloth : alk. paper) —
ISBN 978-0-253-22076-9 (pbk. : alk. paper)
    1. Vietnam War, 1961–1975—Foreign public
opinion, Vietnamese. 2. Vietnam War, 1961–
1975—Influence. 3. Vietnam—Foreign
relations—United States. 4. United States—
Foreign relations—Vietnam. 5. Public opinion—
Vietnam. I. Title.
    DS559.62.V5S39 2009
    959.704′3—dc22
                                        2008054488

    1 2 3 4 5 14 13 12 11 10 09

CONTENTS

ACKNOWLEDGMENTS

This has been a difficult book to research and write. Many scars from the war have yet to heal, as the recent 2008 U.S. presidential campaign again reminded us. I have written this book mindful of the ways in which it will impact different groups of people who have very strong emotional attachments to the issues presented here. The stakes in writing such a book are high; over the years I have come to realize just how high from the strong, mixed emotional reactions—both criticism and encouragement—that my work has engendered in the United States. This has shown me that these are issues worth talking about, but I do so mindful of the diverse sensitivities involved all around. It is my hope that this book might open some eyes to the possibility of new ways of thinking about an extremely painful (and, for many people, still raw) past, and to consider the legacies of war, trauma, and recovery (to the extent that it is possible) through very different perspectives than are usually offered in the United States.

I have incurred tremendous social and intellectual debts in the long process of producing this book. I am particularly indebted to Vietnamese and U.S. respondents who shared with me their personal experiences and traumatic memories of the war, as well as stories about their postwar lives and attempts to work through the past, often collectively across national borders. To protect the confidentiality of research participants, I have used pseudonyms throughout the text, with certain exceptions. Because my research subjects included Vietnamese artists, architects, photographers, museum officials, and U.S. veterans involved in humanitarian and reconciliation projects who could potentially be identified through information provided here, I have changed slight details to avoid revealing their identity to readers who might be familiar with their work.

I first express my profound gratitude to friends, colleagues, and research interlocutors in Vietnam who devoted much of their time to my project over the past decade. I would especially like to acknowledge Lê Thị Nhâm Tuyết and Phạm Kim Ngọc at the Research Centre for Gender, Family, and Environment in Development in Hanoi for their continued academic support and research assistance. I am grateful to Nguyễn Mạnh Thắng for his passionate efforts to teach me about Vietnamese commemorative practices, and for our many field trips to secular and religious spaces of memory. Phạm Thị Vui, an anthropologist at heart, offered her keen insights and friendship during fieldwork in Ho Chi Minh City. I also thank Nguyễn Thị Ngọc, Ngô Văn Tài, Vũ Thế Khôi, Nguyễn Hữu Thông, Trần Kim Ngọc, Linda Mogul, Phan Thanh Hảo, Phan Huy Lê, Huỳnh Ngọc Vân, Hoàng Tuyết Hương, and staff members at the Vietnam News Agency, all of whom went out of their way to assist me in my fieldwork. Mai Nam, Đoàn Công Tính, and the Vietnam Association of Photographic Artists provided me with valuable support in my work on Vietnamese war photography. I also owe much to my research assistant in Hanoi, Hoàng Hồng Nga.

The ideas presented in this book were originally developed while I was a graduate student at the University of California, Irvine (UCI). My deepest gratitude is extended to my dissertation committee for the time and energy they invested in this project. I have been fortunate to work with generous advisors who were, and continue to be, remarkable intellectual mentors and role models. I express deep appreciation to Liisa Malkki, Bill Maurer, and Tom Boellstorff for their unfailing enthusiasm, intellectual creativity, and theoretical precision that greatly shaped this project. I am also grateful to Jim Ferguson for his critical comments on several chapters, which pushed me toward more ethnographic clarity. Thank you to Teresa Caldeira, Robyn Wiegman, Laura Kang, Susan Greenhalgh, Karen Leonard, and Victoria Bernal for their contributions to the development of this project in its earlier stages. Kim Coles, Megan Crowley-Matoka, Jennifer Heung, Rhonda Higdon, Amanda Moore, Marty Otañez, and Kiki Papageorgiou also provided helpful comments on chapter drafts.

My colleagues at the University of California, Riverside (UCR) in the Department of Anthropology and the program in Southeast Asia: Text, Ritual, and Performance (SEATRiP) have provided much academic support and camaraderie, including Wendy Ashmore, David Biggs, Piya Chatterjee, Derick Fay, T. S. Harvey, Mariam Lam, Henk Maier, Sally Ness, Susan Ossman, Paul Ryer, and Anne Sutherland. I am grateful to Tom Patterson and the Department of Anthropology for providing me with time off to finish this book. I especially thank my colleagues Lan Duong, Tammy Ho, Juliet McMullin, and Chikako Takeshita for their insightful ideas and comments on various chapters. I also extend my thanks to graduate students in the History and Memory class, where many ideas were fine-tuned in the later stages of writing, and to my research assistant, Sarah Grant, for her work on the bibliography.

This book has benefited from the insights and suggestions offered by numerous people over the years in ongoing conversations and intellectual exchanges, some more prolonged than others, all of which have contributed to my thinking about this project in important ways. In particular, I thank Victor Alneng, Ann Anagnost, Erica Bornstein, Juliet Feibel, Jennifer Foley, Tuan Hoang, Kate Jellema, Anne Marie Leshkowich, Lynn Meskell, Ken MacLean, Tema Milstein, Lien-Hang T. Nguyen, Julie Pham, Claire Sutherland, Hue-Tam Ho Tai, Philip Taylor, Steve Wuhs, and Peter Zinoman. Diane Fox, Jennifer Ruth Hosek, Nora Taylor, Jessica Winegar, and Julia Zarankin all read and provided helpful suggestions on earlier chapter drafts. Valuable research and other assistance were also provided by Horst Faas, Richard Lennon, Doug Niven, Kerstin Lommatzsch, and Katherine Thornton.

Various conferences and speaking invitations have given me the opportunity to present this work and receive valuable feedback from diverse audiences both inside and outside academia. In particular I thank Nguyen Ba Chung and the William Joiner Center for the opportunity to present my work on Vietnamese photojournalism; graduate student organizers of the James Young conference at UCR for a keynote invitation that allowed me to present new ideas and a new chapter; George Marcus at the UCI Center for Ethnography for my participation in a workshop on fieldwork methods; and Laurie Beth Clark and Leigh Payne for the opportunity to present on "trauma tourism" at the University of Wisconsin, Madison. I also thank Geoff White and an anonymous reviewer for Indiana University Press (IUP) who read and commented on this book in its entirety. Their much appreciated comments helped me to clarify many of my ideas. Thank you to Bob Foster, the series editor of Tracking Globalization, for his guidance and suggestions, and to Susanna Sturgis, Brian Herrmann, Miki Bird, and Rebecca Tolen for their editorial support at IUP.

Many close friends, family members, and colleagues have supported me and my research endeavors over the years in other important ways, helping to keep things in perspective, particularly while finishing this book. I thank for their valued friendship Damon Kupper, Tom Douglas, Selim Shahine, Michelle Otañez, Elfriede Schütz, and many others. My family, especially Scott Schwenkel, has also provided encouragement over the years. I extend limitless gratitude to Rudi Schütz for putting up with it all and for sharing years of companionship in Vietnam and elsewhere.

Research for this book conducted between 1999 and 2001, and in 2004, 2005, 2006, and 2007 was financially supported by numerous sources. A Foreign Language Area Studies (FLAS) grant provided funds for language training at the Southeast Asian Summer Studies Institute (SEASSI), University of Oregon. I thank the University of California Pacific Rim Research Program, the Association for Women in Science, and the German Academic Exchange Service (DAAD) for dissertation research support. A University of California Regents Dissertation Fellowship allowed me to focus on writing. Subsequent research was made possible by a Rockefeller Fellowship from the William Joiner Center for the Study of War and Social Consequences at the University of Massachusetts, Boston, and a Mellon Foundation Fellowship that provided me with two quarters of research leave from the Introduction to Humanities Program at Stanford University. A Regents Faculty Fellowship and other funding from UCR supported research in 2007.

Chapters 2 and 3 were previously published in modified form as "Exhibiting War, Reconciling Pasts: Journalistic Modes of Representation and Transnational Commemoration in Contemporary Vietnam," in the *Journal of Vietnamese Studies* 3, no. 1 (2008): 36–77, and as "Recombinant History: Transnational Practices of Memory and Knowledge Production in Contemporary Vietnam," in *Cultural Anthropology* 2, no. 1 (2006): 3–30. Sections of chapter 6 are forthcoming in *American Anthropologist* 111, no. 1.

NOTE ON USE OF DIACRITICS

Vietnamese is a tonal language written in an adapted version of the Latin alphabet with additional diacritical marks to signify particular tones and vowel qualities. Without these diacritics, the meaning of a Vietnamese word is ambiguous. For this reason I have chosen to include diacritical marks in this book to most accurately represent terms, locations, and people's names. However, at the same time, I recognize that diacritics may prove distracting to those unfamiliar with the conventions of the language. Taking into concern both specialists and generalists who may read this book, I opted to keep all Vietnamese diacritical marks with the exception of widely known geographical names such as Vietnam, Hanoi, Ho Chi Minh City, and Saigon. I also removed the diacritics for familiar Americanized phrases, such as "Viet Cong" or the "Ho Chi Minh Trail." Vietnamese who have migrated to other countries often drop the diacritics from their proper names. I thus refer to individuals according to their own practice, and according to their choice in name order (in Vietnam surnames are placed first). While I recognize potential inconsistencies in my own practice here (for example, Ho Chi Minh City versus President Hồ Chí Minh), I feel this is the most reliable solution for making the text accessible to all audiences.

ABBREVIATIONS

AP	Associated Press
ARVN	Army of the Republic of Vietnam
BTA	bilateral trade agreement
DMZ	Demilitarized Zone
DRV	Democratic Republic of Vietnam
LNA	Liberation News Agency
MCI	Ministry of Culture and Information
MIA	missing in action
NGO	non-governmental organization
NLF	National Liberation Front
PAVN	People's Army of Vietnam
POW	prisoner of war
RVN	Republic of Vietnam
UPI	United Press International
UXO	unexploded ordnance
VOA	Voice of America
VOV	Voice of Vietnam
VNA	Vietnam News Agency
VNAT	Vietnam National Administration of Tourism
VNĐ	Vietnam đồng (currency)
VUFO	Vietnam Union of Friendship Organizations

THE AMERICAN WAR IN
CONTEMPORARY VIETNAM

Introduction

Remembering (in) Vietnam

Friday evening, November 17, 2000. Returning from an art performance on the outskirts of Hanoi, I came upon large crowds of people lining Trang Tiến Street in the city center, a sea of people stretched from the colonial-era Opera House down past Hoàn Kiếm Lake several blocks away. There was no way through; the entire area was blocked to traffic. I parked my motorbike and joined a group of people to wait for the spectacle to begin. The excitement mounted. People grew anxious. A few minutes later the crowds began to stir. "Here they come!" someone yelled. Slowly, in royal fashion, the motorcade approached. People began to cheer and applaud. Like everyone around me, I strained to get a good look through the dense pack of spectators. The cheering grew louder. People waved and shouted hello. Inside the black limousine flying the U.S. and Vietnamese flags at either front end, Bill and Hillary Clinton smiled and waved back through closed windows.

The bystanders remained fixed in place watching the remaining vehicles drive by. I looked around me. The predominantly young onlookers appeared most awed by the opportunity to see the U.S. president, while older crowd members acted more ambivalent. I turned to a middle-aged man next to me. "I'm only here because the roads are blocked and I can't get home," he told me defiantly. "No one wants to see the president of the United States. We only want to see the security forces we've heard so much about. Your country spent over two million dollars on security! That's what I want to see. Never before has there been such security in Vietnam, not even when the French president was here." An elderly man who had approached us stood by listening, and then turned around and slowly walked away. He had no comment.

The security apparatus had indeed been the topic of much conversation and speculation over the previous week: how many people were accompanying Clinton for his three-day visit to Vietnam (hundreds, it was rumored, including two chefs), at which new five-star hotel would he stay (conflicting reports, but most assumed the newly opened Hilton Hanoi Opera), how many large black security vans, limousines, and other vehicles had been flown over the ocean in Air Force One? But there was more that drew the crowds than just the spectacle of U.S. wealth and power. The younger spectators around me saw it differently. Clinton's celebrity excited them ("he's so handsome!" one young woman exclaimed), as did his message: a global capitalist future with freedom and prosperity for all was the only path for Vietnam.

As the first U.S. head of state to visit Vietnam since the end of the war, and the first ever to officially visit the capital city, Clinton's journey was considered by many to mark an historic moment, a "new chapter" in postwar relations between two former rival countries. In the televised speech Clinton gave before a large crowd at the National University in Hanoi a day after his arrival, he carefully broached the topic of the war, at times diverting significantly from conventional U.S. political discourse, emphasizing, for example, the "common" and "deeply intertwined" histories and "shared suffering" that bonded the people of both countries into "a relationship unlike any other." His carefully crafted words even made note of Vietnam's "staggering sacrifice" and its millions of "brave soldiers and civilians" who perished in the war, a much elided topic in U.S. public memory, which continues to see the war as traumatic for *American* society. Despite Clinton's conscientious approach and gestures toward Vietnamese historical memory—he even referred at one point to "what you call the American War"—he also fell back upon more standard American paternalist roles and moral scripts of history. He commended the humanitarian efforts of U.S. veterans who had returned to Vietnam to "work on behalf of the Vietnamese people," and the crucial role they had played in improving bilateral relations. Likewise, Clinton praised the Vietnamese people for their diligent efforts to help locate the remains of U.S. forces listed as "missing in action" (MIA). In an interview in Ho Chi Minh City on November 19, he reflected on an emotional visit to a MIA site:

> It was overwhelming . . . And we watched all those Vietnamese people working with the American people, up to their hips in mud, digging in the ground and taking these big chunks of mud over to sifters, and watching other Vietnamese sift through the mud for any kind of metal object or any cloth object, anything that would give us a clue to whether this was, in fact, a crash site, and whether there's something more down there. It was profoundly moving to me.[1]

The image of Vietnamese and U.S. citizens searching for bodily remains alongside one another in difficult working conditions is an emblematic image of postwar reconciliation, one that on the surface seems to suggest mutual cooperation, but underneath reveals particular postwar relations of power that shape and inform "normalized" relations. The search, for instance, was for the remains of missing *U.S.* combatants, not Vietnamese, of which there are an estimated 300,000, more than five times the total number of U.S. forces killed in the war. Vietnamese participation, moreover, is not wholly voluntary. As Clinton's remarks at the National University made clear, Vietnam's future depends upon a particular engagement with and resolution of the past: "Your cooperation in that [U.S. MIA] mission over these last eight years has made it possible for America to support international lending to Vietnam, to resume trade between our countries, to establish formal diplomatic relations and, this year, to sign a pivotal trade agreement." In other words, the United States has been able to extend the "gift" of global capitalism and U.S. neoliberalism to Vietnam as a reward for its collaborative efforts to resolve unsettled U.S. postwar issues.

This comment got to the heart of Clinton's unprecedented visit to Vietnam: to sell the virtues of American capitalism to a country that had chosen its own graduated path of "market socialism." The timing of the delegation had been carefully planned. Only months before, in July 2000, the United States and Vietnam had signed a controversial bilateral trade agreement (BTA) that would accelerate and establish a more transparent legal and economic infrastructure for privatization and reintegration into a global market economy. The BTA, in Clinton's words, gave "Vietnamese people expanding rights to determine their own economic destiny," while to many in Vietnam it signified a threat to their nation's economic sovereignty. Six years after the U.S.-led trade embargo on Vietnam was lifted, the investment landscape had become rocky. Many U.S. investors, initially excited at the prospect of high profits from a "new" and unsaturated market, pulled out of Vietnam on account of what the *New York Times* identified as a "morass of red tape, corruption, and capricious rules" (Mydans 2000), and controls that "choked" the economy (Sanger 2000). Clinton's visit, then, was intended to create more favorable and profitable conditions for U.S. investment by tapping into the reformist energies of Vietnam's entrepreneurs, especially the youth. His speech at the university celebrated the dismantling of socialism and the fast-paced development of a burgeoning neoliberal economy that had saved Vietnam from malnutrition and other social and economic ills—"impressive proof of the power of your markets." It also hinted at a subtle warning: Global capitalism, he proposed, is an inevitable and natural evolutionary force that cannot be stopped, but can be harnessed for its offerings of wealth, freedom, creativity, knowledge, and democracy, terms that peppered his speech. "It is the economic equivalent of a force of nature—like wind or water," Clinton informed the audience, adopting a language that "*naturalizes* globalization by making it analogous to the natural process of flowing water" and gusting wind (Ferguson 2006, 47; emphasis in the original). "[T]here is no point in denying the existence of wind or water, or trying to make them go away. The same is true for globalization," he insisted.

Clinton's words were met with skepticism by many government officials and residents in Hanoi. Although he is generally held in high regard in Vietnam on account of his work to abrogate the economic embargo in 1994 and normalize diplomatic relations one year later, there was much ambivalence toward his visit and his push toward a less regulated free market system. Enthusiasm was tempered by suspicion of intent—"Let's wait and see why he is really here," one woman suggested to me—and by memories of the war, particularly the lack of redress. In meetings, officials acknowledged the significant "steps toward new relations" that had strengthened mutually beneficial economic and political ties. But they also emphasized to Clinton that while Vietnam anticipated and welcomed a more collaborative future, the country was still mired in the devastating social, economic, and environmental consequences of the war. They also firmly maintained that *Đổi mới*, a series of economic reforms instituted in 1986 that allowed for limited liberalization, was a strategy to strengthen the cause of socialist nation building through selective market mechanisms, what is often referred to as a "market economy with socialist orientation" [*kinh tế thị trường với định hướng xã hội chủ nghĩa*]. As Party general secretary Lê Khả Phiêu reminded Clinton in his remarks at the official welcome ceremony on November 18: "The future of Vietnam is national independence and socialism."[2]

I use the story of President Clinton's visit to Vietnam in November 2000 as a springboard to introduce several key issues that this book will explore. First and foremost are the ambivalence, anxiety, and cautious optimism that underlie postwar reconciliation processes and Vietnam's graduated reintegration into a global capitalist economy. A clear tension emerges here between discrepant visions of economic futures; one still firmly rooted in socialism, in all its mutations, and another still bent on its demise. Clinton's speech, in particular, reflected contemporary U.S. imaginings of Vietnam that continued to reinscribe Cold War capitalist/socialist binaries of difference, and the possibility of transcendence: a free, creative, and open world of choice and knowledge that could, if Vietnam played by the (U.S. economic) rules, replace its controlled, closed, naively uninformed society bursting at the seams with constrained desire and creativity. One of the central arguments of this book is that this tension between, on the one hand, pressures to adopt and institute more broadly U.S. free market capitalism and its attendant moral ideologies of freedom, rights, and democracy and, on the other, Vietnam's determination to negotiate and delimit the extent of liberalization and to maintain its hard-won economic and political sovereignty plays out in the shifting and contested fields of history and memory. As the chapters in this book will show, the expansion of political and economic relations is explicitly linked to "proper" practices of memory and engagements with history, as Clinton reminded the Vietnamese nation when he praised and linked their cooperation with U.S. MIA initiatives to trade benefits and diplomatic developments.

Clinton's visit also demonstrates another central point of exploration in this book: the commingling, and at times the clash, between disparate transnational memories of war in Vietnamese public spaces of history. Despite Clinton's attempts at historical relativism (such as using the term "American War"), a conflict over historical memory erupted during a meeting when a government official referred to U.S. imperial ambitions as having driven its military intervention in Vietnam. Clinton's defensive retort—that the United States was not an imperialist country and had fought the war to contain communism, not to advance imperialism—baffled the Vietnamese as much as the official's allegation irked the Americans.[3] It is perhaps unsurprising that people from opposing sides in any war will construct very different historical narratives based on discrepant interpretations, meanings, and images to represent the past. At issue here is not which narration is "correct"—both explanations, highly charged with emotive sentiment and meaning, were believed to embody "truth." Moreover, neither is wholly uncontested in its respective domain of knowledge production. Rather, this study asks: What happens when contrasting knowledge and images from separate spheres of memory converge in joint spaces of history? Can such competing and contradictory memories coexist to tell new stories about the past? Or does one set of representations, bound up in broader relations of power, serve to reframe or silence another? What was unexpected about this tense exchange was not its occurrence (contending memories are bound to collide), but the criticism it provoked in Hanoi toward the Vietnamese official. It was not in good taste to call Clinton an imperialist to his face, one city resident bemoaned to me. Why did he rely on outdated scripts of history? another asked, pointing to postreform changes in official discourse that had reinscribed American "enemies" as "friends." And still another resident pondered: What impact might this have on U.S. investors and their decision to come to Vietnam? Might there be a concern that they, too, would be called imperialists? I use this story to point to a central ethnographic concern in this book: how shifts in the validity and the production of history in spaces of competing memories intersect with global market capitalism and attempts to discipline and regulate other knowledge practices and representations of the war.

History as Transnational Process

The momentary (yet revealing) tension over memory that surfaced during Clinton's visit overshadowed larger efforts on both sides to maintain peaceful coexistence between discrepant national histories. Clinton's public recognition of the situatedness of historical knowledge, his reference at one point to "the conflict we call the Vietnam War and you call the American War," suggests a broader politics of naming at work in shaping dominant ideological paradigms and productions of memory in their respective contexts. In the United States, the "Vietnam War," a reductive term that Khatharya Um argues has silenced traumatic experiences of war for Cambodians and Laotians (2005, 136), indexes a particularly violent "stage" in a larger Cold War trajectory of fighting communism, as Clinton remarked to Vietnamese officials. This narrative made little sense in Vietnam, where the Anti-American Resistance War for National Salvation [*cuộc kháng chiến chống Mỹ cứu nước*] is considered part of a thirty-year struggle (1945–75) for national independence from both French colonialism and U.S. occupation. There is a marked absence of Cold War discourse here since the "American War" in official Vietnamese history was not fought for communism, but against imperialism (and thus was not a "civil war"). Like the "Vietnam War," the "Cold War" reveals itself to be a western historical construct that has meaning when inserted into particular capitalist frameworks and modes of narrating history. This is important to recognize because it influences how transnational practices of memory and truth making unfold in the following chapters.

Walter Benjamin once wrote, "History is the subject of a structure whose site is not homogeneous, empty time, but time filled by the presence of now [*Jetztzeit*]" (1969b, 263). As frames for the "now" change, so does our framing of the past, as Clinton's visit to Vietnam demonstrated. History, Michel-Rolph Trouillot (1995) has shown in his work on Haiti, is then a *process* in which knowledge is continually remade and repositioned in relation to new truths and memories endowed with meaning and authority in shifting temporal and political orders. The study of a body of knowledge that constitutes "history" reveals more about present power configurations and systems of validation than it constructs a "real" representation of the past. For the past is just that—a representation, an intentional fusing and ordering of fragments of "fact" from history (H. White 1978, 125). The ways in which an increasingly transnational and capitalist "now" in Vietnam, with new social and global concerns and alignments, has come to reconstitute "the past" are a central focus of this book. I make no effort to create my own historical "truth" about Vietnam's past or present. Like Trouillot, I am more concerned with "how history works" (1995, 25). "What matters most," he has argued, "are the process and conditions of the production of [historical] narratives . . . and the differential exercise of power that makes some narratives possible and silences others" (ibid.). With the intent to decenter the nation-state and its production of modernist metanarratives of history, this study analyzes *transnational* processes and conditions through which historical truths and knowledge are remade, and the accompanying struggles over power, authority, sovereignty, and ownership of history.

Two primary research questions motivate this book. I first ask: What does memory of the American War look like in Vietnam? How is it remembered, represented, debated, and contested? Through which words, images, events, and experiences does official history of the war take shape? How is suffering given representation? Where are the silences and exclusions from these dominant narratives? Given that there is little information in U.S. public discourse on the war and its diverse memory and meaning in postwar Vietnamese society, one of my central aims in this text is to introduce the reader to Vietnamese paradigms and practices of memory at public sites of history in which I worked and visited, in and around Hanoi and Ho Chi Minh City predominantly, including museums, war memorials, martyr cemeteries, art and photography exhibits, and former battlefields remade into tourist attractions. To do so, the text employs emic terminology that is commonly used in Vietnamese contexts of official and unofficial history. I do not use the term "Cold War" or other expressions that have currency in the capitalist West unless I am referring to specific western productions of knowledge. I employ words such as "the liberation" of Saigon, rather than "the fall," not to politically position my alignments, but to dislodge common U.S. (including Vietnamese American) perspectives in order to take the reader on an ethnographic journey through dominant modes of narrating and representing Vietnamese history.

To accomplish this, it is important to head off any possible misconceptions from the start: Vietnamese historical memory—the common and repetitive set of images, ideas, and texts that construct and represent a national past—is not fixed, nor is it uniform. It is not uncontested and only produced by the state.[4] It does not exercise control over its population any more than American historical memory shapes the thought processes of U.S. populations. Memory work in socialist contexts is no more ideological or propagandistic than in capitalist societies. There are no docile socialist bodies here, only active agents of history who reconfigure and reinterpret state historical projects, even as they actively sustain them (Watson 1994; Verdery 1991). As David William Cohen (1994) has shown, silences are always central to the production of history, but even histories that have been officially forgotten are not absolute and may at some point in time be publicly re-remembered. Official history in Vietnam has selectively silenced certain pasts that fall outside the dominant paradigm of revolutionary history; for example, histories associated with the U.S.-allied Republic of Vietnam and the people who participated in and supported its institutions. Though, as I show in this book, this is also not fixed and definitive, as new stories about the past from silenced voices are now shared and circulated in public spaces of history and memory. Hue-Tam Ho Tai has linked such changes to *Đổi mới* economic reforms instituted in the late 1980s: "[T]he decline of High Socialist orthodoxy, relative prosperity, and prolonged peace have encouraged other actors besides the state to try to occupy the space of memory. . . . The deconstruction of the official past is thus an untidy, somewhat surreptitious, seldom openly confrontational by-product of economic reconstruction" (2001b, 3). While scholars have long noted that Vietnamese discourses of history have never been uniform and have constantly undergone shifts (Giebel 2004; Pelley 2002; Tai 2001a), I argue that to understand changes in historical memory currently taking place, it is also imperative to look at the realm of "globalization" and to identify the various *transnational* forces involved in the diversification and transnationalization of knowledge, memory, and meaning.

The second research question that motivates this book returns to the commingling of situated memories and historical knowledge that occurred during President Clinton's visit. What happens when discrepant narratives, images, and truths of history converge and intersect in spaces of transnational encounter? My usage of the term "transnational spaces" in this book links Anna Lowenhaupt Tsing's "zones of awkward engagement" (2005, xi) to a condition of transnationality, described by Aihwa Ong as "cultural interconnectedness and mobility across space— which has been intensified under late capitalism" (1999, 4). This work traces the transnational mobility of memory embodied in images, objects, people, and knowledge; its multidirectional, and highly uneven, movement across national borders, primarily between and within Vietnam and the United States, but also transgressing other nation-states that were drawn into the social imaginary of the war through mass-mediated representations. I focus on knowledge frictions, that is, contestations over the past in transnational spaces of recollection and reconciliation, and the resulting efforts—particularly by U.S. citizens, including returning veterans—to define and maintain particular visions of historical truth, knowledge, and objectivity.

Like my use of "Vietnamese" historical memory, when I mention "U.S." memory in the following chapters, I refer to dominant social imaginaries, logics, and paradigms for thinking about and representing the war. This does not mean that certain groups or individuals do not possess "other" memories. Yet it is not within the scope of this book to represent all communities of memory here in relation to the war. For example, a sustained focus on Vietnamese American memory is not included in this text but would be a project of great importance, particularly with the increasing number of diasporic Vietnamese who are now traveling to Vietnam. Nonetheless, there are also intersections between the memories of different populations and dominant U.S. interpretations; for example, referring to the conflict as the "Vietnam War" or to the "fall" of Saigon. As in the case of Vietnamese memory,

I point here to general trends, aware that the work of memory is complex and always involved in acts of silencing. There are clear divergences between commemoration in the United States and Vietnam that this book will explore in the realm of visual practices. What new visual histories and narrations of the past have emerged through transnational encounters, for example, when U.S. veterans donate war relics and photographs to Vietnamese museums? And what do such changes reveal about current global relations and anxieties concerning the spread of neoliberal capitalism on the one hand, and the continuity of socialism, on the other? The book outlines a pivotal force of change in contemporary Vietnam: global capitalism and how it shapes and is shaped by Vietnamese knowledge practices and representations of history.

Scholars have argued that struggles over the Vietnam War continued to play out in postwar American society in cultural representations and in U.S. foreign policy that prolonged the "American War on Vietnam" through other means (Martini 2007; Jeffords 1989). This book looks at how such struggles over the past persist in Vietnam today in transnational spaces of history where U.S. and Vietnamese memories and scripts of history intersect and at times conflict. How can a U.S.-claimed victory be celebrated as a defeat in Vietnamese history? How can torture be remembered as acts of compassion? How can an iconic photograph convey important historical knowledge in one context and propaganda in another? Vietnamese historical memory thus becomes a contested terrain for larger ideological and moral struggles to define, discipline, and control unruly socialist histories. Though I link these contemporary conflicts to global capitalism (as efforts to regulate the economy and historical memory are not disconnected), I should remind readers that globalization is not new to Vietnam, nor is it only linked to capitalism, as there is an equally long history of socialist internationalism that has also shaped current economic and memorial landscapes. In the chapters that follow, I situate neoliberal globalization in relation to emerging practices of transnational remembrance and representation. Neoliberalism, as an economic doctrine that advocates free trade and the market as key to "development" and "progress," as conveyed by President Clinton in his speech, is never a uniform set of practices (Harvey 2005; Ong 2006). How it is accommodated, rejected, and reworked in "market socialist" contexts of memory underpins my inquiry.

The Mobility of Memory

This book is an ethnography of knowledge production and memory-making processes under globalizing conditions in contemporary Vietnam. At the same time, it is also an ethnographic examination of commemorative processes of reconciliation between Americans, Vietnamese, and other people connected to the war through lived experience and through mass-mediated global memory. The stories I present here shed light on cross-cultural complexities involved in coming to terms (or not) with traumatic pasts, and debates over which memory and knowledge shape the present historical, geopolitical, and socioeconomic landscape. I take a processual approach to thinking through knowledge production and memory that examines its mobility, mediation, and multiple intersecting practices and meanings. My study draws upon a large and growing interdisciplinary body of literature that constitutes the field of "memory studies." I offer here observations on general trends in this diverse scholarship, which has shaped my thinking about memory in particular ways.[5]

Much of this current scholarship has its theoretical precedent in the work of Maurice Halbwachs (1992 [1952]), who in his foundational text, *On Collective Memory*, was one of the first scholars to argue that memory is more than a cognitive faculty for retaining and recalling the past. Memory does not exist in relation to the individual self only, he argued, but is a profoundly social process that is also produced and maintained by social groups, such as the family, and shaped by shifting temporal and spatial contexts. This observation opened the door to a new methodological approach to locating and studying memory that went beyond fixed recall in people's minds and bodies to also examine memory as embodied in, for example, objects, images, and landscapes. Scholars have adopted a range of terms to identify and deindividualize processes of memory and link them to broader social and cultural practices: cultural memory, national memory, collective memory, social memory, political memory, official memory, and so on. These terms often precede the word "in" followed by a bounded territorial space, most often a nation ("cultural memory *in* the United States"), but also in localized ("social memory *in* a village") and institutionalized spaces ("national memory *in* a museum"). In other words, like people and culture, memory is often imagined as rooted in place, residing in fixed and bounded spaces (Malkki 1992; Gupta and Ferguson 1992).

In this study I draw upon the work of scholars who "uproot" memory and follow its mobility as it journeys across multiple borders—cultural, political, gendered, ethnic, historical, and territorial. Memory is shown to be an active, constitutive force; it moves, mobilizes, produces, and transforms, rather than simply dwell and exist. As Svetlana Boym has observed: "Memory resides in moving, traversing, cutting through place, taking detours" (2001, 80). In this study I track how memories move and come to constitute transnational knowledge practices. Andreas Huyssen has linked the "intensity of border-crossing memory discourses" to what he terms a "globalization of memory" that connects disparate geographies through multiple and intersecting "cultures of memory" (2003, 12–13). Yet like other global processes, the globalization of memory is beset with disconnections, inequities, and unevenness; it does not flow through but hops across global spaces (Ferguson 2006, 47). This text explores how and which memories travel, in which directions and forms, as well as the implications for their integration in new cultural contexts. As the following chapters show, traveling memories are carried and transmitted by people, objects, images, and technologies that often confuse, disrupt, expand, and recombine with other regimes of representation and their truth making practices. Mobile memories are thus traveling mediations of knowledge that are entangled with larger projects of power and claims to ownership of history.

There is also an underlying assumption in much of this scholarship that fundamental contradictions exist between history and memory. Concerned with ways in which the past is ordered, Pierre Nora, for example, offers a modernist narrative of temporal differentiations between the stagnant "real memory" of "archaic societies" and the progressive "history" of "hopefully forgetful modern societies" (1989, 8). While "real memory" is characterized by "primitive remembrance," modern "history" is marked by distanced forgetfulness. At the crux of change where history replaces a "tradition" of memory, Nora locates *lieux de mémoire*, sites in which traces of memory are found to linger as "reconstituted objects beneath the gaze of critical history," for example, in public monuments and commemorative ceremonies (1989, 12). For Nora, there is little place for memory in modernity as it signifies the backwardness of cultures that are enmeshed in the past, rather than "modern" nations that are facing and progressing toward the future. There is an implicit assumption here that cultures "frozen" in past memory and engaged in ritual remembrance are unmodern and do not possess what Habermas (1987) has called "the historical consciousness of modernity" that advocates a forward-oriented rupture with the past (see also Appadurai 1996).

Another trend in this scholarship has been to map presumed binary oppositions onto divisions in modern society, namely between official and nonofficial practices. Not unlike Nora's paradigm, history belongs in the objective realm of the state, constituted by "facts," and driven by a will to truth. Memory, on the other hand, remains "with the people" in their subjective experiences, laden with emotion and sentiment. This is seen for example in the distinction made between the *objective* processes of historiography and *affective* commemorative practices. A host of binaries emerge here, with public, official, and national history assumed to contradict and be in conflict with private, vernacular, unofficial memory (see, for example, Bodnar 1992). Though attentive to processes of contestation and negation, this approach tends to reinscribe and delimit borders between dissimilar arrangements of memory; for example, between groups of individuals (such as different communities of memory), individuals and the state, or even individuals and the media. In this study I draw upon the work of scholars such as Zemon-Davis and Starn (1989), Sturken (1997a), and Yoneyama (1999), who reject the discursive and epistemological opposition between history and memory, and their respective bounded categories, and insist upon their intersections. I employ the term "historical memory" throughout the text to signal the blurring of borders and the mutual constitution of memory categories: individual, local, global, national, official, vernacular, and so on. In other words, all memory is mediated by other knowledge flows, including that of the mass media. A key difference here, however, is that my work transcends locally and nationally bounded units for the study of memory to examine transnational truth making and knowledge practices. Geoff White's (1995) work on transnational memory making has been key to this agenda. Examining commemorative ceremonies organized by the United States in the Solomon Islands to mark the fiftieth anniversary of World War II battles fought in the Pacific, he demonstrates how public spaces of national memory became sites of disjunctive memories and conflicting truths with the influx of international tourists, a process that is also apparent in Vietnam in spaces of transnational encounter. Attention to transnational history making is often overlooked in studies of "national" histories, but it is not new. The much-cited work of Eric R. Wolf, for example, not only bestows historical subjecthood upon "people without history," but also analyzes the "global interconnectedness of human aggregates" as a means to encourage scholars to "think in more processual ways about the notion of society," and, I would argue, notions of history (1982, 386–387). Recognition that projects of history are also transnational processes compels a more nuanced understanding of the global entanglements and relations of power involved in memory work.

I refer to such entangled, historical scripts and memorial practices as *recombinant history*, a term that suggests the interweaving of diverse and frequently discrepant transnational memories, knowledge formations, and logics of representation. I borrow from David Stark's (1996) work on postsocialist Hungary and his use of *recombinant property* to identify newly diversified and redefined property relations that blur the lines between capitalist and noncapitalist, public and private economic practices and modes of organization. As a response to economic and organizational ambiguity, recombinant property poses a challenge to the narrative of absolute capitalist triumph over socialism as it demonstrates the "fuzziness" of borders under postsocialist conditions and its overlapping economic practices (Burawoy and Verdery 1999), a process parallel to what is occurring in Vietnam with "market socialism."[6] I transpose Stark's idea of recombinant property to think through the complexities involved in the transnationalization and diversification of memory at historical sites in Vietnam. I use the term "recombinant" not to re-inscribe the nation as a bio-organism, as the metaphor might imply, but to signify its condition as a "geo-body" with shifting borders of knowledge that delimit and expand "national" history (Thongchai 1994). Recombinant history highlights how the reorganization of knowledge in Vietnam does not simply emerge from the intersection of diverse national and transnational memories or from the defeat or replacement of one historical narrative over another, but from an active, asymmetrical remaking and rearranging—a kind of co-production that is bound up in uneven relations of power and competing claims to historical authority and truth. To borrow from Benjamin, recombinant history is not additive but dialectical (1969b, 263–264), resulting in a recombination of oft-competing representations that complicates viewing history as composed of distinct national memories.

Recombinant history also provides a framework for examining how knowledge is transnationalized in Vietnam under conditions of "market socialism" and global capitalism. Foucault (1977, 1980) has linked the production of knowledge to operations of power that discipline both knowing and known subjects through the circulation of validated truths. As scholarship on feminist epistemologies has shown, knowledge is always relational, situated, partial, mediated, and perspectival (Haraway 1988; Harding 1991; S. Franklin 1996), as well as in conflict with other regimes and frameworks of truth and objectivity (Daston and Galison 2007). In this text I examine U.S. neoliberal capitalism, in particular, as a knowledge project that comes into conflict with other modes of truth making and understandings of objectivity. This was clearly demonstrated in Clinton's remarks at the National University in Hanoi, with his repeated call for open access to knowledge as a means to glean the benefits of a global economy, namely technology, freedom, and prosperity. The invalidation of existing noncapitalist knowledge systems at work in Clinton's remarks begs the question: Whose knowledge economy is he referring to? In this study I outline and trace new geographies and geopolitics of knowledge and power that are forged in spaces of renewed connectivities (Rafael 1995, xvi). I am concerned with the dialectics of "distinctive confluences of knowledge" that give shape to and underpin projects of memory and reconciliation in transnational spaces of history (Tsing 2005, 113).

Transnational Ethnographic Practice

Critiques of ethnography have identified "the field" as a site for the reproduction of a normative set of discourses and values that define and delimit the parameters of anthropological knowledge. Central to this discussion has been a politics of lo-

cation that rethinks the separation of "the field" and "home" and turns the ethnographic gaze inward (Gupta and Ferguson 1997, 12–15; Visweswaran 1994, 101–
104). Reconfiguring "the field" also suggests the need to rethink our relationships
to, and engagements with, sites that are embedded in ethnographic journeys. Insofar
as many researchers have reconfigured "home" as "the field," my fieldwork suggests
a reversal: how to take "the field" and make it into "home." In other words, how
to reenvision fieldwork immersion in its conventional sense of deep ethnography
so that it instead embraces a practice and condition of long-term and cyclical return
to "the field." This book is a result of such an effort. The material I present here is
based on extensive "patchwork" research (Tsing 2005, x) over a period of ten years
that began with preliminary field trips to Vietnam in 1997 and 1998, when I first
started to observe visual representations of history in museum, memorial, and tourist spaces. In September 1999 I returned to Vietnam to conduct dissertation research
and remained until December 2000, moving between fieldwork sites in Hanoi, Ho
Chi Minh City, and, intermittently, Huế and Vinh cities. I returned again in 2001
for follow-up research. In April 2004, soon after filing my dissertation, I moved to
Ho Chi Minh City with my partner and continued to carry out fieldwork for this
book. Certain changes had occurred during my two-and-a-half-year absence that
made follow-up research imperative, namely, implementation of the bilateral free
trade agreement between Vietnam and the United States and international events
that occurred in the aftermath of September 11, 2001. In 2005 we relocated to Hải
Phòng and Hanoi, where I continued research (also on a new project) and maintained a "home," through the completion of this book at the end of 2007, even while
teaching in California. My movement back and forth between research and work
spaces in Vietnam and the United States has enabled a long-term engagement with
my field sites, rather than a conventional one-year immersion of intense attach-
ment and subsequent detachment. This meant that the lines between "home" and
"the field" became increasingly blurred, as did the standard division between
data collection in "the field" and its translation, interpretation, and write-up at
"home."

Research on the mobility of memory across national borders demanded a particular transnational methodological practice that engaged with multi-sitedness not
as distinct, individuated spaces of encounter—what Mary Louise Pratt (1992) has
called "contact zones"—but as locations and networks of interconnectedness and
mobility (Hannerz 1998b). While multi-sited fieldwork has become a fairly standard mode of ethnographic practice in recent years (Marcus 1995), there is still a
tendency to reproduce notions of the field as territorially bounded and observable.
The emphasis on fixed and contained field locations (albeit multiple ones) persists in

much ethnography and affected the way I initially shaped this project as I struggled to delimit its scope and to make my research appear as conventional as possible. At first I made a concerted effort to "fit the mold" and adopt a Malinowskian approach to fieldwork methodology—for example, my careful preparation for the field, intensive language training, concern with immersion, reliance on participant observation, and use of both formal and informal interviews. However, the usefulness of these fieldwork techniques proved limited for a project that tracked the movement of images, commodities, people, and knowledge between Vietnam, the United States, and other countries (such as Germany, where many socialist-produced images of the war are archived), and my dispersed research engagements made it difficult to demarcate the field and produce a thick ethnography in the Geertzian sense of traditional, bounded sites—rural or urban—that still dominate much ethnography. Anthropologists have increasingly challenged these conventional field models and engaged in what Hugh Gusterson (1997) has called "polymorphous engagements," fieldwork that moves away from its dependence on participant observation to engage with a host of sites, diverse groups of people, and interdisciplinary methodologies. This requires looking at a range of sources, cultural productions, documents, and media representations, as well as interacting with people in spaces outside designated field sites (see also Anagnost 1997). As Ara Wilson has pointed out, fieldwork in multiple locations requires "separate, if overlapping, research strategies tailored for each case" (2004, 26).

The transnational design and focus of my research left me with several methodological and moral quandaries that also required that I remain flexible with my fieldwork strategies and engage in more improvisational ethnography (Cerwonka and Malkki 2007). Because multi-sited, transnational research poses significant challenges to conventional ethnographic practice I struggled to maintain a balance between depth and breadth (Hannerz 1998b, 248–249, and 2003; Marcus 1998, 245–247). Since I could not inhabit my field sites in the more traditional sense of immersion, but continuously traveled to and from and between them, my opportunities to engage in "deep" participant observation were more limited and necessitated a different kind of field immersion that had less to do with absorption and inclusion in fixed sites than with recurring encounters over the long term in spaces through which historical memories flowed and intersected. A conceptual shift in making "the field" more like "home" also allowed for a less rigid methodological practice that in vernacular terms might be called "hanging out." Paul Stoller has demonstrated how this technique proves more effective than "plunging into the field with a barrage of demographic surveys or plans for intensive participant observation" (1997, 70). Writing of his long-term intermittent fieldwork "hanging out" with

Harlem street traders, he reflected: "[H]ad I adopted a less open-ended and more intensive approach, the results would have been far more limited" (90). In my research, this practice also meant relying more on informal and spontaneous interactions, in addition to planned interviews or routinized visits to specific locations. Instead of seeking out historical memory, I also went about my daily activities and observed the unplanned, everyday flows and interconnections between people and their diverse engagements with history.

For example, because my home in Hanoi was outside the tourist circuit and far from the more upper-class districts in which foreigners typically resided, my presence in the neighborhood elicited reactions from residents, especially during early morning jogs in the park. "Are you Soviet [*Liên Xô*]?" I was often asked. My answer, "No, I am American," would either be dismissed as a joke, acknowledged with a cautious nod of the head, or met with surprised enthusiasm. My response at times sparked conversations about the war (especially with older men), or questions about why the United States invades poorer countries (usually young adults), or even sing-alongs to the *Titanic* soundtrack (teenagers). The spontaneity of these interactions, and the subtle way I guided the direction of these discussions without assuming the lead, invoke what Wayne Fife has called "fortuitous interviewing" (2005, 102). Fife argues that directed dialogue runs the risk of inhibiting unprompted exchanges of information. Fortuitous interviewing, then, "takes advantage of the topics initiated by those with whom we are doing our study. Stated another way, this method makes use of the 'lucky breaks' that occur in naturalistic conversations and turns them to our own advantage as researchers" (ibid.).

Such interactions at times proved more fruitful then structured interviews. My subject position in Vietnam as a younger, white, female graduate student from the United States studying historical and visual practices of memory posed certain ethical dilemmas insofar as the war understandably remains a sensitive and still painful topic that most people would prefer not to remember. Fortuitous interviewing then allowed Vietnamese respondents to raise the topic and guide conversations about the past if they so chose, without my insistence. Historical animosities and suspicions of U.S. global economic intent also created particular fieldwork challenges for me, such as acquiring information from certain research respondents, namely government officials who saw me as a representative of the United States. Despite my age, I was not unconditionally afforded historical distance from the war. As James Clifford reminds us, the images and knowledge we construct about ethnographic others are constituted in "specific historical relations of dominance and dialogue" (1988, 23). So, too, are our fieldwork practices implicated in and influenced by these power dynamics.

Interviews often form the backbone of ethnographic fieldwork, particularly in transnational research projects where immersion and sustained participant observation in fixed sites are not an option. Yet there are certain cultural and methodological assumptions and relations of power implicit in this mode of ethnographic practice that might make this research technique also less practical: that of the authoritative interviewer directing questions toward, and receiving a flow of information from, a receptive interviewee. These assumptions and power relations were at times inverted in structured interviews with museum officials in Hanoi, who tended to provide incomplete and ambiguous information (and to evade certain topics), and with whom I faced the dilemma of role reversal. Some museum officials had their own agendas in mind when I arrived at the interview accompanied by my research assistant. After business cards were exchanged and green tea poured, male officials in particular assumed control of the interview and redirected the anthropological lens away from themselves, recording information in their notebooks about me and my research. Interviews would begin with an extensive summary of the work and history of the museum, leaving little opportunity for me to interject and pose my own questions. In the end, I became the interviewee and the subject of knowledge, my presumed ethnographic authority undermined on account of my age, gender, ethnicity, and nationality, all of which rendered me with less power and authority in Vietnamese society.

In the end, both evasion and role reversals were productive failures. The silences required that I pay close attention to what was *not* being said, as well as to the specific questions that were glossed over or entirely shunned (see Hart 2002, 203). Ambiguity proved increasingly significant in my work as I went from one official to the next, never getting to the heart of the matter, but collecting a host of interesting non-answers. This also made me more self-conscious about the quest for truth that was driving my own project, the very will to knowledge that I was critiquing in my work. I understood these power struggles to signify important postwar frictions that increasingly motivated and now constitute the main focus of this book, frictions that shape and inform cautious exchanges and lingering suspicions that are present in reconciliation processes between Vietnam and the United States.

Layout of the Book

Like the discipline of history, the project of ethnography requires a careful arrangement and crafting of knowledge, meaning, and "fact" (gleaned through fieldwork "data") into a cohesive story of ethnographic truths and interconnections that remain "inherently partial—committed and incomplete" (Clifford 1986, 7). This book is then a contribution to ethnographic "fiction" that does not seek to pose particular historical or ethnographic "facts" so much as it aspires to interrogate knowledge production and raise critical questions concerning its relationship to subjecthood, voice, authority, and everyday practices of memory (Visweswaran 1994, 62). Tracing the specific operations of power and knowledge in the transnational co-production and management of history, I explore knowledge frictions—contestations over historical truths and changes in visual and memorial practices—and link them to broader global economic and geopolitical transformations that have occurred in Vietnam. The transnational dynamics of remembrance and representation play a central role in the following chapters as the story moves between sites for the visual and material expression of memory in art, architecture, parks, museums, tourist performances, photography, and other memorial productions, and the people who traverse and make sense of these sites in their everyday lives.

The chapters are arranged into three parts based on larger thematic concerns, images, and tensions that emerged during President Clinton's historic visit to Vietnam in 2000, including reconciliation work, landscapes of memory, and competing moral histories. The first part examines joint U.S.-Vietnamese memorial projects that are shaped by discourses of "common bonds" and "shared suffering." Chapter 1 examines the postwar journeys of U.S. veterans to Vietnam and their efforts to "heal the wounds of war" and mitigate suffering through humanitarian interventions that reinvoke gendered rescue narratives. Collaborative efforts between citizens of both countries to reconcile and build postwar relationships through transnational memorial practices have produced unconventional monuments such as peace parks and friendship forests. Based on visits to sites and interviews with U.S. veteran returnees and others, the chapter demonstrates how these transnational initiatives carry different meaning for U.S. and Vietnamese participants who have discordant cultural understandings of "healing" and "reconciliation." Moreover, while for U.S. citizens these reconciliation projects were steeped in imagery and memories of the past, often for Vietnamese participants the same projects were also recognized as key to a more prosperous and globalized future. Despite these differences, both U.S. and Vietnamese discourses revolved around notions of shared experiences and fraternal camaraderie that identified U.S. veterans as fellow victims of imperialism, rather than simply wartime enemies.

Chapter 2 is a detailed examination of a transnational reconciliation project called "Requiem," a photography exhibit that displayed the works of more than 130 photojournalists from all sides killed in action in the Indochinese wars between 1945 and 1975. Based on my attendance at the opening in Ho Chi Minh City and numerous subsequent visits to the exhibit, as well as interviews with Vietnamese photographers and exhibit organizers, the chapter investigates photojournalism on the revolutionary side of the war and its relationship to transnational practices of memory that have transpired in recent years since the normalization of U.S.-

Vietnamese relations. While scholarly research has focused primarily on U.S. cultural productions of the war, this chapter brings much-needed attention to Vietnamese photographic practices and logics of representation. Distinct and often conflicting visual records of war emerged at the exhibit that demonstrated very different relationships to suffering and its visual objectification. Notably, the exhibit broadens the scope of reconciliation projects by honoring the memory of nonrevolutionary, southern Vietnamese photojournalists in a public space of history. The chapter shows how "Requiem" shifted unsteadily between new memories (images from "other" sides) and old histories (standard historical interpretations) and how it became a site of symbolic acts of reconciliation that also reproduced certain political-historical ideologies that were central to the war and are now reproduced under certain conditions of global capitalism.

In part 2, I approach the Vietnamese landscape as a diverse and embattled terrain for the material production and performance of memory that entails reworking the history of imperial pasts and its commodification of the present. Chapter 3 examines tourist attractions that invoke and commercialize the history of the American War, such as the Củ Chi Tunnels, and the way such sites diversify historical knowledge, memory, and meaning through capitalist consumption of mediated memories. Based on repeated tours to war sites and interviews with guides, employees, agents, and tourists, I show how commodification of sites, objects, and imaginaries associated with the war has engendered certain rearticulations of the past in the public sphere as the terrain of memory making has become increasingly transnational. Variously positioned actors engage in diverse embodied practices of memory that complexify dominant modes of historical representation. These tourist productions and performances are consumed primarily by international visitors and, conversely, are largely rejected by domestic tourists, especially Vietnamese youth who reinvest such sites with new meaning that is largely disconnected from the war. The complex memory work that transpires at war sites in Vietnam suggests that commodification does not simply lead to the trivialization of history or the loss of memory and meaning.

Chapter 4 focuses on the monumentalization of Vietnam's landscape and new trends in public commemorative art and architecture. Based on fieldwork and interviews with artists and architects in Hanoi, it traces shifts in the aesthetic processes of nation building at the intersections of socialism and free market capitalism and shows how state memorial projects have undergone significant transformation in recent years as socioeconomic reforms and increased flows of capital have permitted the reconstruction and beautification of memorial temples, martyr cemeteries, and other national monuments. Central to these efforts have been renewed discussions about how to represent the past in monumental form and how to imbue state memorial sites with more historical, cultural, and commemorative meaning. As sites for the visual and artistic expression of national ideals and dominant values, monuments exhibit "foreign" styles and practices in contested spaces that invoke imperial histories and their aesthetic and commemorative legacies. Efforts to traditionalize and "Vietnamize" memorial sites through the incorporation of cultural symbols and iconographies demonstrate efforts to reclaim a unique "Vietnamese" aesthetic identity. The chapter shows how the movement to recast old monuments into new aesthetic creations, including the construction of peace monuments as part of the agenda of joint reconciliation work, signifies diversified ways that cultural producers reimagine the national past and negotiate their aesthetic and artistic agency.

Part 3 probes more closely the incommensurability of U.S. and Vietnamese historical memory, and tensions involved in extending the status of victimhood to suffering Vietnamese bodies. In chapter 5, I trace emerging frictions between museum officials and foreign, namely U.S., visitors who have assumed a self-ascribed role as the guardians of historical truth and objectivity. Museum representatives have proactively responded to international criticism by changing exhibits and expanding narratives to give representation to differing transnational voices of history. Yet such attempts at "democratization" and historical inclusion did not always assuage critiques. With cries of one-sidedness and accusations of propaganda, many U.S. visitors strove to safeguard the sanctity of "their" war and "their" history, challenging Vietnam's historical authority and memory. Drawing upon sustained fieldwork observations in Vietnamese museums, and interviews with directors, employees, and visitors, the chapter examines how struggles over history have manifested in the realm of photography and desires for "proper" contexts of viewing. Traveling images that traverse international borders and are inserted into new social, cultural, and historical contexts have produced "matter out of place." The impulse to challenge historical representation and narration in Vietnam by imposing democratic truths upon misled people can be more broadly seen as a manifestation of the ongoing desire to democratize, and hence civilize, a socialist country even after the end of the Cold War.

Chapter 6 examines how competing regimes and representations of human rights are mapped onto historical and visual memories that travel between and within Vietnam and the United States, but are also informed by and given new currency and meaning in relation to images of the abuse of Iraqi prisoners at Abu Ghraib. U.S. allegations of human rights violations in Vietnam have strained economic relations, as have charges of "dishonest" neoliberal practices. Drawing upon interviews and examination of congressional documents, I explore representations of Vietnamese humane and inhumane acts that have shaped reconciliatory projects and processes, in particular, the resurfacing of John McCain's torture claims. Neoliberal rhetorics aimed at "saving" the Vietnamese economy and its allegedly poor human rights record through free trade and market capitalism are countered by discourses and images that lay claim to an essentialized Vietnamese "tradition" of humanitarianism and compassion toward enemies that also demand U.S. historical accountability for imperial violence and its aftermaths.

The conclusion calls for more attention to transnational studies of Vietnamese history and memorial practices that are not bounded by, or confined to, the nation, as renarrations and re-presentations of the war suggest. A transnational ethnographic approach to war and remembrance allows for a deeper recognition of how empires of memory and knowledge production operate through entanglements with neoliberal capitalism. I return again to the concept of the recombination of history as a means to understand the unequal relations of power that underlie coproductions of historical memory. A notable point of divergence emerges in this case study: in the postnormalization era, while Vietnam has forged ahead—albeit apprehensively—in its diversification of memory in particular transnational spaces, the United States has remained more stagnant and reliant on its conventional scripts of history.

PART 1

Reconciliatory Projects

Return to Vietnam

Redemption, Reconciliation, and Salvation

CHAPTER ONE

While wandering through an exhibit on the "U.S. Special War in the South" at the Museum of the Vietnamese Revolution in Hanoi in the fall of 1999, an inquisitive, middle-aged museum employee named Hà approached me. "Are you a journalist?" she queried, eyeing my notebook and camera. When I explained my reasons for visiting the museum, she invited me to sit down and talk with her. Hà became even more excited upon learning that I was a U.S. citizen and abruptly hurried off, telling me she had something to show me. Moments later, she returned with a thick notebook filled with handwritten English words, phrases, and questions pertaining to Vietnam's history of war and revolution that she had collected during conversations with international visitors. In the back of the book were several names and addresses of U.S. acquaintances she had befriended at the museum, some of whom had also come to Vietnam for research purposes. In an paradoxical twist of ethnographic agency, Hà, with her notebook containing "native" phrases and contacts, was just as interested in talking to me, her "Other," about history, as I was in talking to her.

Hà and I sat together on a bench in the hallway for over an hour that day, discussing in Vietnamese with a smattering of English (words for the notebook) pre- and postwar relations between Vietnam and the United States, a topic that continued to animate many of our conversations over the next eight years. Like most urban Vietnamese with whom I spoke, Hà possessed an impressive knowledge of U.S. history and policy and displayed a warm enthusiasm toward U.S. citizens. On account of her employment, she was familiar with differing perspectives that tourists brought to the museum, and her notebook helped her to prepare responses when confronted with what she felt was misinformation (for example, about Vietnam's intentions in Cambodia) or a general lack of information. She knew, for instance, that many U.S. visitors lacked knowledge of Hồ Chí Minh's brief residency in New York City, of U.S. economic and military support of the French War, and of Norman Morrison's self-immolation outside the Pentagon in 1965 in protest of the war—information she felt was essential to understanding the history of and current status of relations between the two countries.[1]

I continued to visit Hà on a regular basis during my fieldwork. At one point in a conversation in early 2000, I asked her to describe, in her opinion, the general sentiment in Hanoi toward the postwar return of increasing numbers of U.S. citizens twenty-five years after the reunification of the country. Hà smiled upon hearing the question—she had been asked this many times before—and replied:[2]

> In 1997 we had a special exhibit marking the fiftieth anniversary of the founding of War Invalids and Martyrs Day [July 27]. There was an American woman who came to the exhibit. I saw her standing there crying. When I talked with her, she told me her memories of going out into the streets to protest the war. You see we know many people in your country did not support the war and tried to help Vietnam . . . U.S. soldiers have now started to come back to Vietnam. A group of them went to the War Remnants Museum in Ho Chi Minh City and upon seeing the displays, they wept and went down on their knees to repent (hối hận). I also met a Swedish journalist at the exhibit. He asked me if we Vietnamese hate Americans. I told him, "No, we do not. We understand that the U.S. government was responsible for the war, and not the people." That is why, when you ask me today how people feel about Americans coming back to Vietnam, I tell you we have no problem with them. Between the people there is no hate. No mother wants her son to be a hero. No mother wants to send her son to war.

Hà's statement provides several insights into the role of the traumatized body of the U.S. veteran in postwar memory and reconciliation processes. First, her words underscore a classic socialist construct of "war between governments" and "solidarity between people" (see Lenin 1952), a standpoint that in linking Vietnamese and U.S. suffering (particularly between mothers), also recollects the U.S. soldier as enemy *and* fellow victim of U.S. imperial ambitions. However, at the same time, Hà's quasi-religious imagery of the apologetic, kneeling veteran served to construct specific moral positionings of historical accountability: namely, repenting U.S. veterans who express remorse and exonerating Vietnamese who offer forgiveness. Hà and others in Vietnam are well aware that U.S. veterans often return to the former battlegrounds of their youth to work through their traumatic memories of the war.[3] The image of the remorseful U.S. veteran on his knees asking for—and ultimately being granted—forgiveness from the Vietnamese nation has emerged from the postwar embers of U.S.-Vietnamese relations to symbolize a moral victory for Vietnam and the beginning of the end to ideological warfare and U.S. historical unaccountability. Yet, as this chapter will show, the relationship of returnees to questions of guilt and responsibility is often more complex than imagined here.

In addition to representations of U.S. trauma and repentance in media and popular discourse, the suffering and defeat of veterans are celebrated and turned into spectacle for tourists and other viewers at historical sites of memory. At the Củ Chi Tunnels, their emasculated and penetrated bodies are displayed in murals as wounded by "primitive war technologies" (bamboo spikes). In museums, war photography documents the capture of POWs by female enemies, their bomber aircraft—symbols of U.S. phallic technology—shot down and destroyed, at times by older men or female youth. Taken as a whole, such feminizing images and discourses of loss, regret, guilt, trauma, and failure resonate with representations in U.S. cultural memory of the "Vietnam vet" who similarly suffers from the specter of an emasculating defeat and compounded victimization by the U.S. government, the Vietnamese population, and larger U.S. society. As Marita Sturken has argued, "The Vietnam veteran has thus become an emblem of the American male's crisis of masculinity . . ." (1997a, 70).

In her book *The Remasculinization of America: Gender and the Vietnam War,* Susan Jeffords examines the project of rectifying that crisis and of restoring a morally pure, authoritative "American manhood" that had been "lost" in the theater of war in Vietnam. This dual project can be seen, for example, in *Rambo: First Blood, Part 2* (1985) when the veteran (in this case John Rambo) returns to the site of emasculation, Vietnam: "[B]ecause American manhood seemed itself to be on trial, with soldiers fighting and frequently being killed by women, children, and an often poorly equipped and nutritionally depressed enemy, it is important to revive the image of American strength through Vietnam, the place where it was, apparently, 'lost'" (Jeffords 1989, 135). While Jeffords refers to "Vietnam" here as a representation in U.S. popular culture, I argue that the regeneration of masculinity also demands the "real" Vietnam—that is, the physical return to the place of presumed masculine loss. Like U.S. popular cultural representations, through return journeys, "the veteran takes his place as an experienced leader and spokesperson for a conjointly revived morality and social politics that will regenerate America itself" (Jeffords 1989, 116).

In this chapter I examine how projects aimed toward redeeming the morality and masculinity of U.S. veterans, and by extension the United States as a moral and benevolent nation, play out in the field of humanitarian practice and joint com-memorative practices in post–*Đổi mới* Vietnam. I argue that the healing journeys of many U.S. veterans who travel back to Vietnam are concurrently moral jour-neys often imbued with paternalistic meaning, convictions, and desires to rescue Vietnam from the privations of communism with capitalist models of development, progress, and aid as their tools. Discourses and practices of "witnessing peace," of "sharing sorrow," and of "giving back" to Vietnam as a means to "heal the wounds of war" and "bring closure to the past" are integral to the remasculinization proj-ect and its entanglement with a hierarchical global capitalist order—that of poor Third World Others and enterprising First World actors. There exists, however, the threat of reemasculation when the paternal protector and provider to a presumed needy Vietnam again confronts discourses and representations of his loss and de-feat, and an expected admission of guilt as seen in the tale of the repenting veteran submitting to the once-feminized enemy who now assumes an authoritative role as victor and parental figure who may or may not grant forgiveness. The resulting tensions between shifting metaphorical and gendered kinship roles index ambiva-lences toward accountability and reconciliatory processes, and competing claims to power, legitimacy, and a moral masculinity.

U.S. Veterans: Return to Vietnam

After the normalization of diplomatic relations in 1995, the number of U.S. visi-tors to Vietnam has progressively increased, including tourists, investors, schol-ars, development workers, overseas Vietnamese, and returning veterans, to name but a few of the overlapping U.S. populations who reside in or make journeys to Vietnam. This chapter is concerned primarily with the latter, former members of the U.S. military who served in Vietnam and have revisited the country and its battle-fields since the war's end. U.S. veteran delegations began traveling back as early as the 1980s, at which time they constituted the largest population of U.S. citizens in Vietnam (Curtis 2003, 8). U.S. veterans who return to Vietnam are, of course, a di-verse group of men and (to a lesser extent) women with differing ideological and po-litical positionings. The fieldwork respondents I discuss below were predominantly white, male, middle-class, able-bodied veterans who represented various ranks in all branches of the military. They were in Vietnam during my research for a mul-titude of reasons, some of which required long-term residency or frequent trips: as tourists, philanthropists, missionaries, project coordinators, politicians, civil ser-vants, engineers, corporate managers, and so on. In what follows, I do not intend to reduce the complexities of the category "U.S. veteran returnees" to a set of pre-sumed generalizations or motivations, which are admittedly multiple and multifaceted. I am also aware that my analysis precludes the perspectives of veterans who cannot or will not make a return trip. My intent here is to highlight certain commonalities that emerged in the narratives of veterans who journeyed back to Vietnam and its former battlefields, and the complex ways they attempted to reconcile and work through the past, including tensions that resurfaced between and among enemy and allied troops. Reconciliation is thus shown to be a highly ambivalent process that complicates notions of "healing" for all involved.

In her ethnographic research on U.S. veterans and their postwar travels to Vietnam in tour groups, Paulette Curtis (2003) argues that such journeys signify efforts to reclaim a place in U.S. history and to reinsert one's experience and voice into what some veterans consider an ambiguous historical record that has denied them accurate representation and agency. In this chapter, I highlight other motivational dimensions, pointing to discourses of the suffering body and to mechanisms and modes of action considered therapeutic and healing. Travel to Vietnam is frequently marketed to veterans as a healing journey, through which a transformed moral state is achieved (see Das and Kleinman 2001, 23) via their participation in commemorative and charitable work ("we heal ourselves by healing others"), collaborative memorial projects (which bring former adversaries together), or the act of witnessing the country at peace.[4] Release from trauma and traumatic memory is envisioned through the physical process of return and reintegration into a social milieu in which everyday relations, interactions, and activities are marked by an absence of the sensorial dimensions and violence of war.

The frequent emphasis on "healing" and "working through" the past set veterans and their family members apart from other tourists, who are also drawn to battlegrounds as described in chapter 3, though as non-witnesses who possess "prosthetic memories" of Vietnam and the war through consumption of mediated images in popular culture (Landsberg 2004). On account of their traumatic and experiential relationship to the war, U.S. veterans were thought at times to have more in common with non-tourists, such as Vietnamese nationals, than they did with other travelers who were not veterans. Veterans were also dissimilar to tourists, particularly backpackers, insofar as they usually did not travel independently or with groups of non-veterans on the main tour circuits, but preferred to travel with other returnees, often from the same military unit, in organized reunion packages that have become popular with tour agencies and nonprofit veterans' organizations in the United States and, less successfully, in Vietnam (see Curtis 2003; Bleakney 2006). Tour programs generally provide a range of commemorative and historical-cultural activities, such as trips to former military bases and other war sites, meetings with veterans from the "other side," attendance at Vietnamese cultural performances, and participation in humanitarian projects. As Valene Smith has observed, military reunions have occupied a strong niche in U.S. and European tourism industries since the post–World War II era (1996, 261). In the case of the Vietnam War, their success rates in attracting participants have varied, for reasons I note below. For those veterans who do join military and other tours—some of which sell themselves specifically as healing and recovery journeys, such as Tours of Peace[5] and the faith-based Open Hands and Hearts—sharing the return experience to a site of trauma with other "pilgrims" has "tremendous potential for generating catharsis," as Kugelmass (1996, 202) has argued in the case of Jewish group tours to Nazi concentration camps. In interviews and conversations, veterans recounted crucial support they and others received from fellow returnees in uncertain and emotional moments, such as landing in Vietnam, impulsive flashbacks prompted by certain smells or noises, and initial encounters with Vietnamese citizens, as veterans were often unsure as to how they would be received. In addition to reestablishing certain bonds of camaraderie between U.S. veterans (Curtis 2003, iv), as I highlight below, fraternal linkages also materialized between U.S. and Vietnamese veterans in discourses of shared memories and shared sorrow that paradoxically resonated with Vietnamese configurations of solidarity.

It is worth noting that despite the gradual increase in U.S. veterans who have made the journey back to Vietnam, there are complex historical, economic, and psychological barriers that limit their numbers. In interviews, veterans often pointed out that many former combatants were not yet ready to return and still often harbored ill feelings toward Vietnam. One woman in the United States confided in me her desire to visit Vietnam as a means to help a family member: "I have a cousin who served in Vietnam and refuses to think about going back. He can't even fathom it. He has a deep dislike for the Vietnamese people. So I want to go there and bring back photos and mementos to help him heal." This tense relationship with the past, what the Vietnamese media has referred to as "the ghosts of Vietnam that continue to haunt the U.S.," was also recognized by many of my Vietnamese respondents. Tài, a veteran of the People's Army of Vietnam (PAVN), similarly argued that "U.S. veterans are not ready to come back," and cited as evidence the largely unsuccessful attempts by the Vietnam Association of Veterans to organize commercial tours to battle sites for former U.S. troops. A tour guide in Hanoi speculated about what he saw as a general absence of U.S. visitors in Vietnam: "I have read many books and know that the war is still a bad memory for the Americans because they spent a lot of money, lost many lives, and then lost the war . . . I read they call it the 'Vietnam syndrome.'" The wounded body and psyche of the U.S. veteran is thus marked in multiple ways as suffering not only in U.S. popular culture, but also in Vietnamese public discourse and the mass media. As David B. Morris has argued: "Suffering . . .

is not a raw datum, a natural phenomenon we can identify and measure, but a social status that we extend or withhold ... depending largely on whether the sufferer falls within our moral community" (1997, 40). This status of suffering conferred upon U.S. veterans in *both* the United States and Vietnam suggests their inclusion in differing moral communities across "enemy lines," a status that is conversely denied to certain Vietnamese victims of the war, as I discuss in chapter 6.

Witnessing Peace: Images of Renewal and Regeneration

For many U.S. veterans with whom I spoke, journeys to postwar Vietnam were linked in diverse ways to cathartic and memorial processes of healing, reconciliation, and, at times, historical understanding. One retired officer who had made several trips back to Vietnam spoke to me about the therapeutic and reconciliatory powers of returning to confront a painful and still raw past: "I love the country, love the people. They have been so kind to me. I'd go back again tomorrow if I could ... I've coached a number of people to go back. I tell them, 'You should not die angry—you need to go.' I convinced one man, an alcoholic, to return. When he got back to the U.S. he told me, 'That was the best therapy I ever had.'" Return testimonies posted on the internet, printed in tour and mission brochures, or published in memoirs also frequently convey a recovery component to veterans' return with mention of "unloading baggage," "finding peace," and finally "ending the war." What is it about "the return" that presumably enables veterans to mitigate their suffering and psychic pain? To be traumatized, Cathy Caruth has argued, is to be possessed by the past, seized by traumatic images or events that continually intrude upon the person who has lived through and experienced them (1995, 4–5). Postwar travels to Vietnam disrupted for many the cyclical repetition of images of violence, providing new sights of Vietnam not as a war, but as a country, to paraphrase the Vietnamese government, with a rich cultural and historical legacy that extends beyond the tumultuous years of U.S. occupation.[6]

Metaphors of vision—of *seeing* and *witnessing* the country not at war but at peace—emerged as a common theme in narratives of healing and reconciliation, and in knowledge production about postwar Vietnam. One veteran who served in the 3rd Marine Division in 1969 and 1970 and now returns to Vietnam annually to volunteer for humanitarian projects reflected: "Going back to Vietnam ended the war for me. Before I could never see that the war was actually over. But now the weapons are gone and I no longer have to duck gunfire." The visual absence of weaponry and the veteran's displacement from zones of danger allowed him to visually and experientially *know* the definitiveness of the end of combat. From his new position as a nonthreatened (and nonthreatening) U.S. civilian who could go about his daily activities without the fear of violence, the war was "finally actually over." At the same time, a tension emerged in veterans' narratives regarding the absence of the visual as a tool for healing and a longing for its presence as a means to recollect and reconnect with the past. "I wanted to see again those places where I fought to see what they are like now," a retired lieutenant who returned to Vietnam in 2000 shared with me. "But there was nothing left to see," he added, disappointed at the lack of visual cues of his time served during the war. A transformed Vietnam thus should not become too unrecognizable or risk displacing (and obliterating) U.S. memory and claims to history.

In veteran narratives, acts of seeing Vietnam in peacetime were closely entangled with images of regeneration and rebirth, tropes also commonly found in U.S. representations of the war that Jeffords links to a the project of restoring masculinity (1989, 134–138). In the words of a former U.S. Air Force pilot who spent several years in Hỏa Lò prison (dubbed the "Hanoi Hilton" by U.S. troops): "Every veteran wants to return one day to the battlefield. They want to see how the site has changed; how it's no longer a part of war. They need to have new images and see that life continues." Images of renewal and regeneration thus come to replace memories of death and devastation, disrupting the "insistent return" of the past in the present identified by Freud as constitutive of both war and accident trauma (Caruth 1995, 5; Kaplan 2005, 29–30).[7] This is also evident in the following quote, which draws upon ecological imagery of abundance in nature to signify renewal and recovery of both environment and self: "When I go home and think of Vietnam, I'll no longer think only about the war. It helps to see [previously devastated] areas now filled with rubber trees and coffee plantations. It shows how life carries on." Suffering bodies and desolate landscapes have thus come full circle: from life to war/death and then rebirth. The veteran's quote suggests that the recuperation of the (male) veteran body is intertwined with the regeneration of the (female) fertile landscape, a process to which veterans and others directly contribute.

Bearing witness to peace, however, did not always engender a greater understanding of postwar Vietnam, nor did it enable in all cases a greater sense of moral responsibility that scholars have argued is essential to acts of witnessing (Laub 1992, 85–86; Kaplan 2005, 122–125). Witnessing, Kyo Maclear argues, conveys but a "limited vision" of trauma and its aftermaths, as there exists an "incommensurable gap between perception and reality" that makes knowing the unknowable all but impossible (2003, 234). In witnessing peace rather than the legacies of war, veterans voiced in their narratives a selective and partial knowledge of Vietnam's postwar recovery that elided ongoing trauma in both bodies and landscape. W. D. Ehrhart's 1987 return memoir provides yet another example of this displacement. Drawing upon nostalgic and orientalist visions of a timeless and unscathed Vietnam country-side, he writes:

> Now when I think of Vietnam, I will not see in my mind's eye the barbed wire
> and the grim patrols and the violent death that always exploded with no warn-
> ing. Now I will see those graceful fishing boats, gliding out of the late afternoon
> sun . . . and the buffalo boys riding the backs of those great gray beasts in the
> fields along the road to Tay Ninh. Now I will not hear the guns, but rather the
> gentle rhythmic beat of rice stalks striking the threshing mats. (1987, 180)

In their embrace of peace and restored social normalcy, veterans have at times in-advertently glossed over the war's enduring legacies of poverty, environmental dev-astation, and bodily contamination. It is not that they are oblivious to the insidious threat of unexploded ordnance, for example, that continues to maim or kill Viet-namese children and adults.[8] They are also not unaware of the long-term effects of Agent Orange (see Fox 2005), which are also painfully felt in the United States. Rather, their lack of voiced acknowledgment of Vietnamese trauma suggests that their own processes of healing are frequently in tension with the conferment of the status of suffering upon Vietnamese bodies. In the next sections, I examine how such tensions play out in the field of humanitarian practices and transnational com-memorative projects, which demand recognition of traumatized, victimized bod-ies, while raising apprehensions and disquieting questions about historical com-plicity and responsibility.

"Giving Back": U.S. Humanitarianism or Rescuing Vietnam, Again

The return to Vietnam of increasing numbers of U.S. veterans has coincided with a substantial growth in U.S. humanitarian practices and collaborative projects, many of which have aimed to reconcile and work through the past through acknowledg-ment, rather than denial, of Vietnamese trauma. After prohibitions on U.S. aid to Vietnam were lifted in 1992 and U.S.-Vietnamese diplomatic relations were reestab-lished three years later, U.S. humanitarian efforts in Vietnam grew substantially in number and in scope, according to a representative of the Vietnam Union of Friend-ship Organizations (VUFO)–NGO Resource Centre in Hanoi in 2000. As reported in the center's yearly publication, in 1999, 35 percent of the approximately 350 offi-cially registered international non-governmental organizations (NGOs) in Vietnam were from the United States (VUFO and NGO Resource Centre 2000), a number that does not include smaller bootstrap organizations that attempt to remain below the radar of the Vietnamese government, for example, NGOs with proselytizing missions. At the time of my fieldwork, U.S. projects in Vietnam included, but were not limited to, the construction of schools, clinics, peace parks, libraries, housing, friendship forests, and friendship villages, as well as the donation of food, medical supplies, computer equipment, and funds to provide microcredit and small loans to women and other small-scale entrepreneurs. U.S. citizens who felt the need to "give something back to Vietnam," often war veterans or family members of fallen soldiers, commonly initiated or volunteered in these projects.

Belief in one's capacity to "help" Vietnam transformed a veteran's healing journey into a moral and salvation mission in which the long-delayed fantasy of rescuing Vietnam was finally realized (Turner 1996). As a savior from poverty, oppression, and ultimately communism, the Vietnam veteran reclaims his place as the paternal protector of the Vietnamese nation. It is not always enough just to go back, I was told. In order to "move forward" in life, one needs to act and to assist, thus reinscribing gendered, hierarchical relations of power between (re)masculinized providers and feminized recipients of aid. As Vietnam veteran and poet John Balaban wrote, "Go visit Vietnam, I'd tell the troubled vets. Go visit, and do something good there, and your pain won't seem so private, your need for resentment so great" (1991, 333). "Doing good," however, required that veterans grapple with their own roles and complicity in the war, and with Vietnamese expectations of guilt and repentance.

Yet some veterans resisted these representations of traumatized and guilt-ridden Americans, and they deflected Vietnamese suffering away from individual wrongdoing to U.S. governmental responsibility (resonating with Hà's observation that wars are between governments and not people). This was the case with Jack, a self-proclaimed leftist who was "sympathetic to the Vietnamese cause," though it took him "several years to reach this point." Since his first return trip in 1989, Jack has been involved in medical humanitarian activities, traveling to Vietnam at least twice each year to distribute hospital equipment and other supplies. Jack was aware of, and firmly rejected, ideas in Vietnam that returning U.S. veterans were on a quest for redemption and absolution: "I have absolutely no guilt. I didn't come back here to resolve my sins or to repent. I didn't do anything wrong during the war. I only carried out my job. The people who are guilty are Johnson or Nixon, not me." Despite Jack's assured moral distance from the issue of complicity, his charitable actions showed a more complex and conflicted relationship with unresolved questions of historical accountability. As we sat together drinking *bia tươi* [draft beer] at a popular restaurant in Hanoi, he recollected his recent return to a village in central Vietnam where his unit had engaged in a day of fierce combat in 1969: "We found one woman still living there who remembered the fight. I introduced myself and apologized for scaring her. She said, 'No problem,' but immediately asked for money to repair her roof that was damaged in the crossfire." Jack acquiesced, took out his wallet, and handed her money, not unlike his action earlier that night in the streets in Hanoi as we walked past an impoverished, disabled veteran, to whom he impulsively gave a five-dollar bill. Though Jack denied any affect of guilt, his impulse to give (money or medical supplies) suggests he has assumed the unfulfilled moral and financial obligations on the part of the United States to provide unpaid reparations to Vietnam, though here we find that the veteran "pays" his moral and economic debts not to the Vietnamese government (to which he has no direct social obligation), but to its people.

For other veterans, the burden of Vietnamese suffering was effectively shifted from both individual *and* U.S. historical responsibility to the presumed inadequacies and corrupt practices of the communist government. At the time of our interview in 2001, Paul, a veteran who served in 1969–1970 in Quảng Trị, had returned to Vietnam every year since 1995 to participate in humanitarian activities for two to three weeks at a time, traveling under the auspices of a Christian organization that was involved in several veteran humanitarian projects, such as the construction of schools and libraries ("with American books") in the countryside, as well as humanitarian work in leper colonies and orphanages. Like Jack, Paul denied any sense of individual guilt on account of his "honorable intentions," though he differed from Jack insofar as he situated himself ideologically in opposition to the Communist Party and the Vietnamese government. He told me: "The only guilt I have is that the U.S. didn't succeed. We were in the right . . . I would give my life for freedom and that's what we were fighting for." His ideological construction of a benevolent and well-intentioned United States contrasted with his portrayals of an unfree and undemocratic Vietnam with its deprived and needy populace whom he could "help."

For Paul, the fight to bring freedom to Vietnam continues, with the communist government, again, the principal obstacle to achieving his goals. "I follow my heart in Vietnam, not the government's rules and regulations," he informed me, explaining that his organization chooses not to register with the government in order to carry out its work clandestinely. As a participant in "faith-based humanitarianism" (Bornstein 2005), Paul engages in what might be described as *haphazard* religious-charitable activities. For each trip, he maxes out his baggage allowance and packs his luggage full with donations—food, clothing, medical supplies, candy, and Bibles (wrapped as gifts)—and then distributes the goods in Vietnam in a random fashion from a van in which he travels. Not unexpectedly, this approach has engendered conflict with local authorities who have taken away donations at customs (especially Bibles) and shut down his mobile distribution operations. "I've been run out of places and had my missions stopped," he admitted, though he understood such actions as politically motivated: "The Communist Party is getting weaker . . . And they want to ruin the image of the U.S. and returning veterans by not allowing us to fulfill our promises to help the people. So we look like the bad guys, not them." In other words, Paul believed that communist anxieties over losing the hearts and minds of the populace to the United States impeded his work, rather than his own legally and culturally questionable practices.

Framed in a discourse of "helping others," Paul's narrative oscillated between his work as therapeutic guide and as rebuilder of the nation, two subject position-ings that Jeffords has identified as key to regenerating American masculinity (1989, 238). After his first return trip to Vietnam in 1995, Paul began encouraging oth-ers to make the journey back: "I've helped many veterans return to Vietnam, like my good friend Rob. He was one of the first amputees to return. I helped him and others go back and put down the rock of anger they'd been carrying for years." Paul's work in the U.S.—raising project funds, collecting donations, and recruit-ing veterans—facilitated his efforts to rebuild Vietnam and rescue its people from economic and emotional privation. "Healing and helping go hand in hand," he told me, hinting at the dual project of material and spiritual salvation that underscores Christian-influenced notions of development (Bornstein 2005, 48–49). "When I handed a bag of rice to a girl in Khe Sanh, she had a tear in her eye. Showing people you care helps them more than money. It makes people feel good to know you care. It also lightens your own load, but I try to keep the focus off myself." Paul's role as both paternal provider and healer, believed to engender the girl's material and spiri-tual transformation, allowed him to recuperate his moral manhood, and by exten-sion, to redeem the moral rectitude of the United States by winning the hearts and minds of the Vietnamese people not with weapons, he told me, but with love.

The narratives of Paul and Jack show the diversity of ideological positionings of U.S. veterans who return to Vietnam and engage in charitable practices. Yet despite their differing political persuasions and sympathies, both unequivocally shifted larger questions of historical accountability from the individual to the state (U.S. or Vietnamese). They were both inclined to explain that they had carried out their jobs reasonably and responsibly under the orders of the U.S. military. They also similarly rejected images of traumatized returnees, with Jack specifically point-ing to and contesting Vietnamese constructions of repenting veterans seeking forgiveness—representations that to him suggested admissions of misconduct and unlawful activity. Such moral claims notwithstanding, their humanitarian work revealed more ambiguity concerning these complex issues as both men used their own personal time and money to rehabilitate Vietnam, the self, and the image of their country.[9] Gestures of aid and charity, moreover, were in tension with Viet-namese feminizing portrayals of remorseful and weeping veterans, though working through the trauma of return was a pronounced focus of Paul's journeys: "Bring a towel, you'll cry," recommended a brochure from his organization that he gave me. By assuming moral positions of paternal providers and healers, Jack and Paul made the past right through more triumphant and satisfactory encounters with Vietnam that reestablished the dominance and benevolence of American masculinity and, more broadly, the United States (Jeffords 1989, 135).

American Triumphalism and Post-Aid Debris

U.S. humanitarian interventions in Vietnam have been received with cautious am-bivalence by Vietnamese authorities as well as by certain U.S. veterans who are themselves involved in such activities, but also recognize that effective postwar humanitarianism requires a "greater engagement with the subjectivity of the ac-tors involved" (R. Wilson 2003, 99). As Liisa Malkki (1996) has argued in the case of refugees, recipients of humanitarian aid are often rendered speechless through particular discursive and representational practices that in silencing historical and political agency attribute greater authority and knowledge about particular contexts of suffering to aid practitioners. John, a veteran and long-term resident in Vietnam involved with several humanitarian activities, made similar critiques of veteran-led projects that he feels "have good intentions, but do not have long-term success rates due to short-sightedness, poor management, and self-gratification." In John's view, the hope for transformation that accompanies the humanitarian "gift" (Bornstein 2007) is more about recovery of self than of Vietnam, as is evident in the slippage between "helping" the girl at Khe Sanh and "healing" the self in Paul's narrative. This tendency toward immediate gratification and the lack of prolonged, engaged dialogue with Vietnamese counterparts have produced in some places in Vietnam a landscape of post-aid debris: "Veterans often fly in, build a school, and then leave, giving little consideration to the building's future upkeep. The countryside is in-creasingly littered with neglected, empty buildings, so local authorities are taking a more skeptical stance towards these projects."

Scholars have demonstrated how western humanitarianism is commonly ar-ticulated within liberal and neoliberal discourses that position the recipient of aid also as the beneficiary of "progress," "rights," "freedom" and capitalist "develop-ment" (i.e., Ferguson 1994; Bornstein 2005; Englund 2006). In Vietnam, when aid intervention was hindered by skeptical officials or shut down for nonauthorized practices, U.S. veterans often responded by accusing the government of excessive communist bureaucracy that stifles reform, denies development, and prohibits the realization of U.S. generosity. According to John in 2000, "The heyday of veteran projects is now over. There were too many problems; they expected things to go fast, and they wanted to do things immediately. They didn't understand you had to be in it for the long haul." Thus a delegation of U.S. veterans, now corporate businessmen, who traveled to Vietnam to discuss investment opportunities (U.S. commerce being another "gift") and a charitable donation responded to John that they would take their money elsewhere, to another poor country, after Vietnamese officials politely declined and insisted that they would need time to consider their offer. Vietnamese ambivalence and skepticism thus frustrated these veterans and their efforts to overcome postwar conditions of *socialist* underdevelopment and poverty (often disconnected from the legacies of the war) with U.S. humanitarianism and neoliberal capitalism.

For some veterans, belief in the necessity of U.S. aid and capitalist development to rehabilitate Vietnam linked their healing and moral journeys to the very conflict that initiated their trauma in the first place: the struggle against communism. Humanitarian missions thus often came to mimic the stated objective of U.S. intervention in Vietnam: to rescue the country from the tenacious grip of noncapitalism. Journeys back to Vietnam helped to end the "Vietnam syndrome" by exorcising the past and reversing the trauma of war through witnessing and participating in Vietnam's "liberation" with tools of economic development, including aid and investment. In the history of American triumphalism, discourses of salvation from "immoral" forces (i.e., communism) have long justified U.S. imperial and capitalist expansion.[10] As Turner (1996) and others have shown, the myth of the United States as a benevolent nation of saviors crumbled during the Vietnam War as the U.S. public (and troops) came to consider that their country was not the liberator of the Vietnamese people, but its enemy. The return to Vietnam of U.S. citizens as humanitarian agents thus signifies the resurrection of the salvation myth as Americans resume a particular role as redeemer and healer (of self and Vietnamese Other) that "assists the continuing movement of American capitalism and Vietnamese reconstruction (to the extent that it is dependent upon American policy), bringing to closure a deep crisis in American culture," and in American masculinity (Nguyen 2002, 124).

"Sharing Sorrow": Transnational Reconciliation and Commemoration

In addition to "giving back" to Vietnam through humanitarian practice, U.S. citizens who journeyed to Vietnam specifically for purposes of healing and reconciliation—terms that signify particular cultural constructs, as I discuss below—also embarked upon and participated in *collaborative* transnational memorial projects. In the previous section, I discussed the trend toward "quick-fix" and, at times, "self-gratifying" humanitarian projects that exploded in the 1990s after restrictions on U.S. aid were lifted in 1992, and showed signs of slowing down toward the end of the decade. These projects, I argued, challenged Vietnamese postwar constructions of emasculated and defeated veterans who seek forgiveness from the parental victor through humanitarian acts that positioned veterans in "remasculinizing" roles as paternal providers of food, money, and material supplies to a needy population (a role not completely unlike that assumed in wartime). In this section I focus on humanitarian work that engenders other metaphorical kinship relations that resonate with Hà's imagery at the beginning of the chapter—those of fraternal (and not infrequently maternal) solidarity that underlie collective Vietnamese and U.S. memorial practices.

The transnational memory projects that I examine here and in other chapters reflect desires to jointly remember, reconcile, and heal wounds of war in body, spirit, and landscape. Often drawing on a discourse of peace, rather than of war, these collaborative and typically longer-term projects have produced unconventional "living memorials" that include peace parks, peace villages, peace monuments, and friendship forests. Like the humanitarianism discussed in the previous section, collaborative memorial projects are typically initiated and motivated by U.S. individuals who seek recovery and renewal. However, unlike the previous interventions, joint U.S.-Vietnamese commemoration is less shaped by hierarchical and paternalistic narratives of salvation than representations of fraternal camaraderie and joint solidarity rooted in notions of "shared" memories, sorrow, and suffering.

PeaceTrees Vietnam is a U.S. humanitarian organization that brings former adversaries together to collaborate on reconciliation projects that locate trauma and healing in landscape, community, and self. Founded in 1995 by family members of a helicopter pilot killed in combat, PeaceTrees mission, as explained to me in 2000 by the regional director, is to "reverse the legacy of war" through community and environmental restoration projects, including landmine and unexploded ordnance (UXO) clearance and education. Its humanitarian vision of "working alongside the Vietnamese people" endeavors to locate decision-making power "not in the hands of the NGO because they have the money, but in the hands of the Vietnamese because it's their country and their government." In PeaceTrees one finds greater reflexivity and a deeper commitment to continuous dialogue and "practices of listening" as a means to work toward postwar reconciliation and reconstruction (Borneman 2002, 293–296). This "local empowerment" approach, according to the regional director, has meant "less red-tape" and quicker implementation of PeaceTrees' programs compared with other humanitarian organizations that maintain control over project finances and activities and subsequently experience problems and delays with local authorities. The emphasis on shared power, however, tended to elide other structural inequalities and relations of power that underlie projects and shape the development and implementation of activities.[11]

Located in Đông Hà town, close to the former Demilitarized Zone (DMZ), PeaceTrees was actively involved at the time of my fieldwork in the twofold project of landmine and UXO clearance of former battlegrounds and their subsequent re-forestation. Joint teams of young men from a local Vietnamese military unit and UXB International, a private American munitions disposal company largely staffed by former U.S. military personnel, worked together on landmine and UXO re-moval. During a visit in 2000 to a munitions clearance site on a former U.S. marine base, young Vietnamese soldiers between the ages of eighteen and twenty worked alongside former U.S. Army experts in two-man teams for brief, but intense, thirty-minute shifts that involved the careful probing of land with a long, thin detector in-serted at an angle up to thirty centimeters beneath the earth's surface.[12] The Viet-namese deminers moved slowly through the "grid" (section of land to be cleared), three centimeters at a time, excavating mines, grenades, and mortars that were sub-sequently identified, recorded, and then thrown in a demolition holding pit to be exploded each Friday.[13] In interviews, the two U.S. deminers on site emphasized the "tremendous team spirit" and solidarity that had been fostered during the coopera-tion on account of the seriousness and danger of the work, and also group weekend activities such as football tournaments against other humanitarian-funded demin-ing units. At the same time, there was a clear hierarchy of technical expertise here: the goal of UXB was to train Vietnamese specialists according to "international safety standards" and to gradually hand over demining operations and equipment to the Vietnamese military.

During the war much of the land in Quảng Trị province, which bordered the seventeenth parallel that temporarily divided Vietnam, was severely devastated and deforested by repeated heavy bombing and the widespread use of chemical de-foliants. Though much of the area has experienced regrowth or reforestation since the end of the war, demining procedures have required the selective redeforesting of land and the clearance of fields used for agriculture. The destruction of crops in impoverished communities was a concern expressed by both Vietnamese and U.S. deminers, who made efforts to minimize the economic and environmental impact of their work; for example, certain lands were cleared only after the harvest period to allow sufficient time for regrowth. Subsequent reforestation projects, organized by PeaceTrees, were supported by volunteers from the United States (often veterans or their families) and elsewhere, who paid a few thousand dollars to participate in a two-week "peace trip" that involved working collaboratively with local commu-nity members to replant trees on lands recently deemed free of munitions.[14]

With the motto "peace, reconciliation, and friendship," PeaceTrees reforestation projects have intertwined reconciliatory rites of healing and renewal (the collaborative planting of trees) with cathartic rites of remembrance directed at commemorating both U.S. and Vietnamese war dead. Take, for example, the case of the
Friendship Forest, an eighteen-acre tract of land (and former battlefield) that was
demined and reforested in 1996 by "former sworn enemies" who "put their history
behind them and became brothers," as written in a PeaceTrees brochure given to
me by the regional director during my visit to the site, invoking images of postwar
fraternal camaraderie that resonate with other circulating discourses of solidarity
found in Vietnamese society, to which Hà alluded. At the outset of the project,
forty-three international volunteers, "post-modern peace campaigners," between
the ages of eight and seventy-six, the majority of whom were from the United
States, came to Quảng Trị province "united by the unquenched urge to do good in
the world" (Douglas 1998), thus reflecting the moral drive toward betterment that
underlies much humanitarian work (Bornstein 2005). International volunteers labored alongside local community members to plant 1,700 native trees, many of
which were sponsored from abroad in memory of a loved one, whose name was
read aloud during the tree-planting ceremony. The anthropologist Laura Rival has
identified the socially symbolic and dualistic signification of trees and their social
lives: while trees embody particular social and historical memories that index the
past, they also metaphorically allude to the future as symbols of life, vitality, and regeneration (1998, 23). In the case of Quảng Trị, the reforestation of war-devastated
lands with native vegetation gestured toward the past and the future in diverse and
culturally significant ways that inscribed the landscape with complex and shifting
social and historical meaning.

Reforestation projects were steeped in metaphors and memories of the past in
U.S. discourses and practices. For example, U.S. volunteers buried intimate artifacts
from the war, including military medals and personal letters, at the base of the trees
during the initial planting of the Friendship Forest. Such ritual acts transformed
the trees from arboreal metaphors of cooperation, reconciliation, and regeneration
(embodying the present and future) to an enduring memorial that drew attention to
U.S. historical memory, meaning, and experience. At the same time, through such
burial acts, reforestation activities worked to heal the landscape and self simultaneously, as the war was materially (in relics) and metaphorically (in memory) laid
to rest, buried under a recuperated forest that "transformed a former battleground
into a lifegiving sanctuary of healing," the co-founder explained to me. In Vietnam,
on the other hand, while trees and tree-planting ceremonies also evoke important
historical memory, they are more clearly linked to discourses and social imagina-

tions of the future. For example, respondents in Hanoi referred to personal memories and images of Bác Hồ [Uncle Hồ], whose annual tree-planting ceremony on the first day of the lunar new year [Tết] served as a symbolic and material gesture toward nurturing the environment and providing "national prosperity" and "happiness for future generations." In the context of the Friendship Forest, however, the wholly symbolic and unproductive tree may not ensure such prosperous futures, according to Vinh, a man from southern Vietnam involved in reconciliation projects: "Peace trees, peace parks, peace forests—it's all so abstract. People want something more useful. They need fruit—not parks. They need hope, hope for enough food, hope for the future. Peace does not follow the end of war. Peace can only come after people have enough to eat."

Vinh's concern with healing the larger social body of the nation through the elimination of endemic poverty reflects some of the ambivalence in Vietnam toward U.S. humanitarian and joint commemoration activities. The meanings attached to these acts clearly differ: while U.S. citizens linked such projects to desires to reconcile with the past and lay painful memories to rest, for Vietnamese they were also understood in a more forward-looking way—as a bridge to a desired prosperous future. During my research, the clichéd sentiment that Vietnam looks to the future [hướng về tương lai], while the United States remains haunted [ám ảnh] by the past, often surfaced in the Vietnamese press and in interviews; a binary opposition that inverts conventional modernization theory and its belief that "nonmodern" (and nonwestern) peoples are immersed in tradition and memory practices, whereas "modern" societies—beset by historical acceleration and amnesia—are forward-thinking and future-focused (Nora 1989). Moreover, as I outline in the next section, Vietnamese ambivalence also reveals specific cultural assumptions that inform joint project discourse and objectives that emphasize the need and desire to heal and to reconcile.

Vietnamese Perspectives on Reconciliation and Healing

What does it mean to reconcile? What specific cultural, political, and moral dimensions and understandings underlie, influence, and perhaps inhibit such processes? As Richard A. Wilson has shown in his ethnographic study of South Africa's Truth and Reconciliation Commission (TRC), the normative values, classifications, and discourses espoused by the TRC came into conflict with broader popular norms and practices, as well as competing agendas and meanings attached to "reconciliation" (2001, 98–99). In Vietnam, although collaborative peace projects embodied rites of remembrance that were meaningful to both U.S. and Vietnamese participants, albeit in differing ways, the quest for healing and reconciliation that was so central to U.S. journeys was largely absent from Vietnamese perspectives. Tài, a veteran of the PAVN who has participated in these activities, suggested that the oft-employed terms "healing" and "reconciliation" in the context of the war reflect American cultural constructs that have different connotations in Vietnam:[15]

> The word *hòa giải* [to reconcile] is not really used in Vietnam. It implies a compromise, that both sides are wrong. We use this word when talking about mediating relations between a husband and wife, not between Vietnamese and U.S. citizens. But I know for the Americans this word, like the word *hàn gắn* [healing], is very important.

In Tài's understanding, "reconciliation" is not a politically neutral process or mutually inclusive negotiation in the sense of John Borneman's use of the term: "to render no longer opposed" (2003, 199). Rather, it is a morally charged subject position that also signifies acknowledgment and confession of historical and individual wrongdoing. Insofar as national memory in Vietnam emphasizes a long history of recurring invasion and victimization by foreign aggressors (see Pelley 2002), the Vietnamese nation is in a position not to reconcile but to forgive those who express remorse and desire to make amends for past transgressions and injustices.

"Healing," a concept that shapes return journeys and humanitarian work, was also complicated by my Vietnamese respondents who pointed to differing cultural, historical, and economic meanings attached to the term. Vinh, who had been a student protester in Saigon during the war, again alluded to desires for more prosperous futures: "You Americans came here to fight, then left Vietnam suddenly. So you had no closure and now desire healing. But for the Vietnamese, [these projects] aren't about healing, but hope. What motivates people to reconcile is hope for the future." The idea of economic betterment as a driving force behind reconciliation (as well as forgiveness) also surfaced when Tài reflected on usage of the term "healing" in Vietnam: "Healing is used occasionally, but not in the same way that Americans use it. The government might use 'healing' to refer to relations with the United States, but only if they are trying to attract investors. More often we use the phrase 'build friendship' [*xây dựng tình hữu nghị*]." In both points of view, material gains and national development were considered important incentives for swallowing anger and rebuilding relations with the United States. Moreover, Tài's observation on the selective use of American constructs by Vietnamese officials was confirmed in my own analysis of Vietnamese press discourse: while the English-language *Việt Nam News* commonly employed stock phrases such as "heal the wounds of war" and "reconcile with the past" when referring to U.S.–Vietnamese relations, such terminology was rarely employed in Vietnamese-language newspapers unless quoting an American source.

In addition to aspirations for economic betterment, differing cultural understandings of healing emerged during interviews with men and women involved in collaborative projects and programs. Tuyết, a professor who works with U.S. exchange students in Hanoi, used the example of pilgrimage to former war sites to elucidate divergent healing practices: "[Vietnamese veterans] return to battlefields in search of missing bodies.[16] They want to bring the remains of the war dead home so that their families and others may heal. U.S. veterans return for different reasons; they want to see the battlefield again, or give money to rebuild the location where they fought." Drawing a diagram, she illustrated what she saw as incommensurable cultural practices of healing:

> Americans heal by returning to build things for Vietnam, such as schools or hospitals. Vietnamese, on the other hand, heal by going to the front to search for missing remains. When they return the remains it helps the family to heal, which in turn helps the veteran to heal. So U.S. healing is very direct, while Vietnamese healing is indirect.

Yet, despite these different conceptual approaches to "healing" and "reconciliation," both U.S. and Vietnamese perspectives involved reworkings of the past that relied on similar tactics and practices of memory, that is, veterans from both countries have returned to the battlefield. Moreover, both perspectives revolved around experiences and discourses of shared sentiments, trauma, and camaraderie.

Tình Cảm: *Sentimental Solidarities*

In this section I return to Hà's suggestion of solidarity and her idea that "there is no hate between people, only governments." This is, of course, a broad gloss that oversimplifies extremely complex, unresolved, and ambivalent feelings in Vietnam toward the United States and its citizens. During my fieldwork, when animosity and indifference surfaced, it was often in nebulous, indirect, and sometimes contradictory ways that revealed personal struggles between forgiveness (as official discourse) and resentment (as personal sentiment).[17] The role and form of such ambivalence at public sites of memory will inform many subsequent discussions in this book. Here, I examine not expressions of animosity, but the opposite: pronouncements of camaraderie, particularly between U.S. and Vietnamese veterans, based on a sense of connectedness at having both experienced and lived through the trauma of war. Like Clinton's speech at Hanoi National University, research respondents in Hanoi often referred to the "shared sadness" [*chia buồn*] between people in Vietnam and the United States that resulted in a unique and sympathetic relationship. "No one can understand Vietnam like Americans," Văn, who had been a university student during the war, explained. This sentiment was most often expressed in the words *tình cảm*, used by interviewees to signify strong emotional and heartfelt ties among citizens of both countries. For example, *tình cảm* was used to suggest an especially close affinity that bonded Vietnamese and American women who suffered the loss of sons or husbands in the war.[18]

Tình cảm was often used by respondents to explain the seeming lack of public animosity toward U.S. veteran returnees. However, as Tuyết, the college professor, pointed out, such sentiments and attempts at empathy are relatively recent. Since the mid-1990s, the Vietnamese press has contributed to growing public awareness of joint U.S.-Vietnamese reconciliatory meetings and activities between veterans. Such coverage reflects a greater accessibility to, and interest in, diverse transnational perspectives on the war that have prompted new ways of thinking about and under-standing the past. For example, a series of articles (sometimes translated from over-seas sources, such as the Associated Press [AP]) published in newspapers and maga-zines in the months leading up to the twenty-fifth anniversary of the end of the war in 2000 focused on topics including reasons why U.S. soldiers fought in Vietnam, the postwar lives of U.S. troops, returning veterans involved in humanitarian proj-ects, and delegations of "former enemies" who have met again on the battlefield, this time as friends.[19] Images that accompanied these latter reports showed aging, smiling veterans sitting alongside one another and sometimes shaking hands. Ac-cording to Tuyết, there was almost no coverage of U.S. veterans in the Vietnamese press before normalization in 1995, when it became a more common media trend:

> You can now find many articles that discuss the war from a U.S. perspective. In the past this was never possible; articles only criticized the United States. Now journalists try to see and present the other side. These days we read many sto-ries about how U.S. soldiers suffered and were forced to come here when they were young. We know that most did not want to fight in Vietnam.

An ironic discourse of solidarity emerged here, not unlike that suggested by Hà at the beginning of this chapter—the idea that U.S. soldiers, akin to the Vietnamese people, were victims of U.S. imperial designs, first forced to fight in a war against their will, and thereafter subjected to difficult and impoverished living conditions. The broad circulation of this information via the mass media influenced how U.S. veterans were received as they journeyed through the country. In interviews and conversations, U.S. returnees frequently commented on feeling overwhelmed and deeply moved by what they felt to be a nonhostile and welcome reception in Viet-nam, which they understood as the exceptional capacity of Vietnamese people to forgive.[20] Unexpectedly warm interactions with local residents (at times contrasted with lingering hostility back home) emerged as key to veteran healing narratives. A seemingly forgiving stance was explained by U.S. and Vietnamese respondents as the outcome of having experienced and lived through similar traumatic events.

In the words of John: "You see, only vets understand the pain of fighting a war. So a close bond is formed with the Vietnamese that other Americans cannot have."

Shared memories of a particular moment of violence, for example, bound veterans together in unforeseen ways. Rob, a veteran involved in a U.S.–Vietnamese theater project that used the performative arts as a medium through which to reconcile the past, recounted a story of attending a party in the United States for the Vietnamese cast at the end of the U.S. tour. Rob and another U.S. veteran had been talking to a Vietnamese actor, also a veteran and a former performer for liberation troops during the war, when the topic switched to an event that had taken place during a battle in the district of Củ Chi. Abruptly, Rob's friend and the Vietnamese veteran realized that they had witnessed the same incident, though as adversaries from opposing sides: "It was really weird. They stopped talking and just looked at each other like, wow!" John's and Rob's expressions of sharedness and unity in a *transnational* community of traumatic memory is unique in its constitution *across* former enemy lines and *across* national borders, thus contributing to shared imaginings of fraternal camaraderie and sentimental solidarity (Erikson 1995, 186).

Yet if it is true that certain bonds are formed between people who have collectively experienced traumatic events, as scholars have suggested, then in the case of the war in Vietnam, we should expect to find sentiments of empathy and expressions of unity not only between U.S. troops and revolutionary forces, but also with the soldiers of the Army of the Republic of Vietnam (ARVN). Yet this was not necessarily the case. In fact, ARVN veterans were conspicuously absent from most of these reconciliation projects and healing endeavors. They were not, for example, represented in the Vietnamese mass media in articles or images of reconciliation gatherings and delegations. They were, for the most part, excluded from veteran recollections of working on collaborative projects or meeting former enemies. In effect, they were disregarded participants in a war that is often framed and reductively remembered as a conflict primarily between the United States and "North Vietnam" (also eliding southern revolutionary memory). This relative absence serves to maintain a dominant historical discourse and memory of the past as a war between communism and anticommunism (in U.S. historical memory) or, in Vietnamese official memory, as a war against American imperialism in which ARVN soldiers served merely as puppet troops.

The degree to which trauma or sorrow can be shared across cultural, national, political, and other divisions raises a host of complex questions. To what extent can trauma be co-experienced? How do we take into account different subject positions in the production of experience, subjectivity, and situated relationships to the past (Scott 1991)? Research on trauma has examined both the incommunicability of pain and suffering (see Scarry 1985) and its transmissibility (Das 2006). What does it mean to "feel" or "understand" the pain of others? While there are clearly important personal and social reconciliation processes at work when Vietnamese and American respondents pointed to the sharedness of experience and memory; yet, in doing so, they also elided vast inequalities that underpin wartime and postwar suffering. The "Vietnamese Heroic Mothers" [*Bà Mẹ Việt Nam Anh Hùng*] exhibit at the Military History Museum in Hanoi conveys to viewers the immense loss of human lives and its impact on women, namely mothers. Small portraits of elderly women arranged according to province are displayed on the exhibit walls. Under each image is the honored mother's name, the district where she lives, and the number of children sacrificed [*hy sinh*] in the war. Heroic mothers represented in the exhibit on average lost three to four sons or daughters, though several list eight or more children, with special attention given to a mother who lost eleven.[21] In the accompanying text it is pointed out that Hanoi alone has 681 heroic mothers, while there are 41,624 throughout the country (as of 1998). The vast disproportion between loss of life in Vietnam and in the United States is further suggested in the estimated numbers of war dead: more than 58,000 U.S. forces and well over 1.3 million Vietnamese troops.[22] What I want to suggest here is that employing a discourse of "sharedness" and *not* taking into account these and other disparities in suffering risks minimizing or neglecting tremendous discrepancies in wartime and postwar trauma and dislocation. It also risks maintaining U.S. memory of war as a specifically U.S. *historical* tragedy from which one can now heal, rather than an *ongoing* legacy in Vietnam that continues to inflict new wounds.

On Moral Memories

I close this chapter with a short story told to me by Hà:

> There was an American soldier who was badly wounded in a battle. He crawled and crawled until he collapsed outside the house of a woman who was living alone because all her sons and husband were off fighting the war. The woman found the soldier and took care of him until he died. Then she dug a grave and buried him. Twenty years later, the parents of this soldier came to Vietnam and visited the woman. She was still alone; all her family had been killed in the war. She showed the soldier's parents where his remains were buried, and they dug up the grave to take them home. The parents offered to give the old woman some money but she said, "No! I looked after him like a son. I did not care for

him for money. I am a mother and treated him as my child, as I too lost children in the war." This, you see, is Vietnamese culture. In order to understand Vietnamese history, one must also understand culture.

In the current context of expanding, and yet ambivalent, relations between Vietnam and the United States, Hà's story provides key insights into how Vietnamese citizens construct moral memories of the war and imagine postwar reconciliatory processes. The Vietnamese mother's kindness in tending to the injured U.S. soldier and providing him with a proper burial illustrates both moral acts of remembrance and discourses of shared sorrow and forgiveness that Hà and others referred to. The journey of the American mother to Vietnam and her success in finding the remains of her son metaphorically suggests processes of healing and of finding closure that many U.S. veterans and their family members presumably seek when they travel to Vietnam. Moreover, the story gestures toward the "common bonds" between women who, as mothers, have "shared" the sorrow of losing their sons to war, even while the narrative makes obvious certain discrepancies in suffering (the lone Vietnamese woman who lost her entire family and the American woman who searches with her husband for the remains of one son).

A few years later I came across this same story in the *Vietnamese Literature Review* published with the title "Under the Bamboo Grove" by Trần Thanh Giao (1999). Unlike Hà's narration, Trần Thanh Giao's version emphasized more the disparities in suffering between the two women by contrasting the American mother's closure at finding her son's remains with the Vietnamese mother's anguish and continued search for the missing body of her youngest son. Where one finds peace and brings war to an end, another continues to silently suffer its legacy. Personal reconciliation—coming to terms with the past through locating the remains of her child—becomes a metaphor for national reconciliation with Vietnam. The story ends with the mother's joyful declaration: "It's thanks to this wonderful trip that I now understand better the Vietnamese people and their country. I now understand why you won the war" (Trần Thanh Giao 1999, 184). As in Hà's narrative, a moral victory over the United States is achieved through humane and moral practices that engender historical and cultural comprehensibility. As a symbol of her nation, the American mother symbolically accepts, unconditionally, U.S. defeat; her cultural and historical enlightenment permits her to recognize Vietnamese moral and military triumph, and to realize the humanity—rather than the barbarity—of the Vietnamese people as co-sufferers and not only as enemies.

Yet this moral victory has begun to unravel in recent years with the realization that the United States is not necessarily ready or entirely willing to move in a direction toward historical accountability. The postnormalization image of the repenting and weeping U.S. veteran on his knees, *"với tâm trạng ân hận,"* with the mood of regret, as Hà wrote in her notebook in 2000, has all but disappeared several years later. Ambivalence toward reconciliation and ongoing historical-ideological contestations have contributed to the collapse of moralizing accounts and images of returning U.S. veterans. This shift emerged most clearly in two interviews conducted with Hương, a director at the War Remnants Museum mentioned by Hà at the beginning of the chapter. In 2000, Hương described U.S. veterans who contacted her and visited the museum as traumatized upon seeing the exhibits, often weeping and apologizing for immoral acts committed during the war, not unlike Hà's representation. In 2004, however, Hương had reversed her sentiment: "The number of U.S. veterans who visit the museum is increasing. But they usually deny any wrongdoing . . . They say they were a doctor or nurse or electrician—someone who was not responsible. They are afraid to tell the truth." She then contrasted this embattled relationship with the past and the denial of culpability with the return of other veterans who fought in the war and now return to Vietnam to express their remorse: "More Australian and Korean veterans now come to the museum and contact me. I have worked closely with many of them. They cry, especially the Korean veterans—they cry very hard."

Exhibiting War, Reconciling Pasts

Photojournalism and Divergent Visual Histories

CHAPTER TWO

In April 2000, in celebration of the "twenty-fifth anniversary of the liberation of the south and the reunification of the country" [*kỷ niệm hai mươi lăm năm ngày giải phóng miền Nam, thống nhất đất nước*], the War Remnants Museum in Ho Chi Minh City opened a two-week international photography exhibit, "Requiem—the Vietnam Collection [*Hồi Niệm—Bộ Sưu Tập Ảnh về Chiến Tranh Việt Nam*]." The exhibit displayed the works of 135 photojournalists from twelve nations who were killed in action between 1954 and 1975 in the wars in Vietnam, Cambodia, and Laos. This chapter uses the "Requiem" exhibit as a case study to map out the diverse and often divergent historical truths and visual records of war that the images in the collection produced when juxtaposed with one another. I compare and contrast the representational practices of revolutionary and nonrevolutionary photojournalists, calling attention to the discordant ways in which Vietnamese subjects are constituted (or not) as historical agents, and the ways in which Vietnamese photographic practices challenge and defy many of the assumptions and conventions of U.S. objective journalism.

In what follows, I seek to contribute to a small but growing body of literature on Vietnamese-produced images of war and their diverse social and cultural meanings.[1] Until recently, scholarship has primarily analyzed U.S. popular memory and cultural productions that evoke the Vietnam War.[2] This trend is also seen in research on war and the mass media, which has focused almost exclusively on non-Vietnamese correspondents and their journalistic practices and representations of Vietnam.[3] In recent years there has been growing interest in the United States in stories from "the other side," that is, from Vietnamese, revolutionary photojournalists whose work had previously circulated within transnational socialist networks but was little known in the United States.[4] Encouraged by the mounting international attention to their work, several Vietnamese war photographers subsequently published collections of their own work with Vietnamese publishing houses either in book form or as postcard collections.[5] These bilingual (Vietnamese-English) and sometimes trilingual (Vietnamese-French-English) texts are sold today in Vietnam in city bookstores and museums for upwards of 250,000VNĐ (approximately $15US), thus signifying popular trends in the international consumption of memories of the war, as well as intensified domestic consumption of diverse wartime images and narratives.[6]

Visual images of the war in both U.S. and Vietnamese media have powerfully shaped historical memory, as well as ensuing struggles over meaning. As scholars remind us, all journalistic images of warfare, regardless of the photographer, are produced within certain structural limitations and ideological frameworks that offer only partial and situated historical insights rather than transparent historical truths, understandings, and accuracies. Barbie Zelizer, for example, has examined the limited representativeness of images from the Holocaust that became abstract signifiers of war and atrocity rather than tools to impart substantive and specific historical knowledge (1998, 118).[7] Likewise, photographs of the war in Vietnam (from all sides) provide only fragmented knowledge of wartime violence and select glimpses into its complexities. Moreover, the meanings and significance of such images are never fixed but shift according to new contexts of viewing and new interpretations of the past (Hagopian 2006). It is perhaps unsurprising that photojournalists who supported the revolution told very different war stories through their images than those who did not. Yet analyses of their collections, including photographs on display in "Requiem," show that these men and women were not only involved in the ongoing production of news of the war, but they were also photographer-ethnographers who documented the everyday, routine aspects of lives in wartime. Contrary to representations of violence and suffering portrayed in the United States, and in western media more broadly, Vietnamese photographs reveal to the viewer a broad array of combat experiences that include but are not limited to trauma and the destruction of war. That is, rather than focusing exclusively on atrocities and death, their images also provide insights into more sanguine and leisurely moments in war, and occasionally even fleeting romantic encounters that photographers caught on film. Vietnamese photographers thus bring our attention to the specificities of everyday life under constant threat of violence as the boundaries between the ordinary and the violent became increasingly blurred (Das 2006, 7). This visual history contrasts sharply with the graphically violent photographs of the war that were published in the western press (and also displayed at "Requiem"), thus challenging implicit assumptions that suffering is the fundamental social experience and core representation of war.

In addition, this chapter situates war photography in general, and the "Requiem" photographs in particular, within changing landscapes of memory, entangled in the transnational politics of reconciliation and normalization. Attention to specific practices of historical memory involved in the production of the exhibit reveals subtle and oft-unspoken tensions and ambivalences in reconciliatory processes between the United States and Vietnam. Through its juxtaposition of images from the "winning" and "losing" sides of the war, "Requiem" created a multifaceted, transnational space of historical reflection and knowledge production. Yet this was not an unbounded site for reconfiguring and reconciling the past. Historical memories, knowledge, and sensibilities were shaped and delimited by negotiations between Vietnamese and U.S.-based organizers with regard to the selection, arrangement, and display of exhibit materials. I argue that the diverse visual records produced by revolutionary and nonrevolutionary photographers killed in the wars not only suggest distinct styles of representation and remembrance. When exhibited alongside one another in the context of postreform Vietnam and analyzed against the backdrop of shifting U.S.-Vietnam relations, the images and their accompanying texts also resurrect and reproduce several competing political convictions and ideological beliefs central to the war that continue to circulate in certain public spheres today.

"Requiem—the Vietnam Collection"

In April 2000, scores of international journalists descended upon Vietnam for the twenty-fifth anniversary of end of the "anti-U.S. resistance for national salvation" [kháng chiến chống Mỹ cứu nước] that took place on April 30, 1975. In Ho Chi Minh City, journalists flocked to old wartime haunts, such as the Rex Hotel, previously known for its "five o'clock follies," the daily military press briefing, and the Caravelle, now a premier five-star accommodation. The excitement of the occasion was propelled by nostalgic visions of wartime Saigon and the return of celebrity veteran correspondents. U.S. media were there not only to cover government-organized events marking the anniversary but also to discover what had become of Vietnam since the "fall" of Saigon.[8] For the U.S. press, Vietnam ceased to be a newsworthy country when it ceased to exist as a war.[9] As Nora Alter has suggested, "It is as if Vietnam had no history before the American occupation and none thereafter" (1997, 45).[10] Post-1975 cultural production of social memory in the United States largely revolved around films, memoirs, and other commemorative expressions that reinforced narcissistic myths of the war as a U.S. tragedy, overlooking its devastating and long-term consequences for Vietnam, Cambodia, and Laos, and thus hampering public discourse about postwar reparations and responsibilities (Sturken 1997a, 63). That the Vietnamese people were left to recover from a devastating war and rebuild their nation was forgotten by much of the U.S. public, as well as the press. The barrage of media coverage subsequently put Vietnam back on the front pages of the U.S. press in magazines such as *Newsweek*, *People*, and *U.S. News & World Report*.

Ho Chi Minh City celebrated April 30, 2000, with a series of political and cultural events. Outside Reunification Palace, the former presidential palace of the Republic of Vietnam (RVN), an early morning parade commemorating Vietnam's military victories, as well as its recent economic progress, launched the day's events. Afternoon and evening festivities in the city center marked a shift from political to cultural production, with acrobatic dances, drumming performances, fashion shows, and music concerts. These events predominantly attracted Vietnamese spectators, including families and groups of youths, who gathered in the streets to enjoy the revelry.

On May 5, as part of the ongoing anniversary events, the War Remnants Museum in Ho Chi Minh City opened the exhibit "Requiem—the Vietnam Collection." This exhibition was based on the 1997 book, *Requiem: By the Photographers Who Died in Vietnam and Indochina*, edited by Horst Faas and Tim Page, two photojournalists who had covered the war in Vietnam and who had now returned for the twenty-fifth anniversary.[11] "Requiem—the Vietnam Collection" had been organized and assembled by the Kentucky Requiem Project Steering Committee, chaired by Richard Lennon, a veteran Marine Corps officer who had served in the war in Vietnam in 1968, in collaboration with Horst Faas and the Indochina Photo Requiem Project, Ltd.[12] The exhibit, containing 302 photographs, was first shown at the Kentucky History Center in Frankfort, Kentucky, from October 1 until November 14, 1999, after which it was packed into fourteen crates and flown to Vietnam. Working in conjunction with the Vietnam News Agency and the Vietnam Association of Photographic Artists, the fifteen-person Kentucky Requiem Project Steering Committee secured the necessary financial support to bring the exhibit to Hanoi, where it opened to large crowds on March 10, 2000.

"Requiem" was distinct from other anniversary events taking place in Ho Chi Minh City. As a transnational memorial that honored war photographers regardless of nationality, political orientation, or press affiliation, it presented a united front of photojournalists who died in pursuit of "truth." This is significant insofar as it provided a space for the public recognition and remembrance of nonrevolutionary southern Vietnamese casualties who have been excluded from official historical narratives and state commemorative ceremonies in Vietnam. It was also a space for U.S. viewers to commemorate Vietnamese (rather than only U.S.) fatalities, particularly those of rival forces. Moreover, with its theme of "hope, healing and history" [*hy vọng, hàn gắn và lịch sử*], the exhibit reflected the efforts and desires of the people of Kentucky to reconcile the past and rebuild cooperative relations between the United States and Vietnam. At the opening ceremony in Ho Chi Minh City, Horst Faas announced that the collection of photographs would be presented to the Vietnamese people "as an offering of peace" from the citizens of Kentucky, thus positioning "Requiem" as an example of a transnational healing project embedded in discourses of shared, sorrowful pasts and reconciled, collaborative futures.[13]

The ceremony to launch the exhibit took place in the courtyard of the War Remnants Museum at 9:30 on a hot and humid morning. There were roughly one hundred people in attendance, most of whom were family members of the deceased photojournalists and Vietnamese reporters covering the event. Approximately one dozen representatives from the international press were also present, as well as a few tourists who happened to be visiting the museum at that time. In the front row, under a blue canopy that shielded attendees from the glaring sun, sat Horst Faas and Tim Page between city government officials, representatives from the museum, and an infirm, state-titled heroic mother. Next to the podium was an ensemble of twenty male musicians clothed in starched white uniforms, their instruments at their sides. The first speaker, a city official, reflected on the numerous projects to promote peace that had taken place in recent years. "We must put aside the past," he urged, "but each April 30 the memories return." Mention was made of the 135 war photographers killed and the sacrifices they had made. The official called for a moment of reflection at two different points in his speech; the first for former Prime Minister Phạm Văn Đồng, who had passed away a week before on April 29, and the second, for all the deceased photojournalists. The latter moment was accompanied by a soft and melodious tune in honor of the dead. Horst Faas then took the podium and stressed that the war had taken place not only in Vietnam but also in Cambodia and Laos. The exhibit was not about nostalgia, he told the audience; rather, it was a "permanent memorial" meant to celebrate the photographers and their achievements. References to "us" and "the communists" peppered his speech, reducing the complexities of the war and the convictions of the photographers to polar opposites: communist and noncommunist. At one point Faas spoke of the distinct photographic techniques used by "us" and "them," but "these differences were removed when they shared the fate of death." The collective deaths of the photojournalists thus signified the potential for total reconciliation and transcendence of "difference" to which the organizers aspired.

"Requiem" was hailed as the first international photo exhibition to display "both sides" of the war. The interpretation of the war as a conflict between communist revolutionaries and their noncommunist adversaries, evident in Faas's opening speech, was further buttressed by the division of photojournalists into two categories: those who worked for the western press, for example, the Associated Press (AP) or the United Press International (UPI), and those who worked for the revolutionary press, such as the Vietnam News Agency (VNA) or the Liberation News Agency (LNA). In a system of classification originally espoused in the book by Faas and Page, photojournalists from the revolutionary press were identified as belonging to the country "Vietnam." Nonrevolutionary Vietnamese correspondents who worked for the western press were grouped under "South Vietnam," which was included with a list of foreign countries that lost photographers: France, the United States, Japan, Austria, Britain, Australia, Switzerland, Cambodia, Germany, and Singapore.[14] As will be demonstrated below, the distinct ideological underpinnings of the western press and Vietnamese press gave shape to vastly different subject positions and visual histories of the war.

Paradoxes and Moral Dilemmas in Western Photojournalism

Since the Crimean War in the mid–nineteenth century, cameras have been present to document warfare and record combat (Knightley 2004 [1975]).[15] However, it wasn't until the Vietnam War that photography was identified as a powerful tool that swayed public opinion in the United States. In what was called the "first living room war" (and, it seems, the last), media coverage of dead American—and to a lesser extent Vietnamese—bodies, burning villages, and graphic violence fueled the antiwar movement and arguably reversed public sentiment on the war.[16] Disturbing images from the war proved difficult to forget and many photographs took on a fetishized quality as cultural and political icons, or as symbols of the inhumanity and futility of war. This has been the case, for example, of the haunting photograph by Huỳnh Công (Nick) Út of Phan Thị Kim Phúc—the young Vietnamese girl who ran down the street toward the photographer, screaming as her body burned with napalm. Such cultural representations of war have been imprinted in U.S. minds, and they continue to resurface in new contexts, "subject to a range of appropriations that comprise a continuing negotiation of American public culture" and a "continuing struggle over the meaning of the Vietnam War" (Hariman and Lucaites 2007, 200).[17]

It has often been argued that rather than arousing empathy, repetitive exposure to media images of violence may in fact desensitize and disengage the viewer. The media onslaught of images of human tragedy, they argue, often turns the grief and anguish of others into "infotainment," that is, commercialized and commodified representations of suffering and trauma that dehistoricize and depersonalize violence (Kleinman and Kleinman 1997). Overexposure to these mediated spectacles inadvertently sets higher standards for newsworthy events—more risky, more dramatic, more sensational—eventually culminating in "compassion fatigue" marked by boredom, disinterest, and forgetfulness (Moeller 1999; Sontag 2003, 1990 [1977]). Herein lies the paradox of photography: images of distant suffering intended to elicit compassion and spread knowledge about violence may lead to indifference, inaction, or absence of pity (Boltanski 1999). In his comparative work on television images of the wars in Vietnam and Iraq, Andrew Hoskins links this process to the "collapse of memory." He writes: "[H]arrowing photographs and footage may endure in memory, but the circumstances of those images and the story they once told become detached through their repetition and familiarity" (2004, 11). This is not to deny the power of photojournalism to convey certain knowledges about war or to stir social consciousness and mobilize political subjectivities (J. Taylor 1998; Starrett 2003). However, as a visual modality of power, the camera risks objectifying and depoliticizing its subject (Sontag 1990 [1977], 41)—as I argue below with regard to representations of tormented and abused Vietnamese bodies in the western press—even while its images may also heighten moral awareness and public criticism (see also Klima 2002, 188–198).

The intersections of photography and social suffering inevitably invoke a moral quandary about the political and moral responsibilities of witnessing (Zelizer 1998; J. Taylor 1998). A journalist's decision to photograph a moment of death or to capture terror and anguish on film raises complex ethical issues, as there is a paradoxical participation—taking the picture—through a lack of participation—not offering to help but recording the act. In his ethnography of foreign war correspondents in El Salvador, Mark Pedelty describes reporters' "near-addiction to violence" as they greedily photograph a corpse: "For these 'participant observers' violence is not a matter of 'values' in the moral sense of the term, but instead 'value' in the economic. They need terror to realize themselves in both a professional and spiritual sense, to achieve and maintain their culture identity as 'war correspondents'" (1995, 2). Indeed, combat photographers are often rewarded for their professionalism and ability to maintain composure when confronted with atrocities and devastation. Award-winning photographs of war are valued for their candid, shocking subject matter precisely because the photographer chose for a brief moment not to get involved but to take a picture that could then be widely disseminated as "information." Denise Chong, for example, describes the reactions of the photojournalists who witnessed Kim Phúc's agony and burning body—their desire to help compromised by concerns with deadlines and competition (2000, 68–69).[18] Such momentary expressions of self-interest are indicative of the capitalist cult of objectivity that motivates much western, especially U.S., journalism, reflecting the belief that an "objective" and uninvolved stance is needed to produce informed, "balanced" (and hence profitable) news.[19]

The western journalist's role as detached moral witness is closely linked to a sensationalized idea of war zones as masculinized spaces of risks, thrills, and brushes with death that break with the monotony of everyday life (Pedelty 1995, 136–138; Parameswaran 2006). In Vietnam, this world of "living on the edge" was largely contingent upon the exclusion of female correspondents from the field (only three photojournalists killed in the wars in Vietnam were women: Lê Thị Năng and Ngọc Hương from Vietnam, and Dickey Chapelle from the United States)[20] and upon subjectivities shaped by masculine discourses of adventure, danger, and fearlessness. In literature on Vietnam, this is most apparent in Michael Herr's *Dispatches* (1977), which narrates an archetypal male journalist's zealous immersion in the war. Such journalistic vigor also surfaced at the "Requiem" exhibit in a passage that provided an overview of photography during the war: "Some [western photographers] stayed on for the glory, the money, the thrill. Others returned, again and again, because it was the place to be." Western photojournalist subjectivities are thus represented as closely entangled with the valuation (if not the fetishization) of risk and atrocity, their work dependent upon the suffering bodies that become the photographic object of their "thrill."

Vietnamese Photographic Practices and Representations of War

During wartime, the roles, practices, and subjectivities of Vietnamese correspondents who supported the revolution differed considerably from those of foreign reporters. While most journalists for the western press were in Vietnam on a voluntary basis and could walk away from the battlefield and Vietnam if they so desired, the freedom to leave their country and the war was not an option for Vietnamese photographers, who documented combat and noncombat operations for years at a time, some returning home only after 1975. Moreover, while western press photographers were generally engaged in temporally and spatially bounded, event-driven coverage, for Vietnamese photojournalists, the war demanded a long-term commitment and everyday immersion in dangerous zones of conflict, where they lived, labored, and sometimes fought alongside their photographic subjects, facing severe hardships and often imminent death. Of the 135 photographers killed in action, more than 50 percent (a total of 72) were from Vietnam, a number that does not include four nonrevolutionary photojournalists from the RVN.

There were also differences when it came to the meaning and intent behind their various photographic practices. Unlike reporters working for the western press, most of whom were independent of the war effort and thus regarded as "objective" outside observers, Vietnamese correspondents were considered cultural soldiers of the revolution, whose weapons consisted of pencils, paper, and, in the case of photojournalists, cameras (Hồ Chí Minh 2004, 243; Nguyễn Tiến Mão 2006, 76). In interviews and conversations, photographers stressed the importance of photography to serve [*phục vụ*] the country, denounce [*tố cáo*] the war to national and international audiences, and transmit and propagate [*tuyên truyền*] information from the front. But they also emphasized their multivalent roles as cultural producers immersed in the social worlds of the people who were their subject matter. They endeavored to show the crimes, destruction, and techniques of war, as well as the cooperation, compassion, and social interactions among soldiers and villagers. Vietnamese photojournalists frequently emphasized the close connections they had to the people with whom they lived and worked, and whom they photographed—relations that continue to be important today. Contrary to western journalist discourse, they did not talk about objectivity, yet like their western counterparts, they emphasized their agency and choice in photographing diverse aspects of people's lives and experiences in wartime.

Divergences in conceptualization and implementation of their work influenced the kinds of representations Vietnamese photojournalists ultimately produced. Unlike the graphic images of trauma and death routinely displayed in the global media, images in Vietnam also reflected optimistic and hopeful futures, as well as the everyday, routine present. This broader approach to constituting a visual history of the war differs from western practices of "objective journalism" that find journalistic value and truth in documenting wartime casualties. Such practices implicitly assume that capturing devastation on film is the most authentic manifestation of objective realism—what might be termed "capitalist realism" (Schudson 1984)—based on the belief that free and open access to violence signifies neutral, balanced, and truthful information. When violence is not given adequate representation or is altogether absent, then it is no longer "reality" that is presumed to comprise the content, but "ideology" or "propaganda"—terms that are often applied in the West to artistic and photographic expressions deemed "socialist realist" (an expression rarely used by my research respondents). What drives and shapes much capitalist realism, particularly in times of war, is an attraction to idiosyncrasies and irony rather than to the mundane and routine. This reinforces the belief that suffering should constitute the primary focus of photographic documentation of warfare; indeed, suffering is often assumed to constitute a universal mode of representation. However, during the war, Vietnamese photojournalism was not predicated on violence and disaster alone, but upon the placement of suffering within a broader spectrum of wartime experiences and subjectivities, and it thus produced a more extensive and informative visual history. These differing practices and logic of visuality resonate with Martin Jay's observation that the "scopic regime of modernity may be best understood as a contested terrain . . . [and] may in fact, be characterized by a differentiation of visual subcultures" (1988, 4).[21]

As in many other nations, images of past wars reverberate and continue to circulate in political, social, and pedagogical spaces in Vietnam. Museums, in particular, exhibit Vietnamese photographs of the war that are also reproduced in history textbooks, current mass media, popular culture, and sites of state commemoration. Official narratives of the American War are encoded in images that symbolize national heroism and sacrifice, rather than individual memories of hardship, loss, and trauma. Contrary to the graphically violent photographs that in the United States narrate the history of the war as moral and political failure, images displayed in Vietnamese museums depict the virtues, hopes, labors, and triumphs of the revolution to produce a narrative of progressive and total victory [*toàn thắng*].

With certain exceptions, there is a conspicuous absence of death and suffering in the collections of war photography displayed in Vietnamese museums.[22] When harrowing images are used, they are usually few in number or confined to special displays, such as the "War Crimes" display box in the Military History Museum in Hanoi, where photographs of torture committed by the Ngô Đình Diệm regime are juxtaposed in a montage. More often, museum exhibits provide viewers with ethnographic glimpses into the diverse concerns and creative activities of villagers and soldiers as they went about their daily lives under the persistent threat of wartime violence. Not infrequently, images show optimistic moments of joy or flickers of hope, often captured in smiles that mark special occasions or victorious celebrations (Figure 2.1).[23] Other photographs reveal playful, tender, and leisurely moments, such as music performances in underground tunnels and theatrical events beneath the jungle canopy. Romantic and flirtatious encounters captured on film offer additional insights into the complexity of social and affective relations during the war (Figure 2.2).

In addition to themes of joy, play, and even love, images in Vietnamese museums regularly show acts of labor and preparation for war, providing a visual testimony to Vietnam's historical and heroic "spirit of resistance to foreign aggression" (Pelley 2002, 140–147). Journalists, for example, often photographed antiaircraft artillery units poised to fire or female militia toiling in the rice fields, their weapons on their backs. Other images displayed in exhibits, such as youth volunteer forces clearing roads on the Ho Chi Minh Trail, bring attention to the highly organized and disciplined labor units that assisted in the defense of the nation. Representa-

FIGURE 2.1. Victory smile by the ancient citadel of Quảng Trị. 1972.
Photograph by Đoàn Công Tính. Courtesy of Đoàn Công Tính.

FIGURE 2.2. On the way to war. Undated. Photograph by Đoàn Công Tính.
Courtesy of Đoàn Công Tính.

tions of the diverse contributions of men and women, young and old, as they engaged in agricultural production, covert acts of resistance, or battle campaigns at the front lines offer visual insights into the strategies and workings of a people's war (Võ Nguyên Giáp 1962). Furthermore, these images reinforce discourses of unity and solidarity as central to the war effort, as evident in photographs taken during or immediately after combat that foreground action and victory rather than casualties. Even when injured troops are present, the emphasis is on camaraderie (such as tending to their wounds) rather than on their pain and suffering.[24]

In interviews and conversations, photojournalists explained the displacement of violence and death in their images by referring to the multiple experiences and processes of war and its shifting states of affect. In Ho Chi Minh City, one veteran LNA photojournalist handed me a photograph of a young couple and child relaxing in a hammock in front of a burnt tank, entitled "Happiness." He explained: "Of course there are joyful moments in war. It is not only about fighting battles; there are also quiet times. My images show the many sides of life in war, including entertainment." In Hanoi, a photographer who had spent ten years on the Ho Chi Minh Trail compared his images of Vietnamese troops maintaining roads and transporting supplies with photographs of atrocities in the international press: "Western photographers were interested in the fierceness of war and they photographed many dead people. But why do we need to look at such images? It's not respectful. We know that war is fierce and that people are killed. Do we need to see it over and over again? There is more to photograph in war than death." When I asked Hà, the staff member at the Museum of the Vietnamese Revolution in Hanoi, why, in her opinion, museums tend not to display violent images of war and use terms such as "glorious" to refer to a traumatic history, she also contrasted Vietnamese and western styles of representation: "That is because we were victorious and we were right. You must understand that Vietnam has a long history of foreign invasion. You don't have the same history. Who has invaded your country? So we are very proud to have won our wars. And we were right to fight them. That is the difference with the United States. While you have many pictures of death, we celebrate our victory." The multiple subject and moral positions that Hà refers to here (defenders and aggressors) map onto distinct modes of representing and commemorating the past: while the victors rejoice in their triumph through representations of life, the vanquished mourn their defeat through images of death.

There are also political-ideological motivations for the general absence of images of suffering and death in Vietnam, just as there are such motivations in the United States for including them.[25] Insofar as the Vietnamese state regularly invokes memories of war to commemorate and keep the spirit of the revolution alive, as well as to transmit knowledge of the past to postwar generations, there is political interest in emphasizing victorious achievements and collective acts of solidarity. Historically, artistic and cultural production thought to embody and represent the spirit of the people was deemed central to the Vietnamese revolution and to the project of constructing a new socialist society, as espoused by Communist Party leaders such as Trường Chinh (1997 [1948]) and Lê Duẩn (1977). Today such images are also seen as a necessary means to educate and motivate the youth. A war photographer with the People's Army of Vietnam (PAVN) who held an exhibit at Hanoi's Military History Museum in December 1999 (then called the Army Museum) underscored the pedagogical function of his images: "Photographs from the war carry meaning about the past. . . . I want students who come to my exhibit to learn to hate war, but they should also learn about the brave deaths of those who sacrificed their lives. When they see these pictures, they will understand the need to continue the work to build and develop the country." Photography is thus imagined to bridge the widening gaps between the past and the future, between generations who experienced war and generations born in its aftermath, who are growing up in an era of expanding global capitalist integration and who presumably no longer understand the sacrifices of their elders.

Although images of war continue to have currency among certain cultural-political networks and institutions, such as museums, in other spaces prominent social discourses that disregard the trauma of war are gradually being dislodged as cultural producers rethink aesthetic canons and prevailing artistic and literary modes of historical representation. In contemporary literature, popular novels by Dương Thu Hương (1996), Nguyễn Huy Thiệp (1992), and Bảo Ninh (1993) have contributed to an emerging genre that challenges revolutionary heroism and explores the bleakness and hardships of war rather than its glories. For example, Bảo Ninh's popular novel *The Sorrow of War* (1993) defies the prevalent image of heroic and enthusiastic soldiers in combat. Rather, he explores the horrors of the battlefield—the fear, smell, and taste of death that permeated the solemn air for years—thus giving representation to individual suffering in a broader context of pervasive social trauma.

Knowledge Production and Competing Historical Memories at "Requiem"

After opening formalities had come to a close on May 5, 2000, the doors to the exhibit opened. I entered, made my way through the crowds of journalists, officials, tourists, and family members of those killed in action, and came across a computer-generated, digital presentation that flashed each individual image from the collection as laid out in the book. Because of space constraints and certain political concerns, not all photographs were displayed in the exhibit, and the digital presentation provided the viewer with a more complete overview of the entire Requiem project. Beyond this point, the exhibition extended through two large conjoining rooms that included over two hundred photographs of the war displayed alongside portraits of the photographers, putting human faces on the men and women behind the cameras. The exhibit was arranged into four chronological sections that presented to the viewer the wars with France and the United States from a western historical perspective. The first section, "A Distant War," contained international press photographs from the later years of the Franco-Vietnamese war, or First Indochinese War, as it was called in the accompanying English text. The second section, "Escalation," showed both the earlier years of U.S. troop buildup in Vietnam and photographs from the "other side," that is, from the not-often-seen perspective (in the West) of the revolution. "The Quagmire," the third section, focused largely on U.S. forces in the mid to late 1960s, and was followed by a concluding section, "Final Days," that spanned the years from 1968 to 1972 and exhibited images predominantly from western media sources, with the exception of photographs by VNA correspondent Lương Nghĩa Dũng. At the end of the exhibit stood a small altar with flowers and an urn for offerings of incense between two large memorial tablets that listed the names of the deceased photojournalists, the design of which was inspired by the Vietnam Veterans Memorial in Washington, D.C., according to a U.S. organizer.

In its juxtaposition of revolutionary and nonrevolutionary images of the war, "Requiem" became a site of contrasting modes of visual narration and representation. Although there were subtle variations in the aesthetic qualities of the photographs as a result of financial constraints on the Vietnamese photographers, who had limited supplies of black-and-white film and often developed their negatives under hazardous conditions in the field, there were more noticeable differences in the choice of photographic subjects and settings, as well as the viewpoint and camera angles used to represent them. This produced and presented to the viewer differing subjectivities and visual histories of the war that often contradicted one another. For example, photographs from the western press frequently depicted the brute victimization of Vietnamese suspects. Explicit acts of violence and torture were caught on film, along with tangible moments of pain, anguish, and frustration (Figures 2.3 and 2.4).[26] Fear was an essential element in these images, which were often shot with the camera located above and aimed downward at the subject, conveying a sense of helplessness on the part of the Vietnamese victims while asserting the power of U.S. and RVN forces who are depicted as controlling the situation, and the war.

Photographs from the "other side" contrasted sharply with this dehumanization of Vietnamese bodies in western media and challenged its dominant representations of subjugation. Images taken by Vietnamese photojournalists who had worked with the VNA and LNA typically celebrated resilience and devotion to the nation and the revolution through representations of collective acts of walking, transporting, training, and preparing for war (Figures 2.5 and 2.6). The emphasis on people as active, rational, and creative agents rather than passive, defeated victims served to underscore the humanity, ingenuity, and fortitude of the populace. This was further communicated through the photographers' frequent use of the straight-on angle, with the camera positioned at eye level with the subject to convey a sense of equality, urgency, and authority.

Competing historical truths produced in the exhibit reflect divergent subject positions and memories of the war that are deeply rooted in ideological scripts of history still operative in both Vietnamese and U.S. societies. This was also evident in the captions and texts that accompanied the images, in which U.S. ideological modes of historical interpretation tended to dominate. Written from a conventional western perspective on the war, English-language descriptions of the photographs reproduced dominant historical rhetorics and discourses that diminished the complexities of the war to "two sides" (the us/them, noncommunist/communist dichotomy that was also present in the opening speech) and that reflected at times prevailing anticommunist biases. For example, the word "enemy" was used to describe "the communists," and the pejorative term "Viet Cong" was applied to

FIGURE 2.3. Interrogation of a Viet Cong suspect by South Vietnamese soldiers. 1965.
Photograph by Huỳnh Thanh Mỹ (AP). Courtesy of Indochina Photo Requiem Project.

FIGURE 2.4. Viet Cong prisoners. Undated. Photograph by Terry Khoo.
Courtesy of Indochina Photo Requiem Project.

FIGURE 2.5. A woman soldier of the North Vietnamese army carries an ammunition crate along the Ho Chi Minh Trail. 1966. Photograph by Bùi Đình Túy (VNA). Courtesy of Indochina Photo Requiem Project.

FIGURE 2.6. Viet Cong guerrillas and soldiers of the North Vietnamese army use bicycles to transport supplies. 1968. Photograph by Bùi Đình Túy (VNA). Courtesy of Indochina Photo Requiem Project.

photojournalists who worked with the LNA, the press arm of the National Liberation Front (NLF).[27] The translations into Vietnamese remained fairly true to their corresponding English text,[28] thus circulating among Vietnamese viewers common U.S. and western understandings of the war that differed significantly from their own historical narratives (in which, for example, U.S. troops would be the enemy, not NLF forces).

The predominance of U.S. ideologies and interpretations resulted in an absence of Vietnamese social and ideological perspectives from descriptions of the LNA and VNA photographs. References to the revolution, to optimistic visions of the future, or even to victory—key words and ideas that represent particular revolutionary subjectivities commonly found in Vietnamese museum exhibits—were lacking in this exhibit. In the case of nonrevolutionary photojournalists from the Republic of Vietnam, Vietnamese captions translated from English were void of pejorative words frequently used in official historical discourse to refer to the Army of the Republic of Vietnam (ARVN). In a 1965 photograph by Huỳnh Thành Mỹ, the English term "South Vietnamese soldier" is translated as *"lính Nam Việt Nam"* without the descriptor *nguy* [puppet] that commonly accompanies *lính* in museum texts.

That the exhibit largely represented and reproduced commonly held U.S. beliefs about the war did not escape museum visitors. An English-language entry in the visitor comment book, located at the end of "Requiem" for viewers to share their thoughts, complained about the exhibit's "Western viewpoint" and its use of words such as "enemy," "invader," and "assailant" to refer to the revolutionary troops rather than to U.S. forces, thus resurrecting the popular belief in the United States that "the North" invaded "the South." The critic offered a suggestion: "Why not write from a North Vietnamese view and use words like 'colonizers'?" A quote by journalist David Halberstam that appeared at the entrance to "Requiem" stressed the crucial role these images have played in constituting "modern memory." But as the captions reveal, the "modern memory" produced at the exhibit was not entirely constituted by multiple voices and perspectives on the past but was unevenly shaped by and given meaning through U.S.–western historical interpretations.

Transnational Commemoration and the Politics of Reconciliation

Museum officials were not passive recipients of western historical knowledge, however. A closer look at the choice of site for the exhibit, as well as negotiations concerning the exclusion of certain photographers and the classification of others, reveals ambivalences underlying processes of reconciliation and transnational commemoration. I first turn to the choice of venue for the exhibit, the War Remnants

Museum, a site that offers ethnographic and analytical insights into the shifting parameters of historical memory in the post–*Đổi mới* era of normalizing U.S.-Vietnamese relations.

The War Remnants Museum is a unique museal institution because of its willingness to accommodate and display diverse, often nonofficial and non-Vietnamese perspectives in its exhibits. For example, it is one of the few spaces of official historical memory and history that uses explicitly graphic images to narrate the horrors—not the victories—of war, which contributes to its status as one of the most anticipated stops on the itineraries of foreign tourists in Ho Chi Minh City. Given the focus of many western photojournalists on death and suffering in the war, representations of violence in the museum borrow to a large extent from nonrevolutionary media sources. As a director explained to me, museum officials decided to include more images from international mass media in an effort to "balance" its presentation of the war and appease foreign (especially U.S.) criticism that the museum promotes "propaganda" and lacks "objectivity." Certain exhibits, moreover, contain war relics (such as medals and uniforms) donated by U.S. veterans who have returned to Vietnam in the postwar years. The expanding representation of GI memories in museums, as well as in the Vietnamese mass media, DMZ tourist scripts, and even the trendy Apocalypse Now nightclub points to the various ways in which history is becoming increasingly transnationalized in Vietnam. Even before "Requiem—the Vietnam Collection" opened in its gallery, the War Remnants Museum had already become an international space of memory making and reconciliation that communicated diversely situated, transnational recollections and representations of the past.[29]

The "Requiem" exhibit was not shown in its entirety but was vetted and edited by Vietnamese officials in Hanoi to exclude those elements deemed politically sensitive or unnecessarily explicit that countered the theme of "hope, healing, and history," thus mediating the types of memories circulated and knowledge produced. According to Richard Lennon, despite an agreement to display the entire photo collection, members of the People's Committee arrived the evening before the opening in Hanoi to inspect the recently hung exhibit. A significant number of photographs were subsequently and arbitrarily removed.[30] In Ho Chi Minh City, according to Horst Faas and museum representatives, images of Cambodia were excluded. Officials did, however, allow these images—many of which were taken by Cambodian photographers working for the international press—to be shown in the continuously running digital presentation that surveyed the entire collection as presented in the book.

The exclusion of Cambodia from Vietnamese public sites of national memory is not uncommon. Along with the border conflict with China in 1979, Cambodia remains a conspicuous historical omission from most museums. Like the French and U.S. wars, the Chinese and Cambodian conflicts are remembered as defensive actions in response to border invasions and foreign aggression. Yet social and political discourse in Vietnam regularly asserts the existence of peace since 1975 and elides any references to the violent years in Cambodia (and the intense border conflict with China) that cost an already war-weary population thousands of additional lives. The Cambodian conflict is highly politically sensitive issue in Vietnam, in part, because of international accusations that Vietnam wrongfully invaded and occupied its neighbor, a charge that was repeatedly refuted during fieldwork by Vietnamese research respondents, including government officials who justified Vietnam's actions as protecting its borders and saving Cambodians from Pol Pot. Thus when it came to the issue of war and Cambodia, Vietnamese officials firmly delimited the extent of the circulation and representation of U.S. and other historical interpretations.

Yet, not insignificantly, Vietnamese officials proved more willing to negotiate and suspend official practices of memory and knowledge production within the space of the exhibit when it came to the public recognition and commemoration of southern, nonrevolutionary photojournalists. Though there is rarely open public debate on the matter, the issue of remembering and forgetting the RVN, and the people who participated in its institutions, remains politically, socially, and emotionally charged. After the end of the war, state policies absorbed the area south of the Bến Hải River into a socialist national imaginary of a politically and culturally unified Vietnam. This entailed acts of effacement of nonrevolutionary memories of the RVN, particularly as manifest in its material remains, which included the destruction of public monuments and cemeteries of the former regime, as well as the discouragement of private commemoration of its soldiers (Malarney 2001, 67). Since economic and political liberalization, however, the sociopolitical imperative to forget the "losing" side has gradually eased, and new opportunities have emerged for veterans of the ARVN to communicate their knowledge, memory, and experiences of war, for example, as guides for international tourists, as I discuss in chapter 3.

That "Requiem" provided a space to publicly commemorate nonrevolutionary southern Vietnamese war photographers alongside their revolutionary counterparts is a noteworthy historical occurrence that points to broader processes of reconciliation taking place beyond the scope of Vietnam–U.S. relations and beyond the NLF/PAVN–U.S. soldier binary. Because of postwar memorial protocol and practices that officially recognize and honor revolutionary martyrs only, joint commemoration has been rare. One exceptional instance where combatants from differing sides of the war have been collectively remembered is at An Lộc, approximately sixty miles north of Ho Chi Minh City, where a B-52 air strike in 1972 killed over three thousand civilians and troops. According to the ARVN veteran who took me to the site, the magnitude of the explosions made it impossible to distinguish between the bodies, and victims from all sides were subsequently buried collectively in a mass grave. A monument that stands on location reads: "This grave marks the resting place of three thousand fellow countrymen [*đồng bào*] from An Lộc, Bình Long, who were exterminated by American bombs in summer 1972." In the case of "Requiem," however, nonrevolutionary war correspondents were remembered not as *đồng bào* or fellow countrymen, as they were in An Lộc, but as part of an international contingent of foreign journalists.

Ambivalences about the commemoration of Vietnamese nonrevolutionary photojournalists and, by extension, acknowledgment of the RVN as their country were evident in several aspects of "Requiem." The black, gravestone-like panels that flanked the altar at the end of the exhibit differentiated not only between countries but also between perceived political convictions. To the right of the altar was the "Vietnam" panel, upon which the names of seventy-two men and women who died fighting for the revolution were recorded. To the left, the names of photographers who worked for western press agencies were arranged according to their foreign nationalities. It was here that four Vietnamese journalists were listed under the category "South Vietnam," which, according to a U.S. organizer, Vietnamese government officials from the outset refused to recognize as a country. While the decision to separate "South Vietnam" from "Vietnam" did not lie with Vietnamese exhibit organizers but had already been formulated by Horst Faas and Tim Page in their book, as well as in the initial Kentucky exhibit,[31] this political-conceptual split was further sustained by Vietnamese public discourse surrounding the event. Opening speeches by Vietnamese officials in Ho Chi Minh City avoided any direct reference to photographers from the RVN, mentioning only foreign photojournalists and "Vietnamese revolutionary martyrs who had sacrificed their lives." Vietnamese mass media also typically omitted reference to the four RVN photographers. A May 12, 2000, editorial on the Hanoi exhibition in the daily *Nhân Dân* [The People] listed the nations represented in the collection but neglected to include "South Vietnam." The simultaneous presence and erasure of the Vietnamese nonrevolutionary photographers suggests apprehensions and uncertainties about if, how, to what extent, and in which contexts people from a now-defunct, officially uncommemorated regime might be publicly remembered in Vietnam today. "Requiem" thus demonstrates the interactive mediation of knowledge and memory engendered in transnational spaces of commemoration and reconciliation and the perseverance of certain historical-ideological constraints for all sides involved in the war.

On Becoming *Đồng Bào*

"Requiem" drew large crowds of visitors and received positive accolades from the Vietnamese press, and from those in attendance with whom I spoke. Although the mood was somber at its opening in Ho Chi Minh City with many family members and friends of the deceased present, there was also an air of excitement that the exhibit marked an important era of change in Vietnam—a time of reconciliation with the past and of new possibilities in the present and future. In the words of a military official who was also in attendance at the opening ceremony, the ability to see and reflect on "both sides of the war" marked a "new chapter of modernization in Vietnamese society," with new knowledge and new ways of thinking about the past. Yet as argued above, although the exhibit opened a dynamic space for the expression of diverse historical perspectives and memories of the war, "Requiem" was not a politically neutral site of transnational remembrance, representation, and knowledge production. The competing visual narratives that surfaced in the exhibit through displays of capitalist and socialist realisms—namely, vanquished versus victorious bodies—point to persistent knowledge frictions that permeate reconciliatory processes and play out in the complex and unstable relations between memory and forgetting.

Although "Requiem" marked a significant moment in the development of new relationships between Vietnam and the United States, social and political reconciliation remains an uneasy and ambivalent process, as evident in the afterlife of the exhibit. Presented as a gift and reconciliatory gesture of "hope, healing, and history" from the people of Kentucky to the people of Vietnam, the collection was displayed in Ho Chi Minh City for a total of two weeks, after which the photographs were returned to Hanoi and put into storage, where they remain today (because of space constraints, according to one museum director in Hanoi). Subsequently, a copy of the collection (from an additional set of photographs in London) was made for the War Remnants Museum to keep on permanent display. When I returned to the museum in 2004, several changes had been made to the exhibit. First, retranslations of English captions now presented to domestic museum visitors more standardized, official Vietnamese interpretations of the war. The term "First Indochinese War," for example, was translated into Vietnamese as *"cuộc kháng chiến chống thực dân Pháp,"* or "the resistance war against French colonialism," as it is often called in Vietnam. U.S. ideological undertones evident in the English captions were also tempered in new Vietnamese translations. The term "Viet Cong," for example, remained in use in English texts but was translated for the Vietnamese viewer into the more historically and politically correct form, *"Mặt Trận Dân Tộc Giải Phóng*

FIGURE 2.7. Memorial tablet at the permanent exhibit, "Requiem—the Vietnam Collection," War Remnants Museum. 2007. Photograph by the author.

Miên Nam Việt Nam" [National Liberation Front of Southern Vietnam]. In correcting perceived historical inaccuracies, newly translated captions not only challenged U.S. interpretive frameworks but also diversified subject positions to provide a more informed perspective on the war than the English texts. In Figure 2.5, the misleading title "Soldier of the North Vietnamese Army" was amended in the Vietnamese version to more accurately read *"thanh niên xung phong"* [youth volunteer]. While English captions tended to simplify the war to "Viet Cong guerrillas and soldiers of the North Vietnamese army" (Figure 2.6) on one side, and U.S. and South Vietnamese soldiers on the other, the Vietnamese translations challenged these classifications and brought more attention to the complexities and diverse roles of Vietnamese participants in the revolution.

The memorial tablets placed at the end of the exhibit provided another example of the ongoing negotiation of "Requiem" and the ways in which museum officials first allowed for and then later overturned U.S. (and broader western) interpretations and systems of classification. However, here, official Vietnamese perspectives and modes of representing history were not reinforced in the exhibit, but challenged. In the now-permanent display, a socially and symbolically significant shift in the memorialization of the nonrevolutionary Vietnamese photographers had taken place. That the four correspondents are still listed under the title "South Vietnam" demonstrates a decision by museum officials not to permanently erase their presence or the name of a state that remains officially unrecognized in Vietnam. More notably, their names are no longer classified with their international colleagues but have been re-recorded on a memorial tablet along with the names of photojournalists from "Vietnam" (Figure 2.7). In notable contrast to the initial 2000 exhibit of "Requiem—the Vietnam Collection," where Vietnamese photographers from the Republic of Vietnam were presented as part of the contingent of foreigners, in this reconfigured memorial space they are remembered and represented to museum visitors as *đồng bào,* or fellow Vietnamese citizens.

PART 2

Memorial Landscapes

Commodified Memories and
Embodied Experiences of War

CHAPTER THREE

In the early dawn hours of April 30, 2000, I quickly made my way through the streets of Ho Chi Minh City. The city was beginning to stir as street vendors heated large pots of *phở* broth and residents slowly jogged through the nearly empty streets. I hurried past the neighborhood park, already filled with badminton players, on my way to the official demonstration that would take place at the Reunification Palace. This is also the site where tanks from the People's Army of Vietnam (PAVN) came crashing through the gates on April 30, 1975, signaling the liberation or, depending on one's point of view, the fall of Saigon. The roads were barricaded, but I managed to convince a policeman to let me through to join the various onlookers gathering outside. At seven o'clock in the morning the gates opened and the parade began. Although thousands of participants had been bused in from neighboring provinces and outlying city districts, spectators were rather sparse at this early morning hour—mostly journalists, photographers, and curious tourists who had come to Vietnam for the twenty-fifth anniversary of the end of the war.

The armed forces led the procession, with men and women segregated into different military units. The army first marched past in unison, followed by the air force, the navy, and then a women's militia unit with troops dressed in conventional "guerrilla" uniforms composed of loose-fitting black garments, checkered scarves, and wide-brimmed, floppy green hats. A group of young male cadets carrying the flag of the National Liberation Front (NLF) followed in step. After displaying the nation's military might, the parade shifted to a more jovial civilian-centered phase, represented by members of various Fatherland Front organizations and other social groups. The Women's Union, youth pioneers, gymnasts, farmers, postal work-ers, Buddhist and Catholic organizations, and even children dressed as bumble-bees marched past smiling and waving to the growing crowd. Ethnic minority performers from the Central Highlands region elicited excited reactions from on-lookers when they appeared on stilts dressed in "traditional" garb. The celebration culminated with a festive unicorn dance (similar to the dragon dance in Chinese culture), which wound its way through the city streets, accompanied by the loud, rhythmic beating of drums and the clashing of cymbals.

Finally, a convoy of floats began to emerge through the palace gates, the pri-mary function of which was to advertise and represent local business interests. This capitalist addition to a celebration symbolizing twenty-five years of liberation, re-unification, and socialist transformation is emblematic of current reform policies to develop a "market economy with socialist orientation" [kinh tế thị trường với định hướng xã hội chủ nghĩa]. Several of the floats were advertisements for Vietnam's nascent tourism industry, including one for Ho Chi Minh City Tourism, driven by young men dressed to resemble NLF guerrillas. Another float promoting a popular theme park, Suối Tiên, adopted a similar motif and designed its vehicle in the shape of an armored tank. Young women sporting rubber "Ho Chi Minh sandals" and checkered scarves associated with the NLF rode on its sides waving yellow flowers at the spectators. These presentations exemplified a symbolic and visual mode of commemorating a momentous occasion in Vietnam's history and also clearly indi-cated the expanding role that tourism and capitalism have assumed in Vietnamese society since economic reforms began in the late 1980s. Moreover, the appropria-tion of war-era signs and symbols for present-day tourist displays signified an im-portant trend explored in this chapter: the commodification, representation, and consumption of war memories at public sites of history in southern Vietnam.

Transnationalizing History and Memory through Tourism

Like many nations that are expanding their involvement in the global market economy, Vietnam has adopted tourism as a prime development strategy to pro-duce economic growth.[1] Yet travel to Vietnam is not only about romantic encoun-ters with "natives" or nostalgic colonial fantasies.[2] The icons of war found on the parade floats demonstrate a marketing awareness that Vietnam has more than just the image of the culturally exotic to offer. It has, in addition, the American War. This recognition has spurred in Vietnam a genre of travel that sells memory, history, tragedy, and entertainment bundled into compelling tours to former battlegrounds. Unlike the traveler who seeks the peace, tranquillity, and imagined authenticity of a "premodern" world (MacCannell 1999 [1976]), the battlefield tourist is driven by the desire to see, experience, and understand mass destruction and violence in the modern era. And for people who feel a need to reconcile with a painful and formative past, journeys to former war sites may also serve as a cathartic experience that involves apprehensive and yet performative engagements with memory.

In recent years there has been much scholarly interest in touristic journeys and pilgrimages to infamous sites of death and suffering, a phenomenon referred to in the literature as "tragic tourism" (Lippard 1999), "dark tourism" (Lennon and Foley 2000), "thanatourism" (Seaton 1996), and "trauma tourism" (Clark 2006). Travel to sites of mass death is not a new trend by any means, nor is it confined to more recent spectacles of suffering, such as Ground Zero in New York City (Sturken 2007).[3] Yet the increasing desire and curiosity of tourists—some of whom are intimately linked to the histories of atrocity that occurred at the sites—to journey to places of mass death and tragedy has engendered new tourist destinations and classifications.[4] Like the primary consumers of Holocaust memories who were nonwitnesses to the genocide (Kugelmass 1996; Weissman 2004), the majority of tourists who visit Vietnamese battle sites have no direct experiential connection to the war, but desire to bear witness to the horrors of a past known and felt through "prosthetic memories" that have been shaped and informed by mass commodity culture (Landsberg 2004).

As Vietnam undergoes extensive economic reforms and reestablishes a position in the global market, questions of when to evoke the past and how to remember the war take on renewed significance. In contrast to a perceived U.S. obsession with the war, it is common to hear Vietnamese citizens and government officials regularly assert that Vietnam has "closed the past to look toward the future" [*khép lại quá khứ, hướng về tương lai*]. Yet, as Renan (1990 [1882]) has suggested, the forces of memory and forgetting that constitute a nation's history also shape and secure its collective visions of the future. This chapter examines one specific interrelationship between "the past" and "the future" in Vietnam, when icons of the war are recycled and reproduced in a transnational economy of memory for the sake of "development" and prosperity. Looking at tourist consumption and practices of memory at former battlefields and other social spaces that invoke the history of the war, I argue that the commodification of sites, objects, and imaginaries associated with two historical constructs—the "Vietnam War," portrayed in U.S. history as a battle against communism, and the "American War," represented as a struggle against imperialism in official Vietnamese history—has prompted certain rearticulations of the past in the public sphere as the terrain of memory making becomes increasingly transnational and infused with capitalist values.

Contradictions and tensions between remembrance and forgetfulness commonly surface when public memorials and commemorative projects are transformed into historical sites for tourists and other audiences who at times put these spaces to alternative social uses (Yoneyama 1999; Handler and Gable 1997). In what follows below I demonstrate how the resulting entangled, co-produced, and often contested scripts of recombinant history reveal multiple complexities involved in the transnationalization of historical memory. Diverse actors—including tourism authorities, returning U.S. veterans, international tourists, domestic visitors, and guides—engage in divergent practices of memory that complicate, expand, and often transcend dominant modes of historical representation in new and distinct ways. The complex memory and antimemory work that transpires at war sites in Vietnam attests to the plurality of meanings that people bring to and take away from memorial spaces, and to ways such spaces shape and are shaped by local and transnational engagements with history.

Fashioning the Vietnam and American Wars as Commodities in the State Sector

In the United States, the Vietnam War has long been a commodity consumed by the U.S. public. Thirty years after U.S. troops left the country, reflections on the past and reinterpretations of the conflict continue to drive the publication of memoirs, anthologies, and novels as well as the production of Hollywood blockbuster films and other popular culture trends such as comic books, cartoons, action figures, computer games, and music. These cultural productions sell particular memories and ideological perspectives of the war that are largely devoid of any substantive examination or representation of Vietnamese people, culture, or history and are often steeped in imperial orientalist and anticommunist imagery (Espiritu 2005, 313). With few exceptions, the underlying U.S. ideologies of democracy, freedom, individualism, and moral goodness often remain unchallenged.[5]

With the reestablishment of a market economy in Vietnam, images and artifacts of the American War have become increasingly commodified for public consumption, but with considerably less capitalist vigor than in the United States. State-produced films and plays about the resistance wars against France and the United States are common on television and in theaters. CDs and karaoke videos with "red music" from the revolution are bought and sold throughout much of the country, and Vietnamese memoirs of war, a more recent publishing trend, are in high demand by domestic consumers. In the arts, wartime posters and socialist realist paintings of Hồ Chí Minh are on display and available for purchase in galleries and shops, primarily for international consumption, especially by tourists looking for socialist kitsch. Whereas the cultural production and marketing of the war in the United States often reproduce persistent Cold War rhetoric (such as killing

"VC" in video games), in Vietnam such commodities typically communicate revolutionary values of heroic resistance and sacrifice. Yet, as in the United States, the relationship between these commodities and dominant ideologies is ambiguous at best, and Vietnamese cultural producers are often actively engaged in subverting authoritative historical memory and producing their own counter-representations of the past.

In the early 1990s, state tourism officials in southern Vietnam began to develop a market around the historical construct of the Vietnam War; in other words, they began to use expressions, artifacts, knowledge, and spaces primarily linked to wartime experiences of U.S. troops that have little meaning to the average Vietnamese person. Although the cultural production and commodification of the American War generally targets a domestic audience (revolutionary art notwithstanding), the Vietnam War is predominantly sold to U.S. visitors and other international tourists. As diplomatic relations between the United States and Vietnam warmed, expectations that U.S. citizens, particularly veterans, would return to Vietnam in large numbers inspired the selective re-Americanization of the postwar landscape. International and domestic tour agencies and veterans' organizations constructed tours around events and sites significant in U.S. history of the war (for example, the Khe Sanh marine base, the Rockpile, and Camp Carroll on the DMZ tour) and revived military vernacular such as China Beach and DMZ to attract U.S. tourists familiar with these locations (Gluckman 1997).[6] Tour guides further diversified the historical knowledge communicated to visitors by integrating the recollections of U.S. veterans into their presentations.

Marketing the Vietnam War in Vietnam requires that tourist officials and employees have knowledge of the conflict as it has been presented in U.S. history and popular culture. It also assumes that visitors will possess a certain level of media, historical, and visual literacy to understand tourist spaces and spectacles. Despite such efforts, however, the number of tourists from the United States has remained comparatively low (Biles, Lloyd, and Logan 1999, 215). In the perception of many U.S. citizens I spoke with, Vietnam remains a dangerous and war-torn country rather than a potential travel destination.[7] The primary consumers of these tourist productions have been, therefore, international tourists from western countries other than the United States whose knowledge of Vietnam and memory of the war has been shaped by travel guidebooks (Laderman 2002), popular culture, or live media coverage. In the words of a Canadian man touring the sites of former battlefields:

> I may be Canadian but the war was a big part of my life. I saw it all on TV. That's why I'm here now. It's amazing to finally visit those places I'm already familiar with—My Lai, China Beach, Cu Chi, Saigon, and the DMZ. This evening I'm

going to the Rex Hotel where journalists sat the last night before the liberation troops arrived, and then I'll go to the Apocalypse Now nightclub. Do you
know if the original U.S. embassy is still there?

This man's bond with the past, a common theme that emerged with many interviewees, young and old alike, suggests that the war is not only significant in the
sociohistorical consciousness of the United States, Vietnam, or other nations directly involved in the conflict, but has assumed a unique status in global historical
memory, largely on account of global mass media coverage of the war. Moreover,
such comments reveal that "touristic phantasms" of Vietnam as a war-ravaged place
have driven its exoticization by international tourists who actively and eagerly seek
to discover and experience its tragic history (Alneng 2002).

    Foreigners, including returning veterans, who came to Vietnam searching for
physical traces and remnants of the war were often surprised by the apparent lack
of visual reminders, and they frequently expressed disappointment that there was
"not much left to see," especially at former U.S. military bases, save for the barely
detectable contours of former airstrips. One tour guide reflected on this desire to
find remnants of the past in contemporary landscapes: "Many French and American veterans return to Vietnam because they want to visit the places where they
fought. But they find that there is nothing left!" Complaints about the lack of visual
stimulation to overwhelm the visitor have led to the removal of certain war sites
from tourist agendas. This was the case with the U.S. Marine base Camp Carroll,
which was taken off the DMZ tour itinerary because, according to a guide from
central Vietnam, there was nothing for tourists to see: "It has all been ravaged for
metal!" Diller and Scofidio have argued that an empty battlefield need only be "designated by a marker to become auratic for the tourist. When national narratives
are written directly onto material soil, that surface carries the image of validity"
(1994, 28). Yet as the above comments suggest, verbal and written representations
do not unconditionally validate the authority of the site, nor do they alone constitute the symbolic and historic meaning of landscapes for tourists. Rather, tourists
invest historical authority and emotive value in particular manifestations of material culture, such as artifacts and ruins that embody and transmit traumatic memories, and when viewed in symbolic landscapes, become the "bearer of sensory multiplicity" and surplus meanings (Seremetakis 1994, 11).

    Interviewees contrasted the perceived absence of signs in Vietnam with Cam-
bodia, where many felt the war was more discernible. Winding up a month-long tour
of Laos, Cambodia, and Vietnam, an older man in his late sixties from the United
States discussed the country that had most overwhelmed him with its visual evidence of war:

I was completely shocked by the number of amputees in Cambodia. They were everywhere—people without hands, arms, and legs. I couldn't believe it. It was very disturbing. I was expecting to find that in Vietnam and was surprised how few [amputees] there were. You know there weren't too many signs of the war. I thought there would be more.

This comparison between Vietnam and Cambodia reflects the tendency to evaluate and contrast war sites turned into tourist attractions on the basis of their "realness," with travelers discussing the best places to visit where they could encounter more directly the tumultuous past. War was more tangible in Cambodia, I was told, with the infamous skulls at the Choeung Ek "killing fields." It was more "real" at Phnom Penh's Tuol Sleng Museum of Genocidal Crimes (formerly a Khmer Rouge prison), with stained blood on the concrete floor and thousands of prisoner photographs on the walls.[8] Jane C. Desmond (1999) has argued that tourist practices are less about site-seeing than about embodied sensation and imagination.[9] The "sensing" of Cambodia's history through embodied acts of presence, of "being there" and witnessing firsthand the tangible traces of violence (for example, bloodstains in cells where prisoners were tortured and executed), imbues such sites with an aura of realness and the power to evoke the horrors of the past in the present (cf. Kirshenblatt-Gimblett 1998, 20).

To attract visitors to war sites in Vietnam, tourist officials incorporated "real" traces of history into staged multisensory environments that appear to dismantle historical distance and detachment for close-up viewing and interaction.[10] Visitors joined group tours to battlefields and massacre sites, some of which had been partially reconstructed; they inspected and at times climb onto military vehicles; they crawled through enlarged underground tunnels, fired war-era weapons, sampled "guerrilla" food, and explored the interiors of unreconstructed memorials, such as a bombed church left standing as silent testimony to a violent past. Mingling visual landscapes with smell, sound, touch, and sometimes taste to produce simulated spectacles in which signs and representations of history are consumed, these embodied sensorial journeys forged an "implied" experience of the war that "operates in the realm of the imaginary" (Desmond 1999, 253).

There is often an ironic reversal of desire in the consumption of war and suffering, however, when embodiment loses its "implied-ness" and becomes too visceral, uncomfortable, and potentially unsafe. If history is not adequately aestheticized or if the suffering of others no longer remains at a distance but is inadvertently transferred to tourists, visitors might have an unpleasant or even bitter experience. According to a domestic tour operator, in 2000 the stopover at Xẻo Quýt, an NLF revolutionary base deep inside the forest, was removed from the itinerary of a

Mekong Delta tour after foreigners complained that snakes and insects encountered at the site made it "too dangerous" and taxing. The dilemma for tourism officials is how to make the war a palatable, multisensory experience without making it too real, perilous, or offensive (Lisle 2000, 110).

Selling American GI Subjectivities in the Private Sector

While tourist authorities in southern Vietnam fashioned an industry around the consumption of diverse historical memories of the war, private vendors and entrepreneurs followed suit, expanding the market beyond government-regulated sites. Commodities in the private sector largely drew from U.S. wartime imaginaries produced in U.S. popular culture, especially GI subjectivities. References to the war as represented in popular culture often surfaced in tourism discourse in the names of hotels, restaurants, bars, and signature cocktails, and in war souvenirs and other tourist memorabilia. Yet such co-optation is rarely without resignification. "Good Morning Vietnam" T-shirts, adopted from the title of a Vietnam War film starring Robin Williams, were widely sold by street and market vendors in downtown Ho Chi Minh City. The film's poster image of Williams set against the patriotic backdrop of the stars and stripes had been replaced, however, with an elderly Vietnamese woman in a conical hat next to a Vietnamese flag, signifying the nation's cultural strength and historical resilience.

During my fieldwork, the Apocalypse Now nightclub was one of the more well-known appropriations of U.S. popular culture in Vietnam. Privately owned with branches (at that time) in Hanoi and Ho Chi Minh City, this trendy discotheque attracted a domestic and international clientele with its dark, smoky rooms and 1970s dance music. The extensive use of the war motif invoked the embodied subjectivities of U.S. soldiers engaging in the "corrupt" cultural practices of Western music, drugs, and prostitution—"neocolonial poisons" once targeted for elimination by the postreunification socialist government (P. Taylor 2000; 2001, 23–55). In the Hanoi club, the disc jockey pumped out a loud rhythmic beat from a helicopter cockpit with red strobe headlights flashing through the misty fog on the dance floor. The whirling blades of the ceiling fans, propellers of "Hueys" painted on the ceiling, gave the illusion and breezy sensation of hovering helicopters. GI helmets sheathed the dim hanging lamps over the pool tables and red "blood" trickled over the bulbs of light fixtures on the walls. Sex workers dressed in the latest Vietnamese fashion sidled up to foreign men sitting at a bar designed to resemble a thatched village hut. "I hope a vet doesn't have a flashback in here and take a lighter to this," joked a middle-aged customer from the United States next to me at the bar one night, conjuring media images of soldiers burning village huts with Zippo lighters on search-

and-destroy missions. He continued: "Just look at this place! It's killing and whores just like the war!" Both of these "attractions" (sex and violence) are closely linked to the social imagination of the lives of U.S. troops in Vietnam, as well as to the construction of exoticized and sexualized Vietnamese women, one of the persistent legacies of the war.[11]

However, foreigners were not the only consumers of this spectacle. The Apocalypse Now bar was also a gathering place for certain members of the Vietnamese populace with global social networks, such as artists, gays and lesbians, affluent youth, and employees of international organizations, signifying a Vietnamese cosmopolitan space of conspicuous pleasure and consumption (see Drummond and Thomas 2003). These domestic consumers—dancing, fraternizing, and reveling in spaces that reinvoked the era and culture of U.S. occupation—were the embodiment of recombinant history; their embrace of alternative wartime perspectives and practices transgressed dominant historical models and resisted current social discourses and campaigns to stamp out "social evils."

A fundamental aspect of the union of war, tourism, and capitalist consumption in southern Vietnam has been the war relic or "souvenir of death" (Stewart 1993, 140). With its multiple social lives and shifting valuation (Appadurai 1986), the souvenir of death reflects a unique turn in history as domestic vendors, particularly in the underground economy, profit from the U.S. war machine by recommodifying artifacts and everyday objects that U.S. soldiers discarded or unintentionally left behind, such as dog tags, medals, compasses, patches, cooking utensils, razors, and clothing.[12] Embodying memory and sacredness through its alleged connection to a tragic past, the souvenir of death is an object of fetishized tourist desire that is valued and collected, and at times disdainfully rejected, for its mystique—the unknown but implied fate of the soldier who possessed it (Stewart 1993, 149).

The most iconic and sought-after relic from the war is the Zippo lighter (Figure 3.1). In Ho Chi Minh City, itinerant street vendors, generally children and young adults from the countryside who peddle their wares in the low-budget tourist area, as well as upscale tourist shops in the downtown area, offered a diverse assortment of polished silver Zippo reproductions and tarnished "originals" with such engraved messages as "We are the unwilling led by the unqualified doing the unnecessary for the ungrateful." Sometimes cynical, at other times patriotic, and often sexist and racist, the inscriptions provide discerning insights into the subjectivities and ideological positionings of U.S. soldiers during the war. Tracing the history and social lives of Zippo lighters in Vietnam, Ian Walters points to the paradox of their commodification. What were once used as a tool in the destruction of the country (in setting homes and villages on fire) are now used to contribute to its economic development (1999, 275). Walters situates Zippo lighters in relation to an expanding

FIGURE 3.1. "Original" Zippos on sale in Ho Chi Minh City. Photograph by the author.

market economy, but also significant is the role such cultural artifacts play in trans-
nationalizing historical memory in Vietnam.[13] Like customers who frequented the
Apocalypse Now nightclub, consumers of Zippo lighters reenact particular sociohistorical imaginaries and subjectivities of the war that are largely informed by images circulated in U.S. popular culture. Moreover, as a symbolic souvenir of death
that is more often imitative than "authentic," the Zippo lighter is valued for its mi-
metic qualities and indexed connection to the past (an implied vehicle of memory)
rather than a verifiable cultural biography (Kopytoff 1986).

Embodied Memory and Reconfigured
Meaning at the Củ Chi Tunnels

The Củ Chi Tunnel Historical Remains, Vietnam's most popular war attraction, lies
sixty kilometers northwest of Ho Chi Minh City. In recent years, the notorious Củ
Chi battlefields have been transformed into a commercialized transnational public
space for the consumption of a multisensory "Viet Cong" experience.[14] Wartime secrets are divulged and the invisible enemy revealed as young men dressed as guerrillas escort visitors through a day in the life of a typical fighter living underground.

Local tourist officials, tour guides, domestic visitors, and international tourists, in turning spaces of violence and death into spaces of education, entertainment, and pleasure, transform and diversify the authoritative meanings and memories communicated at Củ Chi. Through embodied, interactive, and choreographed tourist practices, the lines between "the authentic" and "the fake" collapse, and it becomes increasingly difficult to distinguish between a lingering sense of history and a purely imitative hyperreality (Eco 1983; Baudrillard 1994). However, this is not just a tale of commodification leading to dehistoricization or even trivialization (Adorno 1991), as scholars have also argued in the case of Vietnam (Tai 1994, 8; Kennedy and Williams 2001, 145). Rather, similar to the Zippo lighters, underneath the veneer of "inauthenticity" are complicated practices of memory at work that set apart social and historical actors and their diverse engagements with the past.

During the war, Củ Chi district was a free-fire zone of intractable underground warfare, aggressive U.S. military operations, and persistent chemical weapon assaults on largely imperceptible guerrilla forces. A U.S. Navy veteran who had been stationed in the port of Saigon and returned to Vietnam for the twenty-fifth anniversary celebration recalled the formidable reputation of Củ Chi as we toured the tunnel complex together in April 2000: "I had always heard of this place during the war. This was the worst area to be stationed—the worst. Some bad battles occurred here. Those tunnel rats [U.S. soldiers sent underground] came back screwed up." Yet the very reasons that make Củ Chi infamous to many U.S. veterans (and therefore an appropriate place for this navy veteran to work through his trauma) also make it function as a Vietnamese national symbol of courage and heroism. Built during the resistance wars against France and the United States, the two-hundred-kilometer underground network of tunnels has come to signify the nation's resolute perseverance and clever ingenuity. As described in an English language brochure: "The Củ Chi Tunnels represent the will, intelligence and pride of the people of Củ Chi and symbolize the revolutionary heroism of Vietnam."

After the war, most of the tunnels were abandoned and left to decay, although some underground passages and chambers were preserved as a memorial (Mangold and Pennycate 1985, 268). This commemorative site drew government officials, schoolchildren, and gradually, foreign visitors. According to a Củ Chi Tunnel employee, in the early 1990s, in anticipation of an increase in the number of international tourists, tourism officials modified the passageways to allow access to "larger" bodies. The extremely narrow tunnel system was originally designed to accommodate the generally smaller stature of Vietnamese guerrillas. Although Củ Chi combatants easily slipped through the tight entrances, most U.S. soldiers could not fit on account of their broader and often bulkier physiques. Today, few of the original tunnels remain and most of those tourists see today are reconstructions. However,

FIGURE 3.2. Củ Chi tunnel demonstration, Bến Đình. Photograph by the author.

one "original" entry has been preserved; this site marks a pivotal moment in the visit to Củ Chi, where displays of bodily difference serve to authenticate history as well as the tourist experience. As part of the entertaining spectacle, a male guide locates a concealed and indiscernible underground entrance that is camouflaged by forest debris. Viewers gasp and camera shutters click as he descends through the exceptionally narrow opening (25×37 cm) and disappears into the constricted space below, resealing the cover above him (Figure 3.2). After climbing out, he invites observers to try. Adult tourists typically decline, and volunteers who rise to the challenge often cannot make it past their hips or shoulders.

Desmond has argued that international tourism is often contingent on a "visual and kinesthetic basis of codifying 'difference'" (1999, xiii). At Củ Chi, while tourists consume difference as presented and typologized in such spectacles, their participation in the performance further accentuates what are believed to be fundamental dissimilarities between Vietnamese bodies and those of U.S. soldiers. In conversations with Vietnamese respondents, physical difference was frequently used to explain the success and fortitude of Củ Chi combatants. Traits such as small stature, according to one person, bestowed the ability to effortlessly maneuver through the tunnels and to live underground for long periods of time, while another respondent surmised that "round western eyes" hindered vision in the bright tropical sun and ultimately contributed to the defeat of U.S. (and French) troops. Moreover, victory was at times explicitly linked to the idea of a unique Vietnamese "character" that has the propensity to endure immense suffering as a result of sociohistorical adaptation to recurring and protracted periods of war. According to an intellectual from Hanoi: "We won the war because of our character of high perseverance. For over two thousand years we have had a tradition of fighting the enemy." Such discourses of difference reflect a national consciousness that, in linking military success to essentialist notions of race and culture, crafts the Vietnamese nation as historically and culturally distinct.

International Visitors and Embodied Experiences

The Củ Chi Tunnel Historical Remains encompasses 830,000 square meters and is divided into two areas: Bến Đình and Bến Dược. Each area maintains a separate section of the tunnels for tourists to explore, and both underground systems are managed by the central tourist administration in Củ Chi district (an outlying district of Ho Chi Minh City). Although the tunnels at both Bến Đình and Bến Dược have been restored and renovated in one way or another, international tourist discourse differentiates between Bến Đình as "the original" and thus "most authentic" tunnel complex and Bến Dược as merely a reconstruction. Low-budget tours from Ho Chi Minh City take mostly international tourists on day trips to the former, whereas the latter predominantly attracts Vietnamese tourists and residents from nearby urban areas. In an interview, one government tour operator summarized the differences between the two destinations: "Bến Đình has the original tunnels and attracts fewer people. At Bến Dược one finds many Vietnamese visitors and schoolchildren, and there are more things to do there, like go to cafés or restaurants. Bến Đình is more natural and does not have these activities, so that is where we take foreigners." Visitor practices and desires are thus mapped onto naturalized distinctions between "foreign" and "Vietnamese" tastes to produce two divergent tourist experiences (cf. Bourdieu 1984, 174–175): one that promises a "pure" and focused historical journey and another that situates Củ Chi history in a more visibly mediated environment of recreation and retreat.

The modern and arguably western desire for the authentic—for the unmediated "real thing"—has long been linked to commodification and to particular global processes, such as international tourism (MacCannell 1999 [1976]) and transnational flows of cultural artifacts (Clifford 1988, 1997; Errington 1998). In Vietnam, a country where fakes and reproductions are readily available on the market as works of art (N. Taylor 1999), pirated DVDs and computer software, designer clothing and accessories, and war kitsch, the quest for authenticity is often bound up with anxiety about imitations and loss of value or meaning. In the case of Củ Chi, the preference of tour agencies for Bến Đình over Bến Dược is largely a response to international demands for historical authenticity.[15] During fieldwork, I regularly encountered foreigners who were concerned that they would be deceived and taken to the "wrong" tunnels. Although there is some variation in the spatial layout and design of Bến Dược and Bến Đình, the tours generally mirror one another, with only slight divergences concerning the organization and presentation of exhibits. For instance, the Bến Dược tunnels are shorter and wider and therefore, from the perspective of international visitors, they have less historical value, even though in both locations, the lines separating realism from restoration, and history from entertainment are ambiguous at best.

As at Bến Dược, the Bến Đình tour begins in a small theater where visitors are briefed on the design and construction of the tunnels prior to watching a twenty-minute black-and-white film that uses footage from the war to illustrate the everyday lives of Củ Chi combatants. After reconvening with their English-speaking guide who has accompanied them from Ho Chi Minh City, visitors are introduced to a "local guerrilla" (always represented by a young man or woman rather than an actual participant in the war), whose role is to activate and perform in the exhibits. The trek into the once-defoliated jungle under a canopy of tropical regrowth and young eucalyptus trees begins. The first stop is the "Self-Made Weapons Gallery," where guests observe guerrilla defense tactics and weaponry adapted from "traditional" hunting techniques, such as the infamous "tiger trap" and the "spiked folding chair," a device that, when stepped on precisely in the center, flips up to close onto the lower leg, impaling it with metal spikes from both sides (Figure 3.3). A mural depicting scenes of bloodied U.S. soldiers caught in the clenches of bamboo traps or falling onto piercing stakes demonstrates the efficacy of the rudimentary yet inventive defense system and signifies a celebratory form of Vietnamese historical memory: the defeat of the United States.

Visitors then continue along narrow, dusty trails past several discernible bomb craters, as distant rifle shots and machine-gun fire pierce the quietude of the forest and contribute to a contrived sensation of moving through a former battle zone. Tourists soon arrive at the much-anticipated climax of the tour, where the embodied experience of "guerrilla life" culminates with a descent underground to crawl ninety meters through dimly lit and airless tunnels that slope up to three meters beneath the ground surface. There is always trepidation as well as excitement, and visitors are assured that the tunnels have been sprayed for spiders and snakes, and that emergency exits appear every thirty meters for those who choose not to proceed into the deeper and narrower sections. At this moment, authenticity is no longer the issue as safety and comfort take precedence. "Time now to be a hero!" one guide exclaimed with a tinge of sarcasm during a tour in April 2000 as he coaxed a group of foreigners into the widened passageway, which at its narrowest point is

FIGURE 3.3. "Folding chair" trap, Bến Đình. Photograph by the author.

still twice the size of the wartime tunnels (and thus not "authentic" by any means). After emerging, the perspiring and dirt-speckled tourists are invited into the underground kitchen to feast on "guerrilla food": boiled cassava dipped in a mixture of salt and crushed peanuts. As the tour continues, more secrets are revealed: how smoke from the kitchen was dispersed aboveground through a series of small airholes, giving the illusion of lingering jungle mists; and how dead U.S. bombs were sawed open and used for ammunition at a weapons production facility. A brief interlude at a rusting U.S. tank destroyed by Củ Chi fighters then follows. "Go ahead and be Rambo," the same guide joked as visitors climbed onto the tank to have their photographs taken. Such comments and actions reveal the presence of recombinant scripts of Củ Chi history that merge Vietnamese historical memory of the American War with images of the Vietnam War in U.S. popular culture.

The official narrative of history disseminated to foreigners at Bến Đình tunnels, which emphasizes heroic values and acts while eschewing individual pain and suffering (Henderson 2000, 277), is not a uniform and consistent representation of the past. As with concerns for safety and comfort, economic interests tend to override and displace the project of historical authenticity. This is particularly evident at the last stop in the tour—the shooting gallery, a Củ Chi highlight in which discordant historical images, events, and memories coalesce to produce an embodied "journey into hyperreality" (Eco 1983, 8). Demands for the "real thing" produce images that imitate images, obscuring the lines between history and illusion. For some foreign tourists, visiting the shooting range and firing a Soviet AK-47 (or other weapons that the Củ Chi fighters had acquired) is the quintessential virtual guerrilla experience. During one tour in February 2000, a Canadian man expressed the "need to shoot a VC gun just once." Along with other tour participants, he purchased several rounds of automatic rifle ammunition for $1 apiece. Taking aim at painted animal targets in an open field, he fired them all off in less than two seconds and then shared how it felt to shoot an "actual" firearm from the war: "It was more real than the movies; a powerful, but solemn experience. I just had to do it." In relating his experience to U.S. popular culture, this respondent suggested that remembrance through reenactment is dependent on the conflation and simulation of multiple transnational imaginaries of the war, in which the availability of "real" guerrilla weapons evokes U.S. representations of "VC" in film. This merging of historical imaginaries took a new turn in 2004, when I returned to the shooting range to find a glass case containing the uniform, helmet, and shoes worn by a U.S. pilot during the war with a sign that read: "Whole Set for Rent 8,000VNĐ / Shoot / 10 minutes" (approximately $0.50US). This fusion of impersonations, in which foreign tourists wield the Soviet weapons of "Viet Cong" guerrillas while wearing U.S. Air Force uniforms, demonstrates the extent to which modes of historical representation at Củ Chi signify both recombination and transnationalization.

Domestic Visitors and Reconfigured Public Space

In contrast to foreigners who sought to experience the battlefield through recreation and representation, domestic tourists were rarely interested in, and in fact often attempted to avoid visiting, sites associated with the war. In interviews and conversations, Vietnamese tourists typically expressed a preference for traveling to beaches that dot the extensive coastline, cool mountainous areas such as Đà Lạt and Sa Pa, or cultural parks, such as Suối Tiên and Đầm Sen outside of Ho Chi Minh City, that draw on religious, historical, and nationalist imagery not unlike other themed recreational parks in Southeast Asia that present to visitors a "fantasized image of a fantasized [nation-state] polity" (Errington 1998, 222). Although local governments and state-owned companies encourage the populace to visit important sites of the revolution, often through subsidized tours, domestic tourists (a small but growing number of middle- and upper-class citizens) regularly linked their touristic desires to hedonistic pursuits of entertainment and leisure, rather than desires to consume history, trauma, and memory.[16]

If tourism signifies the desire to break from the everyday mundane and the ordinary as MacCannell (1999 [1976]) has suggested, than the general disinterest in

war sites, especially by older Vietnamese, can be understood as the result of a specific subject positioning in relation to the past. As I was often reminded, Củ Chi
is hardly a novelty for the generations of Vietnamese who lived during the war.[17]
To escape U.S. bombing raids, some villagers lived for extended periods of time in
tunnels, such as the one at Vịnh Mốc in Quảng Bình province, now a regular stop
on the DMZ tour in central Vietnam. In Hanoi, those who were not evacuated to
the countryside often sought safety underground when B-52 bombers approached.
Văn, who had been a student at the College of Foreign Languages in Hanoi when
the bombing of northern Vietnam began on August 5, 1964 (a date he vividly remembered), recalled: "When the bombs came we would hide in underground shel-
ters and trenches we had built ourselves. If the alarms sounded, we would move
into our trenches to study. It was that way for years." As we discussed his visit to Củ
Chi Bến Dược, I asked Văn if the tunnels were a popular destination for domestic
tourists. He answered no and explained: "Few Vietnamese go to Củ Chi. The young
people like it, but for people like myself, it is nothing special. Living in a tunnel is
not strange to me because that is how I lived during the war. Older people feel this
way and do not have a desire to visit there. I visited Củ Chi but not as a tourist; the
government paid for the trip."

Văn's comments provide important insights into domestic tourism at Củ Chi,
such as the state functions of Bến Dược and the role of government-sponsored
tours in bringing visitors, especially schoolchildren, to the tunnels. Such groups
typically come from state enterprises, organizations, and educational institutions
(as in Văn's case). The patriotic and pedagogical intentions behind these organized
trips are clearly linked to the emotive and historical messages that officials aim to
convey, namely, that the site should be able to "move visitors" and "stir their pride,"
as well as educate the youth and enhance their understanding of Vietnam's "tradition of revolution" (Trương Như Bá 2000, 38–39). Historical memory and knowledge of the past are further transferred and sustained through state commemorative rituals (Connerton 1989, 40), including public recognition of military war dead
on the side of the revolution. Each year on December 19, local Party officials con-
vene at a memorial temple on the grounds of Bến Dược to light incense at an altar
containing a large, gold-plated bust of Hồ Chí Minh and pay tribute to the 44,357
men and women from the greater Saigon–Gia Định area who fell during the French
and U.S. wars (Figure 3.4). As one temple employee pointed out, the names of the
deceased are inscribed in gold on large slabs of granite in a memorial style reminiscent of the Vietnam Veterans Memorial in Washington, D.C., a parallel that suggests traces of transnational aesthetic influence in official memorial projects.

Văn's comments, furthermore, confirmed my fieldwork observation that in addition to state-subsidized tours, Củ Chi Bến Dược also draws a younger Vietnamese

FIGURE 3.4. Altar in main sanctuary of martyr memorial temple, Bến Dược.
Photograph by the author.

crowd, who often come from adjacent city districts. Yet, as a tour guide was quick to point out, the attraction of Bến Dược for urban Vietnamese youth lies not with the tunnels but with the recreational facilities in the immediate area. Whereas the grounds of Bến Đình contained little more than souvenir shops and a small stand selling coconuts and cola, Bến Dược provided a commercialized leisure park and a respite from urban clamor and pollution. Pool tables, food stands, a mini hotel, and numerous cafés were places where youth gathered to talk, relax, eat, drink, and make new acquaintances. When I asked a guide why Vietnamese visitors go only to Bến Dược, the idea of distinct "tastes" surfaced again: "Because there is entertainment and the Vietnamese like entertainment! They don't care about going through the tunnels. Only foreigners like that. The young people like to go to the cafés, especially on Saturdays and Sundays. I think it's a place for love." This speculation was later corroborated by a female respondent in Ho Chi Minh City who took me to observe one of the latest urban phenomena in Vietnam: *café ôm* (hug cafés). The popularity of these cafés has grown in response to the increasing demand by young couples for private space. In a country where public affection is generally discouraged and there are few places lovers can be alone, hug cafés offer the privacy of a little cubicle and, in more peripheral areas such as Củ Chi, segregated nooks for couples under the trees. Spaces associated with violence and death are thus reinvented as spaces of love, desire, and pleasure.

In his work on public memory in the United States, John Bodnar (1992) argues that the official agendas of memorial institutions are often disrupted by vernacular interests. At Củ Chi, consumption practices do not always resonate with intended meanings, and at times they interrupt the ability of tourism officials to manage public space and the narratives of history they produce. Despite government efforts to retain its historical and commemorative significance, Vietnamese youth, in particular, have transformed the Củ Chi Tunnels into a site of entertainment that is largely detached from the war. In insisting on the irrelevance of the tunnel complex, they are neither engaged in debates over the past nor "reliving" the war and consuming it as spectacle like foreign visitors to the area. Rather, by turning a historical and pedagogical state site into a public space of pleasure, Vietnamese youth have imbued it with new antimemory functions and meanings that suggest their increasing detachment and distance from the nation's traumatic history.[18]

Tour Guides and Unofficial Historical Knowledge

The cultural landscape at Củ Chi is also unique to the extent that it represents a transnational public space in which memory and meaning are reconstituted not only by local youth or global tourists but also "other transnationals" (Hannerz 1998a) whose profession hinges on mobility and interconnectedness: namely, tour guides (Favero 2003). Since the early 1990s, tourism in Ho Chi Minh City has provided new jobs for the marginalized population of veterans of the former Army of the Republic of Vietnam (ARVN). These men are able to use their knowledge of the war and their ability to speak English to their economic and social advantage, as well as to the benefit of state and non-state actors in the tourism industry. As purveyors of specific memories that have been silenced by official history, ARVN veterans have turned their morally suspect experiences, cultural capital, and marginalized knowledge into a marketable commodity.

After reunification in 1975, ARVN soldiers were subjected to discriminatory measures and political reformation to integrate them into the imaginary of a united socialist homeland. Because of state employment policies that gave preferential treatment to citizens who had fought for and supported the revolution, many of these veterans survived economic and social hardship in the postwar period by working in the underground economy. In recent years, the rapid expansion of international tourism has provided these veterans with new employment prospects and career possibilities in the private sector. Take the case of Trung, a former officer of communications in the ARVN. After three arduous years in a reeducation camp followed by ten years in the countryside, Trung migrated back to Ho Chi Minh City in 1988, where he struggled to make ends meet as a pedicab driver until he found work as a freelance guide for an international tour operator. Trung has been able to use his reestablished global connections as a lucrative financial resource, and he currently runs his own private travel agency that specializes in catering to *tây ba lô* (western backpackers) and U.S. veterans. In his view, tourism is a viable option for former ARVN troops, despite their lack of official certification and competition with younger, government-trained and -certified guides,[19] because "foreigners, especially returning U.S. veterans, do not want to hear the party line" but prefer the other side of the story, the side that he has survived and can recall for his audiences. During my fieldwork, guides openly discussed their backgrounds and wartime experiences working with U.S. troops. At the outset of one tour in September 1999, the guide announced forthrightly to a busload of tourists that he was a "South Vietnamese soldier" who would "tell the truth," a perspective, he alleged, we would never hear from younger state guides who knew little of the war. Differing from official historical truth and knowledge, the truth of the ARVN veteran, expressed in his shared public recollections of the past, assumed an exchange value in which rhetoric and memory became commodities and a much-sought-after product for foreigners to consume.

Not unlike other individuals who have suffered political persecution and socioeconomic marginalization, guides from the former ARVN were expected to posses a "quasi-sacred power to represent truth" (Coutin 1993, 119). During tours of the Củ Chi Tunnels, international tourists were frequently interested in the "testimonies" of the veterans, and many were direct in asking about reeducation camps or personal sentiments toward the government and Party officials. Some foreigners, particularly those who harbored anticommunist suspicions, expressed their concerns about the "propaganda" and misinformation to which they were presumably exposed as they traveled through the country with younger, government-certified guides. In the words of one frustrated Australian tourist who felt overburdened by the war scripts that were woven into tours: "Everywhere we went in the Mekong our guide kept telling us: 'This bridge was bombed by Americans, this village was bombed,' and on and on. I finally said that I don't want to go to any more war sites. I'm tired of hearing about it. Besides, they always give you the wrong information anyway." On the other hand, there was the belief that ARVN veterans, as witnesses to certain injustices of the socialist regime, would be more objective, truthful, and forthcoming in their recollections than younger, government-trained guides. Yet, as scholars remind us, narrations of trauma are also fluid and mediated constructions of suffering, rather than transparent, unmediated truths (Antze and Lambek 1996; Douglass and Vogler 2003).

On tours, while some guides voiced their support for the present communist leadership, others used their position to speak out and publicly express their bitterness to an international audience. Standing before a busload of predominantly European tourists, an irate guide instructed me: "Write this down. The government does what it wants. It does not listen to the people. That is the problem here." After condemning Party corruption, he declared to his fully attentive audience: "Anyone with money is a VC because non-VC have no way to become rich." In a society in which public political dissent is largely discouraged, such tour guide discourse can be understood as a "hidden transcript" that recirculates anticommunist historical rhetoric ("VC") and expresses socioeconomic and political dissatisfaction without directly confronting or challenging the state (Scott 1990).

That ARVN veterans are now finding jobs as tour guides demonstrates how the value of knowledge has changed over time, and that a critical renegotiation of historical memory has taken place in which unofficial knowledge and memories of the past are redirected, reshaped, and revalued to benefit the market and the state, as well as the veterans themselves. This shift is significant given postwar efforts to impose historical amnesia on the "losing" side. Even today, there continues to be a lack of public space to commemorate or mourn RVN military war dead, after monuments and martyr cemeteries of the previous regime were destroyed or forcibly abandoned (Figure 3.5).[20] Yet, like the "Requiem" exhibit, it is clear that some

FIGURE 3.5. Former RVN military cemetery at Biên Hòa. While most graves have been abandoned (and the remains removed), some are still discreetly cared for. The cemetery's central monument is visible in the background. Photograph by the author.

measure of public remembrance is permitted and no longer perceived as a threat to social stability. The communication of ARVN veteran sentiments to foreigners, references to popular cultural representations of the war at the tunnels, and the narration of stories about U.S. forces and "South Vietnam," with a peppering of slang phrases and acronyms, such as "VC" and "DMZ," attest to the complex entanglements of diversely situated transnational memories and imaginaries that inform and give shape to knowledge produced and consumed at Củ Chi.

Reconstituting Memory

As capitalist globalization in Vietnam ushers in an era of renewed capitalist projects, reestablished global markets, and "normalized" diplomatic relations, the contours and constraints of historical memory have shifted in new and complex ways. The cases presented here underscore the presence of multifaceted practices of memory at sites where transnational imaginaries of the war are remade into multisensory spectacles. Though traversed by capitalist consumer culture, memory at war sites such as Củ Chi is not necessarily erased, defiled, trivialized, or homogenized, as popular beliefs would hold, so much as it is reconstituted, recombined, renarrated, and resignified by multiple actors, all of whom bring to the site their differing histories and relationships to the past. This does not deny the absence of certain memories and narrations of particular historical actors, but calls attention to the complex memory work that transpires for many at war tourist sites. While some visitors worked through the trauma of defeat, as in the case of the former navy veteran or Trung, the tour guide who retells stories from a difficult past, others engaged in anti-memory activities, such as the young lovers at Củ Chi. Still others were active participants in the re-creation of wartime subjectivities through embodied practices of memory that suggest a reanimation of the past in the present: lighting cigarettes with fake war-era Zippos, dancing till dawn in an apocalyptic ambiance, crawling through tunnels, and firing guerrilla weapons in the contrived and hyperreal atmosphere of guerrilla warfare. In all these cases, memory is a collection of reconstructed images (Halbwachs 1992 [1952]), forged through the intertwining of oral narrations, lived experiences, state representations, popular culture, and the global mass media, thus dissolving the boundaries between individual, historically reconstructed, and culturally produced memories.

Touristic processes that commodify war and, in the process, instill history and memory with exchange value are indicative of larger global trends in which images and knowledge of social suffering are appropriated and consumed in diverse social fields. Yet, if projects of history and practices of memory signify shifting engagements with power, as Lisa Rofel (1999) has suggested, then these processes also provide insights into a global politics and transnational political economy of knowledge production and postcolonial power relations. Assigning value to icons and images from the war reflects historically constituted socioeconomic and geopolitical relations within transnational fields of power. The ambivalence of Vietnamese citizens toward such commodities, in contrast with the engaged consumption by international visitors, alludes to the symbolic violence that occurs in converting the landscape of Vietnamese suffering into an object of consumption. For the state, the marketing of war for transnational tourism not only brings in much-needed foreign capital, but it also contributes to the strengthening of diplomatic relationships to the extent that it denotes a new era of "openness" in the economy and in civil society, with less restricted access to sites, materials, and knowledge about the war. On tours to battlefields and other war sites, the "invisible enemy" is finally made present as military secrets and guerrilla strategies are unveiled and displayed for the visitor. Shifts in both the economy and historical memory thus reflect the Vietnamese state's precarious global position as it negotiates global hierarchies of power and international (especially U.S.) pressure to further implement democratic reforms and neoliberal policies.

Monumentalizing War

Toward a New Aesthetics of Memory

CHAPTER FOUR

Đà Lạt,
December 1997, Chicken Village

Traveled outside the city of Đà Lạt today, into the hills of the Central Highlands, on motorbikes with two ARVN veterans as the guides. The men approached me in the street with a book of photographs and recommendations from previous tourists. I agreed and off we went on their self-made tour. Along the way we stopped at an impoverished K'ho ethnic minority village, which the guides referred to as "Chicken Village" on account of a massive cement chicken statue that greets visitors, reportedly bestowed by the government upon the residents as a "reward" for resettling and abandoning a nomadic lifestyle (Figure 4.1). One of the guides criticized the monument and local authorities for wasting money on an impractical statue that could have been used to combat the area's abject poverty.

Đà Nẵng,
June 2000, Mother Courage

"Put into action our heroic traditions" [*Phát huy truyền thống anh hùng*] read the street signs on my way to view the monument *Mẹ Dũng Sĩ* [Mother Courage] at the entrance to Đà Nẵng city. The taxi driver, whose parents had worked for U.S. troops during the war, called the monumental statue, constructed in 1985 for the ten-year anniversary of national independence, a "symbol of patriotism and liberation" (Figure 4.2). At the base of the monument, city regulations stipulated proper behavior: no petty trade, consumption of alcohol, waste disposal, or sports

FIGURE 4.1. "Chicken Village," outside Đà Lạt, Lâm Đồng province.
Photograph by the author.

should take place in the immediate area. Such monuments honoring "heroic mothers" [*bà mẹ anh hùng*] have been a point of scorn for many who see the government
as having invested money in "useless" things like memorials, instead of support-
ing impoverished mothers who are often without family as a result of the war. "Invest more money in 'gratitude houses'" [*nhà tình nghĩa*], for example, has been a
common sentiment.

FIGURE 4.2. *Mẹ Dũng Sĩ* [Mother Courage], 1985, by artist Phạm Văn Hạng, Đà Nẵng. Photograph by the author.

Điện Biên Phủ,
June 2007, Eating the Statue

Front-page coverage in the Vietnamese press: seven officials in the city of Điện Biên Phủ are arrested and charged with corruption in the 2004 construction of the *Điện Biên Phủ* victory monument that marked the fiftieth anniversary of Vietnam's defeat of the French on May 7, 1954 (Figure 4.3). The bronze, 12.6-meter statue—reportedly the largest of its kind in Vietnam—has since fallen into "serious disrepair," according to the *Lao Động* [Labor] newspaper (Duy Thanh 2007), on account of the embezzlement of project funds (30 percent, it is estimated) and the resulting shoddy and unaesthetic construction of the statue which now urgently requires additional funds for renovation. The case of the "eaten" monument has again engendered calls to halt the construction of costly [*tốn kém*] and unsightly [*xấu xí*] "foreign-style" statues.

Recent years have seen a marked increase in the number of state memorial projects throughout Vietnam with the construction, renovation, and beautification of memorial temples, martyr cemeteries, monuments, and other national sites of memory. In Hanoi new and ambitious monument initiatives have coincided with extensive urban redevelopment projects and large-scale preparation for the upcoming thousand-year anniversary of the city's founding (Nguyễn Vinh Phúc 2000, 13). Against the backdrop of such changes, this chapter examines recent shifts in the visual and cultural landscape of commemorative art and architecture, with an eye to aesthetic practices of nation building and memory making that have taken place in the post-economic reform era. As sites for the cultural and artistic expression of national values, sentiments, and ideals that are neither fixed nor agreed upon, state monuments reflect both the shifting sociohistorical and aesthetic contexts in which they are produced (J. Young 2000, 93). The three field note excerpts presented above span a decade of research interest in the contested terrain of monumentalization; in particular, critical responses to memorial proliferation and its reputed costly and substandard aesthetic production. Central to these debates have been politicized discussions about how to recognize, represent, and memorialize the past in cost-effective and aesthetically proper "Vietnamese" form.

   This chapter examines recent trends in the diversification of monument design and commemorative practices as linked to efforts to define and demarcate a "Vietnamese" aesthetic-cultural identity that is distinct from "foreign" influence. This has entailed, for example, the adornment of modernist monuments with cultural icons that imbue secular sites of collective state memory with more religious and personal significance. Ensuing dialogue about authenticity and foreignness demonstrate intensified engagements with, and anxieties about, the role and constitu-

FIGURE 4.3. Victory monument at Điện Biên Phủ, 2004, by artist Nguyễn Hải.
Photograph by the author.

tion of Vietnamese "traditional" culture in a moment of fast-paced global capitalist change. An analysis of current shifts and debates in the field of commemorative public art and architecture reveals tensions and contradictions that underlie and inform national and transnational memory work at this specific historical juncture. It also provides insights into how people reconfigure their worlds and their relationships to the enduring visual legacies of former empires as the lines between socialism and capitalism, spiritualism and state materialism, local and foreign, are further obscured.

As a technology of rule that gives visual expression to nationalist sentiments of solidarity, state-erected monuments articulate and communicate to the masses hegemonic moralities, cultural-national identities, and political-historical consciousness that are presumed to be shared (Sherman 1999, 7). Yet despite state intentions, which are themselves never uniform, monuments remain contested sites of layered, equivocal meanings and diverse (and often noncommemorative) practices that rework dominant aesthetic and memorial processes (J. Young 1993). National memory, scholars such as Renan (1990 [1882]) and Anderson (1991 [1983]) remind us, depends as much upon remembrance and representation as it does upon forgetfulness. Thus I approach monuments not only as a technology of memory (Sturken 1997a), but also as an instrument of forgetting that silences and displaces particular historical pasts and sociocultural modes of memory making.

As in previous chapters, however, my concern here lies less with confrontations between official and vernacular memory than with moving beyond the borders of the nation to show how seemingly "national" projects such as commemorative art and architecture are entangled with broader transnational aesthetic practices and historical struggles over power, memory, knowledge, history, and meaning. Reading monuments and examining changes to the landscape of memory, including the rejection of "foreign" commemorative styles and the recent addition of transnational peace memorials initiated by returning U.S. and other veterans, show how current debates concerning artistic and commemorative agency invoke and yet simultaneously transcend the nation. I examine how monuments, as disciplinary sites for the management of particular histories and memorial hierarchies, have been reworked in recent years by cultural producers and consumers whose competing agendas of remembrance and representation have produced new forms and practices of memory.

Historicizing Vietnamese Monumentalism

Vietnam's memoryscape is dotted with war monuments, martyr cemeteries, commemorative statues, and other state productions of memory that recognize heroic and virtuous sacrifice [hy sinh] for the socialist nation. Like conventional war monuments in other national contexts, Vietnamese public commemorative art and architecture convey dominant (though often contested) narratives of suffering, sacrifice, indebtedness, and citizenship. As a practice in Foucauldian biopolitics, according to Yves Helias, official memorial processes and their representation in monumental form work to publicly and visually reaffirm the role and the right of the state to conscript citizen bodies to serve in defense of the nation (cited in Winter 1995, 94).

At first glance, the public recognition and commemoration of citizen contribution and loss in wartime with the ubiquitous inscription on monuments "Tổ Quốc Ghi Công" [The Fatherland Remembers Your Contribution] suggests state practices of democratizing death, not unlike European commemoration following World War I (Laqueur 1994, 151; Mosse 1990, 99).[1] This practice is most evident in contemporary "martyr cemeteries" [nghĩa trang liệt sĩ], in which one finds strict uniformity in the size and shape of graves that are ordered nonhierarchically and without attention to rank (Figure 4.4). With few exceptions (see Hồ Trung Tú 1998), this differs significantly from prerevolution Vietnam, when common soldiers and lay participants in warfare were typically *not* ascribed to public national memory, save for prominent military leaders who came to occupy exalted (and sometimes sainted) positions in the pantheon of heroes, such as the thirteenth-century general Trần Hưng Đạo. Yet the democratization of death in contemporary, postreunification Vietnam is also based on a politics and practice of exclusion, as it carefully demarcates proper forms of belonging to the social category of "martyr" [liệt sĩ]. As Shaun Malarney points out, though the term *liệt sĩ* predates the socialist revolution, it became an official (and verified) classification for soldiers who were "sacrificed" [hy sinh] in battle during the revolutionary wars (2002, 173).[2] While monuments and martyr cemeteries acknowledge the collective contribution of *liệt sĩ* regardless of their deed and rank, this memory excludes, for example, war dead from the ARVN, whose monuments were promptly dismantled after the end of the war and who currently have no official public spaces of commemoration.[3]

Despite their ubiquity in Vietnam's landscape, towering monuments and figurative memorials represent an "invented" tradition (Hobsbawm 1983) and a "foreign" aesthetic-commemorative practice that was introduced to Vietnam during French colonial rule (Dương Trung Quốc 1998, 37). Historically, Vietnamese heroes were not publicly honored and remembered via collective and secular monuments [tượng đài], but worshipped at temples [đền] dedicated to "deities, national heroes, or persons who rendered meritorious services to the country or to a particular village or district" (Nguyễn Bá Đang et al. 2006, 36). While temples in Vietnam [đền] are distinguished from Buddhist pagodas [chùa], during my research I found that both have been used in certain—often urban—locations to house small shrines

FIGURE 4.4. Democratizing death: Uniform graves of revolutionary martyrs at Trường Sơn National Cemetery, Quảng Trị province. Photograph by the author.

to *liệt sĩ*, a controversial practice on account of its blurring of the boundaries between *nhớ* [secular remembrance] and *thờ* [worship to ask for protection/favors]. For example, in Hanoi, where there are few large war monuments due to space constraints, it is not uncommon to find newly erected shrines to *liệt sĩ* on the grounds of temples, pagodas, or communal houses [*đình*], in which village tutelary gods are honored.

Both "modern" monuments and "traditional" temples, it could be argued, are *lieux de mémoire*, sites in which the past is channeled and given representation to mitigate the anxiety of memory's displacement in modernity (Nora 1989). Yet differences in memorial intent—honoring the memory of the collective war dead to counter forgetting versus worshipping exceptional heroes to secure their assistance and protection—rendered these memorial acts (and their architectural representation) fundamentally irreconcilable to my research respondents. In interviews, artists and intellectuals repeatedly referred to war memorials and monumental sculpture as "non-Vietnamese" practices of memory.[4] The threat of "foreignness" to displace "tradition" was suggested by one art historian in particular, who hinted at commemorative mimesis and inauthenticity in an interview: "It's a tradition in Vietnam to visit a temple, not to construct large monuments or statues to commemorate war. But then Vietnam started to imitate the West and build memorials. This came from the influence of French colonialism."

William S. Logan has argued that Vietnam's urban landscapes can be read as a layering of past geopolitical and sociocultural domination, from Chinese to French to Soviet influence (2000, 9). Each layer tends to disrupt, dismantle, displace, and yet simultaneously engage and at times coexist with or draw upon past architectural legacies to demonstrate shifting and impermanent ideological regimes of representation. While some material and aesthetic aspects of these imperial legacies have been Vietnamized and appropriated as local "tradition" (such as temples [đền], which Logan claims reflect Chinese practices [2000, 45], yet my respondents firmly identified as Vietnamese), others retain their "foreignness" and are tolerated, if not revalued and reclassified as part of a larger Vietnamese history of architectural heritage. And still other architectural icons were seen as antithetical to, or in the way of, national hegemony, as was the case in postwar Saigon, where the material embodiment of a delegitimized regime in monuments and other historical markers merited their immediate destruction.

This is, of course, also the story and the legacy of French colonial architecture. As Panivong Norindr has argued, French architectural discourses were central to the production of Indochina as phantasmatic imaginary, which served to "reinscribe the colonized subject within a framework that answers to the political and aesthetic needs of an imperialist's appropriation of exotic worlds" (1996, 23–24). Colonial urban design, predicated on the reordering, reconstruction, and, at times, destruction of Vietnamese architecture, became a visual reminder and expression of France's political domination and cultural superiority (Wright 1991). In Hanoi, efforts to recreate Paris in the Orient consisted of large-scale infrastructural projects such as road and bridge works, as well as the construction of extravagant municipal buildings, cultural and knowledge institutions (such as museums), churches, villas, department stores, and other commercial architecture that entangled "modernization" with capitalism. Despite the looming threat of ephemerality, the extravagance of these urban projects attempted to "convey the impression of authority and continuity where they by no means existed" (Wright 1991, 166). As Logan has shown in great detail, French urban projects of "modernization" resulted in the displacement and demolition of significant Vietnamese architectural vestiges, such as temples, pagodas, and other religious and historical sites of memory that interrupted France's civilizing mission (2000, 80–91).

Monuments were another technology of rule meant to assert via the urban landscape French colonial power and the permanence of empire. In Hanoi, monuments and statues were constructed in urban parks and squares, several of which were located in the vicinity of Hoàn Kiếm Lake. In the late nineteenth century, for example, a smaller replica of the Statue of Liberty was built to the west of the lake; on the eastern bank, a statue of Governor-General Paul Bert was erected but a few years later (Dương Trung Quốc 1998, 37). A few kilometers away, a statue to signify French protection of Indochina (entitled *France as the Protector of Its Asian Daughters*) was emplaced before the Governor-General's Palace in 1908,[5] and a monument to commemorate both World War I and the fiftieth anniversary of the founding of the French Republic was constructed next to the Opera House in 1920 (Nguyễn Vinh Phúc 2000, 11). Built upon the French-destroyed ruins of hundreds of years of Vietnamese architectural history, these monuments obliterated sites and practices of Vietnamese memory through the establishment of a new visual commemorative order that placed a higher value on French history, artistic form, memory, and meaning.

In Saigon, similar processes of monumentalization took place. In his late-nineteenth-century memoirs, Pierre Barrelon described colonial Saigon as one of the most beautiful and monumental cities in the Far East: "Public monuments have been built that would embellish whichever city in the world . . . On [Boulevard Norodom] stands the great bronze statue of Gambetta. It teaches our subjects, the Annamese, that at home we erect statues and with good reasons for the courageous who strove to throw a foreign invasion from of [*sic*] our national soil" (1999 [1893], 54, 56). And learn they did! Following the 1945 revolution, many French monuments in Hanoi were razed; some of these were eventually replaced with memorials to honor Vietnamese heroes who helped to overthrow colonialism (Dương Trung Quốc 1998, 38), such as the towering statue to the revolution toward the northern end of Hoàn Kiếm Lake constructed in 1984 on the site where a memorial to the Portuguese Jesuit missionary Alexander de Rhodes once stood on the partially destroyed grounds of the seventeeth-century Bà Kiệu temple (Figure 4.5). David Morgan has pointed out, "When an idol falls, its place does not long remain vacant . . . [A]s Stanislaw Lec more poignantly advised aspiring iconoclasts: 'When smashing monuments save the pedestals—they always come in handy'" (2005, 115).

Iconoclasm, Adrian Forty has argued, not only signifies the collapse of overthrown regimes and the desire to induce forgetting. It is also an act of reclaiming history, and of constituting a new regime of memory (1999, 10–12). Iconoclastic acts, in other words, are as much about the future as they are about the past. With the founding of the Democratic Republic of Vietnam (DRV) in 1945, Hanoi set about creating a new tool kit of national memory to ground and legitimize its project of socialist nation building. National museums and commemorative holidays were established, such as War Invalids and Martyrs Day [*Ngày Thương Binh Liệt Sĩ*] on July 27, 1947. After the defeat of the French in 1954, a cemetery for war dead was constructed at Mai Dịch on the outskirts of the city. Street and building names that commemorated French historical figures were replaced with names of

FIGURE 4.5. *Cảm Tử Cho Tổ Quốc Quyết Sinh* [Determined to Brave Death for the Survival of the Fatherland], 1984, by artist Nguyễn Kim Giao, Hanoi. Photograph by the author.

Vietnamese heroes and revolutionaries (Logan 2000, 216–217). A new postcolonial history was created (Pelley 2002). Monuments and memorials were erected, most notably, the mausoleum of Hồ Chí Minh after his death in 1969, though such projects were hampered as resources and labor were directed toward the escalating war with the United States.

Forging a national aesthetic and iconography are also central to cultural nation building processes (Löfgren 1993, 162). In the DRV, a rhetoric of "newness" guided revolutionary cultural policy and its visions of a socialist order of progressive new socialist men and women, with new revolutionary ethics, new lifestyles, customs, and ideological sentiments (Ninh 2002; Lê Duẩn 1977, 119–122; Ha Huy Giap 1978; Malarney 2002, 53–57). "New culture" [*văn hóa mới*], as advocated by Party officials, however, did not represent a complete aesthetic, moral, and cultural rupture with the past. As culture theorist Trường Chinh stipulated in his 1948 treatise, *Marxism and Vietnamese Culture*, new revolutionary and democratic culture entailed the embrace and preservation of Vietnamese heritage and foreign influences thought to be "good and beautiful," and a rejection of negative and destructive cultural practices (1997 [1948], 139). As Hồ Chí Minh proclaimed: "That which is old and bad, must be eliminated . . . That which is old and not bad, but trouble-some, must be modified and made sensible . . . That which is old and good, must be further developed . . . That which is new and good must be created!" (in Bùi Đình Phong 1998, 218). Practices deemed superstitious [*mê tín*], backward [*lạc hậu*], and feudal [*phong kiến*] that hindered the cultural and scientific development of the na-tion were thus targeted for elimination or modification (Malarney 1996, 542; 2002, 81–83; Trường Chinh 1997 [1948], 140–141).[6]

"New culture" likewise required a reorientation in the arts, a movement away from "escapist" and "aestheticist" French practices (art for art's sake) toward "ob-jective" and "truthful" representation of social development, what Trường Chinh and others identified as the doctrine of socialist realism (Trường Chinh 1997 [1948], 142–143, 163–164; Ninh 2002, 62). As the new aesthetic of the revolution, social-ist realism was understood to be a "method of artistic creation" that would depict the lives, work, and revolutionary spirit of the masses in order to educate, lead, and inspire them (Trường Chinh 1997 [1948], 163; Boi 2005, 135). Twenty years later, Prime Minister Phạm Văn Đồng reaffirmed art as the most effective ideological and cultural tool of the revolution because of its tendency to "delve deep into the thoughts and sentiments of people, sowing the seeds of a great harvest" (1975, 89–90).[7] What is of particular concern to me here is the application of socialist realist practices and methods to the cultural field of monument production, and the ways in which such aesthetic projects, and their communication of political, national, and historical messages to the masses, drew upon and at times merged both colo-nial and revolutionary aesthetics that were strongly influenced by French and So-viet commemorative cultures.

After the end of the war in 1975 and official reunification of the country one year later, monument production accelerated, most notably in areas that supported the revolution. Like their memorial predecessors, monuments designed at this time had much in common with French memorial styles. As in post–World War I France, the obelisk was by far the most common memorial constructed, most likely on account of its low construction cost (Sherman 1999, 171; Winter 1995, 97). Fol-lowing standard memorial convention in France and elsewhere, monuments pre-sented a sanitized and glorified past that transformed devastated "fields of horror" into heroic "fields of Honour" (Kidd 2002, 188). Moreover, in accordance with the secularist tenets of new socialist culture, and echoing western secularized com-memorative practices, memorial sites were constructed as distinctly nonsupersti-tious, national spaces of secular memory in which visitors were to commemorate [*tưởng niệm, tưởng nhớ*], honor [*tôn vinh*], and pay their respects [*tôn trọng*] to the dead, rather than to propitiate and worship [*thờ*] them with incense and other offerings (Hoàng Đạo Kính 1999, 26).[8] As Shaun Malarney has argued, unlike non-state, family customary commemorative practices, public war memorials were *not* spaces for the proper care and nurturance of the souls of the war dead (2001, 68).[9] Rather, as a "modern" [*hiện đại*] architectural form, commemorative practice, and architectural technology, monuments served to materialize the nation, its memory and its history, in spaces that research respondents increasingly came to vocalize as "non-Vietnamese."

At the same time, Vietnamese monuments diverged in particular ways from French memorial iconography. In the 1950s memorial structures, such as Hanoi's former memorial platform and monument at Ba Đình, the obelisk at Mai Dịch martyr cemetery, and the Việt Minh war memorial on Hill A1 at Điện Biên Phủ, incorporated indigenous motifs into design and form (Figure 4.6). This practice gradually diminished as cooperation with the Soviet Union increased, particularly in the postwar years of national reconstruction when architects from the Soviet Union and other aligned countries further marked the urban landscape with distinct socialist architectural styles.[10] Lenin's decree on "monumental propaganda" also had a noticeable effect on Vietnamese aesthetic practices as heroic figurative monuments, with outstretched arms and clenched fists, became increasingly popular.[11] While French colonial and French-influenced monuments were recognized as appropriately sized for the urban spaces in which they were displayed, often true to life forms, statues and memorials that embraced Soviet trends were noted for their "monumental dimensions" [*quy mô hoành tráng*] (Dương Trung Quốc 1998, 38). Yet, significant differences emerged. Female figures, for example, were given diverse and more prominent representation in Vietnam's memorial iconography than in France and the Soviet Union, where women were commonly linked to maternal nationalist imagery (for example, suffering mothers in France and "Mother Homeland" in Soviet cities). While in Vietnam the image of the mother (and grandmother) also "became the cultural vector of grief and memory" (Tai 2001b, 177), monumental statues of young women as active and heroic agents of war and revolution also abound. Additionally, while monument construction in France and the Soviet Union commonly involved higher-quality materials such as stone or bronze, in postwar Vietnam, the materials used—cement or concrete, often watered down, and occasionally yellow paint as a gold leaf substitute—reflected cash-strapped provincial and national coffers.[12] After economic reform, the accelerated rate of monument construction and renovation, with gray, cracked statues replaced with granite or marble copies, attested visually and symbolically to an era of growing prosperity and concern for the maintenance and management of historical memory.

FIGURE 4.6. 1950s obelisk at Mai Dịch cemetery, Hanoi. Photograph by the author.

The Democratic Politics of Monument Production

Monument construction in Vietnam is a multitiered process that involves, at various stages and to differing degrees, multiple state, non-state, corporate, and at times transnational actors. It has often been noted in the Vietnamese media and in art and architecture magazines that public and state expenditures on the design and production of monuments have increased in tandem with economic development. Projects have become progressively larger, more costly, and more ostentatious, as one municipal district attempts to outshine the next, funds permitting. The landscape of monumentalization can be read as a map of increasing prosperity, spread unevenly. In 1983, for example, amid the difficult subsidy period, the provincial authorities of Phú Khánh province in southern Vietnam invested *twenty million* Vietnamese đồng into a concrete war memorial. Six years later, in the early stages of economic reform, city authorities in Vinh City, in the central province of Nghệ An, invested *one hundred million* đồng in a stone memorial to commemorate martyrs. Around the same time, in the wealthier southern beach city of Nha Trang, city officials spent *three billion* đồng on a granite replacement of a victory statue and park. In 2004, *forty-seven billion* đồng was invested in the bronze Điện Biên Phủ fiftieth anniversary victory statue mentioned in the corruption case at the beginning of this chapter. "Our country is still extremely poor," the renowned art critic Phan Cẩm Thượng remarked to the press in 2004, two months after the Điện Biên Phủ statue had been erected in the poorest area of the nation (northwest Vietnam). "We don't have the right to spend money on such luxuries. We need to stop producing these large, bulky, imposing, ugly monuments now" (Thu Hà and Uyên Ly 2004).

As monumentalization intensified, and new actors, such as overseas Vietnamese and returning war veterans, came on to the scene, state regulations established new legal parameters and guidelines for memorial design and implementation. The Ministry of Culture and Information's Decision No. 05/2000/QD-BVHTT of March 29, 2000, on the "Management and Construction of Grandiose Monuments," outlined in great detail a democratic and transparent process that further opened the door to non-state and transnational historical memory and its presentation in diversified monumental forms, without fully relinquishing state authority. Article 3, for example, stipulated that "state bodies, social and mass organizations, Vietnamese citizens, overseas Vietnamese and foreign nationals may build and thereafter must maintain responsibility for the management, renovation, repair, or replacement of monuments." This reaffirmed favorable conditions for citizen-led memorial initiatives and transnational commemorative reconciliation projects, provided that the "ideological contents" did not contradict the "cultural, literary, and artistic policies of the Party, the State laws and the morals and customs of the nation" (Article 2).

At the central level, the Ministry of Culture and Information (MCI) in Hanoi oversees and grants permits for monument construction and renovation in conjunction with the Vietnam Fine Arts Association and a provisional Arts Council that comprises sculptors, painters, architects, and administrators who "have prestige and high professional and moral qualities" (Article 8).[13] At the provincial and municipal levels, local people's committees and local ad hoc art councils work together on project approval and implementation, along with the provincial branch of the ministry. Funding generally comes from a combination of state, provincial, or local budgets, and, increasingly, citizen contributions. For example, Vinh City residents donated five million đồng to the 1989 memorial, 5 percent of project costs, at a time when monthly income in the province hovered around forty thousand đồng (approximately $6) for civil servants ("Khởi công xây dựng" 1989).

In most cases, competitions are held to determine the most worthy and relevant monument design, though an "investor" (the instigator of the monument project) may invite a specific artist, provided that he or she has a university degree in sculpture and has been the designer of at least two large-scale monument projects in the past (Article 6). If no specific sculptor is desired, the investor must organize a design competition, which is open to all artists and architects who have experience in sculpture or propose to work with trained sculptors on the project. Contributors must first submit a sixty-centimeter model of their design, to be evaluated and ranked by the Arts Council. The investor establishes a scoring rubric that the council must adhere to "so as to ensure fairness, honesty, accuracy, and secrecy" (Article 11). Working on the "principle of equality and democracy" among all members, the final selection is made through individual secret ballots. A design must acquire at least 50 percent of the votes for the decision to be valid and presented to the investor and the MCI or its provincial branches for approval (Article 10). After final consent and acquisition of necessary permits, the author and investor select a team of artists and others with whom they will construct the monument. Corporate entities that provide labor and construction materials are incorporated at this stage (Figure 4.7). For example, the services of the Đoàn Kết Bronze Casting Company were contracted to build the 12.6-meter-high, 360-ton Điện Biên Phủ victory statue (the vice director of which was subsequently arrested in the corruption case).

In January 2000, I interviewed Minh, a sculptor and employee at the Military Arts Association, who works on monument and art production that falls under the jurisdiction of the military. Minh has entered several monument competitions, and his designs have won three times. Born in 1960 in Hanoi, Minh is part of a post-

FIGURE 4.7. Monument construction on the grounds of the former Air Force Museum in Hanoi, 2000. Photograph by the author.

colonial generation of artists who grew up at a time when children were evacuated to rural areas to escape U.S. bombing raids. Minh's work is distinct in that he blends revolutionary art themes with abstract and modernist sculptural forms. As we wandered through an exhibit at the Army Museum (now the Military History Museum) that marked the fifty-fifth anniversary of the founding of the People's Army on December 22, 1944, he pointed to a selection of designs submitted to a recent monument competition.[14] While some of the miniaturized models embraced a more traditional socialist-realist aesthetic (such as statues of Hồ Chí Minh), other designs were more unusual, such as the militarized metal bodhisattva with multiple outstretched arms standing on an unexploded U.S. bomb. Other less figurative designs were more abstract in form, including the wing of a mythical phoenix to symbolize the strength and the continuity of the nation. Minh emphasized the growing diversity and imaginative qualities of Vietnamese monumental art, challenging conventional views of socialist aesthetics as uniform and unidimensional (see also Lahusen and Dobrenko 1997).

I asked Minh to explain what a good design needs to merit selection. He answered promptly that submissions should exude monumentalism and possess political and historical significance. At the same time, he continued, artists are also being held more accountable to "art"; that is, they are now called upon by fellow cultural producers and the public to create more aesthetically pleasing public monuments. Minh seemed to believe that the selection process was fair—the best submission to the competition would win. Yet when I asked him to clarify the role of the sculptor in the postselection process, he became more critical. "It's a funny story," he replied. "An artist can submit one small model based on a particular idea, and if chosen, it will be enlarged. The thing is, after the monument is made, the sculptor usually can't recognize the work anymore. During the process, the design undergoes so many changes to make everyone happy that in the end, it often doesn't look the same anymore."

Many postcolonial cultural producers I spoke with expressed skepticism about participating in state-organized artistic competitions. Artists and architects often voiced complaints that such contests were "rigged by officials" or "won only by those with the right contacts." "I only enter international contests," a female architect named Linh who works at the Ministry of Culture and Information informed me. "The jury never takes your work seriously here, and they are never fair. Someone always wins for other reasons, not on account of their work." Concerns with corruption often surfaced, only to be reconfirmed by scandals such as the one that occurred in Điện Biên Phủ. According to a painter named Đức: "I don't know for certain, but I have heard many rumors. When you win the competition, you get a lot of money. Yes, a lot of money is involved. For instance, at my university, after the dean won a monument contest, he suddenly became very wealthy. If your design is chosen, you must have connections. That's how it works here."

Relationships to revolutionary art in general, and the construction of monuments in particular, were mapped onto generational differences by artists I interviewed. To my respondents, older artists who participated in the war and revolution were more aligned with state art production while younger postcolonial generations with new commercial and global opportunities increasingly distanced themselves from the state and the state-run Fine Arts Association. In reality, such divisions were not so neat, as the case of Minh demonstrates. Another postcolonial artist (also born in 1960) pointed out that even state artists who used their skills to support the revolution (for example, creating "propaganda" posters) unofficially produced nonrevolutionary art in the privacy of their homes or elsewhere.

Nonetheless, the ambivalence of younger artists, particularly those who grew up in postwar Hanoi, was often a topic of conversation. One fall evening, in a small café in Hanoi, I sat drinking hot tea with two cosmopolitan artists, both of whom have spent much time overseas: Đức, a male painter born in 1971, whom I quoted above, and Mai, a female performer born in 1974. The conversation shifted to their training in "Marxist-Leninist aesthetics," which they rebuked as outdated and irrelevant for today's more global artists:

Mai (laughing): Even today this is still taught in the university. We had to read this book called *The Road to Culture and the Arts.*

Đức (also laughing): Oh yes—*The Road to Culture and the Arts.* We were told that we have to follow this way . . . Those older artists are so fixed on the past. Not me. I'm independent and have no desire to join the Fine Arts Association. I just can't relate to most of the artists there. They are nice people and all, but I am just not inspired by national themes like them. Take Hồ Chí Minh. Sure, he was a good man. But I just cannot figure out where the inspiration to paint or sculpt him comes from. Nobody forces artists to do it; they do this on their own. I mean I admire him and all, but I don't want to paint him. But for some people he is magic.

Đức and Mai's conversation about Hanoi's art scene and training as polarized between different generations of artists underscores the very different subject positions that cultural producers occupy in relation to history, memory, and the state. Yet, Mai, Đức, and their artist friends are not the only ones critical of such aesthetic trends. As Minh suggested, artists and the public are increasingly demanding new artistic styles, as well as new practices of memory.

Vacant Lots: Reception and Aesthetic Rejection of State Memorials

Vietnamese monuments, thought to embody official (and often conflicting) ideologies and memories of the past, are not unambiguously an expression of state autonomy and power. Rather, as a relatively new form of public art and architecture, monuments also signify a "foreign" aesthetic order and cultural practice that ironically invokes and gives visual representation to histories of domination that complicate the intended narrative of national liberation. Conjuring memories of French and Soviet political and aesthetic hegemony, it is no surprise that memorial aesthetics, and their corresponding practices, have been vociferously critiqued as "nontraditional" and "unfamiliar" by cultural producers and visitors alike.

By and large, state memorial sites, including martyr cemeteries, remain vacant except during state commemorative ceremonies (for example, War Invalids and Martyrs Day) or brief and infrequent visits by family members of war dead, usually on death anniversaries [*ngày giỗ*], lunar new year, and also state memorial holidays. This is, of course, not unique to Vietnam. Robert Musil (1987) has notably written about monuments as conspicuously inconspicuous; they repel, rather than attract attention, and fade unnoticeably into the landscape. In Vietnam, as the monument and its primary significance fade from attention in everyday life,

FIGURE 4.8. Threshing rice at Gia Trấn martyr cemetery, Ninh Bình province.
Photograph by the author.

the open and oft-vacant space in which it rests may be infused with new value and
meaning, and put to alternative social and economic uses, such as feeding livestock
or drying and threshing rice (Figure 4.8).

Hùng, a Hanoi intellectual whose father was a veteran of the August Revolution
in 1945, explained the multiple and fluctuating meanings attached to national sites
of memory as a response to historically unfamiliar, state productions of memory
that contrasted with "traditional" spaces and practices: "For me, temples and pagodas have more meaning than monuments or statues. These only recently appeared
in Vietnam—some after 1954 and even more after 1975—and are important only to
the state. On special occasions our leaders will go to these sites to remember [*nhớ*],
while people go to temples to practice their beliefs [*tín ngưỡng*]." Of course people
do attend ceremonies at state memorial sites and they *do* visit other state spaces of
memory, such as martyr cemeteries, so it would be erroneous to assume that these
sites have *no* commemorative or historical-political meaning. Nonetheless, respondents typically maintained that despite their importance, sites of national memory
had *less* commemorative significance than "traditional" spaces of ritualized memorial activity, including temples, pagodas, and ancestral altars in the home (see
also Malarney 2001; Kwon 2006). A dualistic commemorative order between state
and non-state practices emerged, in which "Vietnamese" memorial customs and

spiritual beliefs contrasted with secular state politics and "foreign" commemorative practices. Yet rather than see this binary as signifying "two distinct communities of remembrance around the war dead" (Malarney 2001, 72–73), which risks reifying cultural practices as fixed, timeless, "of the people," and somehow outside the zone of national politics and memory, I emphasize instead their mutual constitution as evident in the *liệt sĩ* shrines in pagodas and temples and in acts to traditionalize secular sites and state practices of memory, as I outline below.

In addition to cultural unfamiliarity, respondents often commented that sites do not attract a continuous flow of visitors due to the aesthetic unpleasantness or ugliness of monuments. Cultural producers have long probed the relationship and tensions between art and monumental sculpture—between aesthetic demands and commemorative needs—in, for example, post–World War I France (Sherman 1999, 155–170) and post–World War II Germany (J. Young 2000, 92–93). Since the late 1990s, the role of art and aesthetics in memorial projects has become a critical locus of debate in Vietnam. Typically, state monumental art, diversely identified by my respondents as Soviet, modern, Russian realist, and, occasionally, French colonial, was thought to be incompatible with "traditional" Vietnamese architecture: while the former is fraught with conflict and disruptive to the environment on account of its unaesthetic monumental tendencies, the latter is perceived as unobtrusive, harmonious, and in aesthetic balance with its natural surroundings.

This binary between "traditional" and "foreign" modes of representation, and the demand for more aesthetic and culturally meaningful memorial production, formed the basis of numerous articles in architectural journals and fine arts magazines in the late 1990s and through the following decade.[15] In these discussions, criticism was leveled against government officials for the hasty and ill-planned construction of monuments that produced a landscape of failed artistic projects on account of poor conceptualization, design, and implementation. To resolve the "lament that artistic principles are being sacrificed for the purpose of memorializing"—in other words, the sacrifice of artistic form and quality for political content and meaning—over fourteen monument symposiums have been organized in Vietnam since 1997 (Phạm Quốc Trung and Nguyễn Hoàng Hà 2006, 7). In 2004 symposium discussions resulted in an addendum to the MCI's 2000 Decision No. 05/2000/QD-BVHTT, in which the need to merge ideological content with higher aesthetic quality in monument initiatives was affirmed and encouraged.

The Hồ Chí Minh mausoleum is perhaps the most well-known monumental structure in Vietnam thought to represent an unfamiliar and unaesthetic architectural style identified as "Soviet" (Figure 4.9). As a site for the political performance of the nation and the visual embodiment of its memory, the mausoleum's thirty-year history has been shaped by the entanglements of public desires and official practices,

FIGURE 4.9. Hồ Chí Minh Mausoleum, Ba Đình Square, Hanoi. Photograph by the author.

signifying what Hue-Tam Ho Tai (1995) has called as a state of "monumental am-biguity," drawing criticism at the same time as it attracts over one million domes-tic and international visitors annually. A typical scene replayed during my frequent visits: busloads of schoolchildren and civilians from outlying provinces arrived in the capital city and waited in long lines under awnings in the early morning hours before entering the dark and solemn air-conditioned chamber, only to be quickly ushered past the embalmed remains of the former president affectionately known as Uncle Hồ [*Bác Hồ*]. At times people cried, at times they stood and stared, until gently urged on by watchful guards. Historical curiosity also attracted many for-eigners to the site, particularly from China, which provides the largest share of in-ternational tourists to Vietnam. Many American citizens, on the other hand, in-cluding those of Vietnamese descent, and also U.S. heads of state, have refrained from visiting the mausoleum during trips to Hanoi due to its enduring contentious, political-historical significance.

The massive granite and concrete structure, reminiscent of Lenin's tomb (and a few years later the inspiration for the design of Mao Zedong's), stands at the center of Ba Đình Square, an area of great national and symbolic significance that marks the site where Hồ Chí Minh read the Declaration of Independence of the Demo-cratic Republic of Vietnam on September 2, 1945.[16] Built with Russian architectural and technical expertise, the mausoleum merges Soviet aesthetics and commemorative technologies with Vietnamese resources and cultural iconographies. Standing 21.6 meters high and 100 meters wide, its construction incorporated twenty-seven different kinds of granite collected from multiple locations throughout the country. Twenty towering columns emerge from a massive, tri-level foundation to support a three-tiered rooftop designed in the shape of a lotus (Anh Quang 1985, 29–30; Tai 1995, 280). Constructed between 1973 and 1975, the mausoleum opened to the public on September 2, 1975, on the sixth anniversary of Hồ Chí Minh's death. Only months after the end of the war, the mausoleum further signified the unity of a divided, war-torn nation with its ternary symbolism (representing northern, central, and southern Vietnam) and its combination of collected stone resources from around the country.

Despite the mausoleum's historical and symbolic significance in Vietnamese national memory, many Hanoians expressed to me their disapproval of the site (see also Tai 1995, 281). Most angering to respondents was that it had been built in defiance of Hồ Chí Minh's request before his death in 1969 that the government not waste already limited funds on an elaborate state burial, but should cremate his body and scatter his ashes in northern, central, and southern Vietnam, to literally and symbolically instill in the nation his eternal presence. The mausoleum and the display of Hồ Chí Minh's body thus stands as a reminder of an unfulfilled desire and an unnecessary state expense. As I have demonstrated at several points in this chapter, criticism of government spending on monuments has been vociferous and therefore not unique to this context. Moreover, as Eric T. Jennings has shown in his study of French colonial monuments in the 1920s, Hồ Chí Minh himself criticized French memorial projects as wasteful, a view with which Vietnamese journalists also tended to agree as they voiced in the press their loathing for monuments that they perceived to be "artistic flops" and financial drains on Indochinese taxpayers (Jennings 2003, 21–22).

Public disapproval of state expenditures on monumental projects should not be seen as a pointed critique of the socialist regime nor of its intent to commemorate heroes. Most research respondents in Hanoi maintained the importance of building memorials to honor and remember wartime sacrifices, even if they do not regularly visit such sites. They were, however, far more concerned that the government address other socioeconomic priorities, such as poverty alleviation and adequate care for heroic mothers and aging veterans. The painter and art critic Nguyễn Quân, who in 2005 called for a moratorium on monument and statue construction until 2020 on account of poor design and wasted funds, has pointed to the increased economic burden that monuments have had on poor citizens who are increasingly asked to make donations: "Of all poorer countries in the world, the one with the most monuments is Vietnam," he wrote in a pointed editorial (*Lao Động* [The Worker] June 18, 2007).

Another common criticism centered on the "foreign" architectural style of the mausoleum and its overwhelming, monumental presence on the landscape. A perceived lack of fit between structure and environment made the mausoleum project a failure to many. Hùng, the intellectual quoted earlier, pithily summed up his impression of Hồ Chí Minh's final resting place:

> **Hùng:** Unsuccessful! The mausoleum's architecture does not follow the eastern aesthetic and it does not blend with its surroundings. Look at the One Pillar Pagoda that stands behind it. The view is now ruined by the [Hồ Chí Minh] museum and the mausoleum. For sure if Hồ Chí Minh were alive today he would feel the same. These buildings are too tall and not in harmony with the environment. And they are not made of wood, but stone!
>
> **CS:** Then why did the government build them?
>
> **Hùng** (shaking his head): Because the cultural standards of our leaders are not high. The idea of monumentalism just does not fit with Vietnamese architecture. It is not a harmonious aesthetic.

Hùng's comments reveal a concern that came up often in critiques of commemorative art and architecture: that of improper planning and placement. Historically, geomantic concerns and attention to location, topography, and directionality played a key role in Vietnamese architecture (Ngô Huy Quỳnh 1986; Nguyễn Bá Đang et al. 2006). The orientation of a structure and its proximity to waterways and mountainous landscapes, for example, has been of extreme importance in Vietnamese commemorative practice, which sees a direct link between the proper construction and emplacement of memorial structures, such as tombs or temples, and the fate of the dead and that of the living (Nguyễn Bá Đang et al. 2006, 16–17). Research respondents often commented that monuments have ignored these basic tenets of Vietnamese architectural design and now stand in uninspiring and unharmonious locations, such as close to historical and religious sites, as in the case of the One Pillar Pagoda, one of the earliest architectural structures in Vietnam (built in 1049), which is now dwarfed by two massive stone structures: the mausoleum and the Hồ Chí Minh Museum. Monumentalism, with its perceived lack of attention to harmony and geomancy, sticks out from, rather than blends into, the landscape.

Not unlike Hùng, Vinh, a migrant to Hanoi from southern Vietnam who works on transnational memorial projects, also expressed a similar critique of the mausoleum as we drove past on a motorbike:

Vinh (pointing to the National Assembly and the mausoleum): Do you like those buildings? Have you ever visited the mausoleum?

CS: Yes, many times. How about you?

Vinh (surprised): Really—many times? I was there once and that was enough. Do you talk to people about how many times they have been there? It's probably like Paris; the French never go to the Eiffel Tower.

CS: And what do you think about the mausoleum's architecture?

Vinh: People don't like it. They have no connection to it. After the mausoleum was built, it was rejected. We are unfamiliar with this kind of Russian architecture. It has no soul; no feeling. It is quite unlike the Vietnamese style.

CS: And what is Vietnamese style?

Vinh (pondering): Asian, Oriental. Like the pagodas and temples that are built low with curved wooden rooftops. Maybe Vietnamese style is mixed, influenced by China and also by France. We are used to these styles, but not this Russian architecture. The Kremlin is beautiful, but not these buildings here.

Vinh's rejection of the mausoleum—expressed through the subject position of "the people"—reveals a larger ambivalence and uncertainty about Vietnamese architectural identity. It was easier for Vinh, like other research respondents, to define what Vietnamese architecture is by pointing to what it is *not*. It is not monumental, it is not Russian; it is, perhaps, a hybrid, Vinh concludes, a fusion of past architectural legacies that have a lingering visual history in Vietnam. In the examples above, complaint discourse was a means for respondents to express dissatisfaction not with state commemorative meanings, values, and memories attached to the mausoleum and its surroundings, but with the socialist project of "new culture" and its new aesthetic and commemorative order that further rendered the landscape "foreign." In her work on Vietnamese fashion and the resurgence of the *áo dài*, Ann Marie Leshkowich has similarly identified an enduring historical desire to "differentiate that which is Vietnamese from that which is foreign" (2003, 93). In the section below I move to examine the cultural work to resolve architectural ambiguity in the landscape through efforts to aestheticize and "Vietnamize" monuments and sites of memory.

Aestheticization and Traditionalization: New Trends in Commemorative Art and Practice

Anthropologists, in particular, have pointed to renewed and intensified engagements with cultural practices and discourses of tradition in post–*Đổi mới* Vietnam; for example in the resurgence and resignification of ritual and ceremonial activities (Jellema 2007; Endres 1999; Kleinen 1999; Luong 1993). Philip Taylor has argued that emerging anxieties over national identity and cultural roots that have spurred the revitalization of ritual processes can be linked to intensified global interconnectedness and an increase in capitalist practices (2004, 47–48). The reembrace and reimagining of Vietnamese cultural pasts is also evident in the fields of art and architecture, where cultural producers are grappling with ideas about Vietnamese national identity and its relationship to the global market and to transnational imperial histories (N. Taylor 2004, 114–115).

During my fieldwork, artists and architects often voiced a sentimental yearning to rediscover a uniquely Vietnamese culture and aesthetics set apart from foreign cultural and artistic influence, a trend that Jessica Winegar (2006, 96–100) has similarly observed in postsocialist Egyptian art. One Vietnamese artist, who upon our meeting stressed his deep connections to and prolonged residency in France, described to me his idea of making "Vietnamese" art. After staging a performance art piece in Hanoi that entailed killing live eels and laying them into French baguettes to eat, the artist explained that he had left France and returned to Vietnam to found a new kind of Vietnamese performance art that was distinctly *not* European. As Nora Taylor has argued, *Đổi mới* signals a moment in which cultural producers are reinterpreting what it means to be Vietnamese. But how Vietnamese identity, tradition, and culture are constituted is not clear: "[A]lthough there does not seem to be a consensus among artists over what constitutes Vietnamese art, their talking, writing, and discourse about art indicates most feel it necessary to qualify their work as such" (2004, 115). Yet as the example of the performance artist shows (with his French bread and extensive links to France), "Vietnamese-ness" is caught between the national and the transnational—it embraces, consumes, reinvents, yet simultaneously reworks, rejects, and detaches itself from that which is "foreign," not unlike the architectural ambiguity to which Vinh referred. Such recombinant art highlights how cultural production has become a site to work through desires to embrace (and perform) "modernity" without loss of historical and cultural specificity (Winegar 2006, 96).

Debates over art and culture were often described by my respondents as a struggle led by a younger generation of cultural producers who seek to redefine the parameters of art and reclaim a "Vietnamese" aesthetic identity they feel was lost in the "new culture" years. Linh, the architect in the Ministry of Culture and Information who was suspicious of monument competitions, shared with me her vision to aestheticize and Vietnamize the city center by ridding it of unsightly illplaced memorials:

In my proposal to redesign Hoàn Kiếm Lake I suggested destroying the monument to the French resistance [see Figure 4.5]. It's just terrible! And it's not a suitable location. A war memorial does not belong there next to the temples. I proposed to build a new dragon monument, but no one paid any attention to my project.

Linh's proposal to raze one of the city's central monuments and erect nine large dragons that would encompass the perimeter of the lake reconfigured dominant modes of political and historical representation. Given that the removal of monuments has "become the central idiom for explaining the fragilities of power, [and] the changing of the guard" (Grant 2001, 332), as in the case of the Soviet Union and, more recently, Iraq, it is not surprising that her approach was considered controversial. Yet Linh's aesthetic vision, which suggests the impermanence of monuments and the shifting of power to a younger generation with different visions for Vietnam's economic and social future, should not be read as a call for a new political regime or a rejection of official historical memory. It is rather an appeal for a new regime of representation that reproduces and conveys similar visual knowledge and narratives of the past—both the statue and the dragons similarly represent the nation's power, valor, and fortitude—but through very different iconography and aesthetics.

Aestheticization was not only a process initiated by a younger generation of cultural producers with different aesthetic ideals that have been met with resistance from an entrenched older cultural guard, as respondents often suggested. In fact, some of the most vocal critics of monuments have come from within this artistic guard, as seen in the controversy that surfaced during the renovation of the Trường Sơn National Cemetery in central Vietnam for troops killed on the Ho Chi Minh Trail between 1959 and 1975.[17] The dispute centered on the cemetery's main monument, a three-sided structure representing cooperation between Vietnam, Cambodia, and Laos, standing sixteen meters high (for sixteen years of mobilization and combat on the trail), and the proposal by board members of the Association of Architecture in Hanoi to replace it with a new and more aesthetic memorial design (Figure 4.10). A war veteran and former leader of Unit 559, which began construction on the Trường Sơn Road, the Vietnamese name for the Ho Chi Minh Trail, adamantly protested its removal and demanded that the monument be preserved as a historical relic [di tích lịch sử]. What transpired was not a conflict over historical memory but its signifier (the monument), which became an important signification of postwar memorial and representational practices of the late 1970s. In other words, the older monument came to symbolize for the veteran a historical memory not only of the war, but also of a particular chapter in the history of postwar aesthetic and commemorative culture. In his call to preserve the monument as an historical relic, the veteran did not contest the shift to new standards of memorial aesthetics and design, but would not consent to the obliteration of Vietnam's architectural

FIGURE 4.10. National monument at Trường Sơn National Cemetery, 1977, Quảng Trị province. Photograph by the author.

heritage. Regardless of aesthetic devaluation, "these monuments are a part of our architectural history," Minh, the military sculptor, maintained.

Desires to aestheticize the memorial landscape did not always result in the proposed destruction of monuments and statues, but more often in their enhancement through material upgrades and architectural embellishments. This engendered a more hybridized style of monumentalization in which "foreign" structures (such

FIGURE 4.11. Unrenovated martyr cemetery, Nghệ An province. Photograph by the author.

as the obelisk) were "Vietnamized" with the addition of cultural motifs and objects considered "traditional." Such changes were particularly evident in commune-level martyr cemeteries located throughout much of the country in areas that supported the revolution.[18] In the more prosperous years of the 1990s, affluent communes embarked upon the cultural and aesthetic renovation of these important memorial sites, which has included the replacement of cement tombstones and monuments with granite, the addition of commemorative stelae, and the beautification of the landscape (Figures 4.11 and 4.12).

One of the more common styles of monuments found in martyr cemeteries is the obelisk. Occupying the center of the memorial site, usually on a raised platform, Vietnamese obelisks are tall, slender pillars that typically rise to a blunted apex topped with a yellow, five-pointed star as found on the national flag (Figure 4.13). In an effort to traditionalize "modern" monuments and create spaces of remembrance that are seemingly more "Vietnamese" and less "foreign" or "unfamiliar," architects have increasingly added cultural icons to standard obelisk designs, including dragons, lotuses, bronze drums, or crowns resembling sloped pagoda rooftops (Figure 4.14). Other designs have replaced the obelisk altogether with a temple-style memorial as the central monument (Figure 4.15). In one martyr cemetery I visited outside the port city of Hải Phòng, a large ochre-painted temple structure had been built in 1999 following ancient [cổ truyền] architectural styles, the grounds-

FIGURE 4.12. Refurbished martyr cemetery in Thắng Lợi commune, Hà Tây province. Photograph by the author.

keeper informed me. With some economic support from the local government, residents from neighboring villages raised $2,000 for the renovation project, which entailed the replacement of a crumbling and aged concrete obelisk with a "traditional and more meaningful memorial," he explained.

Another recent commemorative trend in martyr cemeteries informed by historical practice has been the addition to of a pair of black, marble stelae [*văn bia*]. These "martyr memorial stelae" [*bia tưởng niệm liệt sĩ*], often sheltered by a curved roof in temple style, are symmetrically positioned to either side of the central monument toward the rear of the cemetery behind the mass of gravestones which face the entrance (see Figure 4.14). Biographical information engraved onto the marble slabs, such as name, village, and years of birth and death, are either arranged chronologically according to "year of sacrifice" or listed under one of three periods of war: Against the French [*Chống Pháp*]; Against the United States [*Chống Mỹ*]; and Protecting the Nation [*Bảo Vệ Tổ Quốc*], a category that refers to post-1975 conflicts with China and Cambodia.

Scholars have identified the historical significance of new naming practices that emerged in post–World War I European commemoration. While Laqueur (1994) has linked large-scale state efforts to find, bury, identify, and mark individual bodies in military cemeteries to new memorial processes of individualization and democratization, Sherman (1998) has localized such practices to argue that the inscription of the names of war dead on local stelae and monuments signified new

FIGURE 4.13. Hội An martyr cemetery, Quảng Nam province.
Photograph by the author.

commemorative expressions of personal grief and private mourning within collective memorial contexts. In Vietnam, though the widespread use of memorial
stelae to collectively name martyrs appears to have emerged as common practice
as recently as the 1990s, it draws upon a much longer history of *văn bia* in multiple
commemorative contexts, including ancestral tablets in family ritual practice and
historical markers of heroic deeds. As an important vehicle for historical knowl-

FIGURE 4.14. Juxtaposing "traditional" and "modern" aesthetics in Văn Từ commune martyr cemetery, Hà Tây province. Photograph by the author.

edge production and transmission in precolonial Vietnam, stelae inscribed in historical memory particular events or the biographies of people deemed notable for their contributions to Vietnamese society, such as the life histories of royalty or individual patronage of spiritual institutions, including financial and other meritorious contributions to pagodas (Ban Hán Nôm 1978).[19]

The roles and functions of *văn bia* in Vietnamese history are not unlike those

FIGURE 4.15. Temple-style martyr cemetery in Hà Tây province. Photograph by the author.

of monuments in other parts of the world. One historian, in an interview, referred to memorial stelae as "original Vietnamese monuments." Like their counterparts in Europe and elsewhere, *văn bia* were meant to signify permanence and continuity, and to anchor specific historical memory. And not unlike contemporary monuments in their varied forms and meaning, *văn bia* were also sites for the expression of diverse and contested histories; for example, at the Hai Bà Trưng temple in Hanoi, two adjacent stelae from the mid–nineteenth century engraved with Chinese characters offer differing interpretations of the events and significance of the Trưng sisters' uprising against Hán invaders between CE 40 and 43.[20] Moreover, similar to monument destruction as a symbolic act of regime change, so too were *văn bia* destroyed by Hán and other invading forces in an effort to overthrow Vietnamese power and authority, and to forge a new cultural and political legacy. As powerful signifiers of Vietnamese historical knowledge and memory (though influenced by Chinese practice [Ban Hán Nôm 1978]), the recent addition of *văn bia* to martyr cemeteries demonstrates efforts to further democratize and individualize mass death, and also to imbue such sites with "traditional" memorial practice and meaning. This is not to argue that the inclusion of Vietnamese cultural symbolism at memorial sites is wholly new (both the mausoleum and the Trường Sơn monument incorporated lotus symbolism into their designs in the 1970s), but to link such trends to post–*Đổi mới* debates about "national style" and to desires for more meaningful (i.e., "traditional") practices of ritual remembrance.

The cultural reshaping and redesign of war memorial sites and cemeteries increasingly confounds the state's intent to remember—not worship—martyrs. This shift is particularly evident in a new form of Vietnamese commemoration that has emerged in recent years: the construction of "martyr temples" [*đền liệt sĩ*]. These ornate ceremonial structures, the largest and most popular of which is located in Bến Dược, Củ Chi district, outside of Ho Chi Minh City, are built to resemble "traditional" spaces of worship, though they retain their state secularist emphasis on recognizing the work and contribution of martyrs to the nation (Figure 4.16). The Bến Dược Martyr Memorial Temple, constructed between 1993 and 1995, receives hundreds of Vietnamese visitors daily and is strikingly similar in architectural design and spatial arrangement to Vĩnh Nghiêm pagoda, built in the late 1960s in central Saigon (then the Republic of Vietnam) and based on the eleventh-century original in northern Bắc Giang province. Both complexes, for example, contain a three-entrance gate, as is common in Vietnamese pagodas and temples. A tiered tower at each site (seven stories at Vĩnh Nghiêm and nine at Bến Dược) stands to the left of the main double-eaved sanctuary that dominates both complexes (also built with three entrances). Inside, however, the sanctuaries differ significantly. At Bến Dược, one also finds a large central altar with offerings of incense, flowers, and fruit, but a large gold bust of Hồ Chí Minh set against the Vietnamese flag replaces the dominating Buddha and other smaller statues found at Vĩnh Nghiêm (see Figure 3.4). Marble tablets line the three walls at Bến Dược, with over forty-four thousand names of martyrs etched in gilded letters. Posted high on the back wall, beneath a row of iconographic symbols from early Đông Sơn culture, the patriotic phrases often found at national sites of memory, such as *Vì Nước Quên Mình* ("Self-Sacrifice for the Nation") remind visitors of state-intended meanings. While it may be a temple [*đền*] implying worship, it is also a place of secular memory: *Đời Đời Ghi Nhớ* ("Always Remember"). Yet visitors at Bến Dược keep the altar "warm" by lighting incense, offering fresh fruit or flowers, and praying at the main shrine. This contrasts with "foreign" memorial sites that often remain vacant and "cold" (without burning incense), demonstrating that traditionalization and aestheticization not only make familiar "non-Vietnamese" commemorative practices and design, but also serves to personalize and historicize acts of memory at state sites in ways that have more cultural, emotional, and spiritual meaning.

Scholars have identified the revival of family- and community-based economies of memory in which practices such as ancestral veneration have assumed a more central and visible role in the maintenance, transmission, and work of his-

FIGURE 4.16. Bến Dược Martyr Memorial Temple, Củ Chi district, Ho Chi Minh City. Photograph by the author.

torical memory (i.e., Jellema 2007; Kwon 2006; Malarney 1996, 2002). Yet diversified commemorative practices should not be seen in all cases as a "shift of attention *from* state-administered sites of hero worship *to* the communal sites of ancestral worship" (Kwon 2006, 26; emphasis added). I have argued above for transcending divisions between state and non-state memory work and for paying more attention to the ways in which secular state recollection and ritual propitiation inform and constitute one another in particular communal and state sites of memory. Intensified family and community practices should not be seen as a dismissal of state sites for the latter are not rendered meaningless, but rather less meaningful as visitors feel disconnected from form and practice. Martyr temples are thus sites where diverse commemorative ritual practices and meanings congeal as the war dead are both remembered for their service and ultimate sacrifice for the nation *and* attended to as venerated souls in need of ritual care.

These merged processes of secular recollection and ritual propitiation surfaced most recently at an elaborate ceremony I attended in July 2007 to mark the sixtieth observance of War Invalids and Martyrs Day at the recently constructed martyr temple in Hồng Bàng district, Hải Phòng. The day's program which ran from 7:00 AM until 10:00 PM, hung outside the temple on a large placard and emphasized the dual purpose of the event: a ceremony of secular remembrance [*lễ tưởng niệm*] and a Buddhist mass for the souls of the dead [*lễ cầu siêu*]. Officials from each ward

in Hồng Bàng district, as well as representatives from the local People's Committee, arrived in the early morning hours to light incense at several elaborate altars
that had been set up outdoors and inside the main sanctuary. Thereafter, Buddhist
leaders, along with local residents and members of "martyr families" [*gia đình
liệt sĩ*], subsequently performed a mass for the dead at the main altar through the
evening hours, calling upon the souls of the war dead to return and receive their
offerings. Underneath the main hall, groups of older women sat on bamboo mats
as they prepared large piles of votive paper offerings to be burned for use in the
afterlife, including military uniforms (hats, shoes, pants, shirts, and medals of
honor), as well as silver coins, pieces of gold, and U.S. dollars. Votive offerings,
which provide for the material needs of souls in the afterlife, were at one time
"vigorously outlawed" as superstitious rites during the era of new cultural policy
(Malarney 1996, 551).[21] Their important role in this ceremony to mark a day of national recognition of citizen contribution to the state confounds the differentiation
between *nhớ* and *thờ—vừa nhớ vừa thờ* [both remembrance and worship], one at-
tendee at the mass explained—and demonstrates how souls of the war dead were
cared for not only as ancestors, but also as heroes, two distinct but intersecting kinship identifications that merge state and non-state discourses and ritual remembrance practices.

Toward a New Aesthetics of Peace

Desires to traditionalize and "Vietnamize" memorial landscapes have engendered
in select monument initiatives a shift from iconographies of war to representations
of peace. Global political trends in memorialization, most notably in the context
of Germany, have given rise to what cultural producers and others have termed the
countermonument [Das Gegendenkmal]. According to James E. Young, a countermonument embodies the dilemma of ambiguity and distrust that engulfs processes
of monumentalization in postwar Germany. In its reversal of memorial conventions, the countermonument signifies unresolved tensions between the moral cer-
tainty about memory work and mounting skepticism toward the underlying aesthetic and political messages that are embedded and communicated in standard
memorial forms (1993, 27). Like the countermonument, monuments to peace also
challenge a nation's aesthetic representation and social configuration of memory.
They undermine what critics identify in conventional monumentalism as milita-
ristic ideologies of heroism that glorify and aestheticize war as a noble, if not sacred, nationalist endeavor (Mosse 1990) by offering less patriotic and less celebratory spaces for historical reflection and recollection. In Vietnam, an emerging
aesthetics of peace, prompted by both national and transnational actors, raises

critical questions about historical knowledge production and its representation in a postreform era of peace, in which the legacies of past wartime violence are still tangibly felt and seen.

Beyond debates about the need for aestheticization and traditionalization of memorial sites, certain research respondents (namely artists and intellectuals) were critical of the use of militarized images and discourses of war to remember, represent, and transmit knowledge of the past. Vinh, who had been a student in Saigon during the war, expressed concern about the effects on youth of expanding monumentalization of the war:

> How should young people understand war monuments? What are they to think when they see all these images of war? In my hometown, there is a large monument of a woman on a pedestal holding a knife above her head standing in fire. For the older generation, they understand the significance of this woman—that she is protecting her village and family from the enemy and will fight if she has to. But what are the youth to think of this woman? This monument instills fear in them: "You had better be good children or else!" So you see, these monuments have very different meanings for younger generations. We need to give them fewer images of war and more of peace. We need to build monuments to teach the youth about peace, not about past wars.

Vinh did not just talk about peace, but put his concerns into action in a transnational peace park initiative he worked on in collaboration with a U.S. veteran-run humanitarian organization. The peace parks the project built in northern and southern Vietnam, he told me, aimed to create a living, viable memorial of shared public space. Vinh envisioned the parks as an alternative to war memorials, which he felt were painful and all too present reminders of the past, rather than regenerative symbols for the future. Like the Peace Memorial Park in Hiroshima, the peace parks "signified post-war recovery—what was positive, future-oriented, and not bound by 'bitter memories' of the past" (Yoneyama 1999, 19). With gazebos designed in "Vietnamese architectural style," they represented a symbolic gesture of friendship and reconciliation between the people of the United States and the people of Vietnam, similar to the "Requiem" photographs in chapter 2. Not unexpectedly, their meanings have differed depending on the visitor.[22] Like the Củ Chi Tunnels (chapter 3), Vietnamese youth have also invested new social meaning in the parks that displaced but did not wholly erase memories of the war. According to Vinh: "The young people are tired of all these war monuments. The peace parks are important to them not as memorial spaces, but as places where lovers can meet." On the other hand, older generations, in Vinh's view, while appreciative of peace memorials and their significance, have more urgent concerns not unlike those that were expressed about friendship forests in chapter 1: "Peace parks have special symbolic meaning. But what people need and want are peace gardens. They are so poor; they are more concerned with having enough food than with having a park. It is important for these peace projects to offer something else as well." Memory work thus insists upon the fulfillment of material as well as spiritual needs.

The movement away from militarized memories and representations of war did not only occur in transnational reconciliatory peace projects, but is also evident in the changing landscape of figurative monuments of national heroes, most notably that of General Trần Hưng Đạo, who twice defeated Mongol invading forces in the thirteenth century. An early 1990s cement sculpture of the sainted general in Hải Dương province, not far from his famous battle site at Bạch Đằng River, follows typical stylistic techniques of socialist realism, with chiseled features, a monumental and squared body form, and a confident militant pose. In 2000, another monument was unveiled in Trần Hưng Đạo's hometown of Nam Định to celebrate the 700th anniversary of his death. This stone and copper monument was considerably different: rather than emphasize Trần Hưng Đạo's military prowess, the sculptor portrayed the national hero as an educated leader with smoother and rounder features that orientalized his body, clothed in a flowing mandarin-style uniform. A sword at his side and a scroll by his heart signified his dual identity as a learned warrior noted for both military and literary skill. "This is a successful monument!" Hùng, who had disapproved of the mausoleum, declared. "Trần Hưng Đạo must not only be remembered for his military victories. We must remember him as a man of culture and morality." The shift from commemorating a heroic warrior to recognizing and honoring a cultured man of erudition marks new ways of understanding and re-presenting wartime pasts that repositions memory in a dialogue with peace.

Rethinking Vietnamese Monumentalism

George Yúdice has pointed to the expanded use, application, and management of culture across transnational circuits in an era of rapid capitalist globalization. Culture, he argues, "is expedient as a resource for attaining an end" (2003, 29), though Leshkowich, in the case of Vietnamese fashion, identifies the ambiguity that commonly underlies cultural production and its rhetorics of identity and authenticity (2003, 29). Likewise, newly articulated and intensified attachments to "culture" and "tradition" in the arts have not been without their critics. In the words of Đức, the young cosmopolitan artist:

> Scholars here argue over what Vietnamese culture is, but no one can define it. Everyone is concerned about Vietnamese tradition. They love that word, but

what exactly is it? Our traditions have been destroyed by artists and officials. There was a time when the government would not allow people to practice their rituals, and many of our traditions died. Nowadays, things we label Vietnamese tradition are only for tourists, such as *Chèo* and *Tuồng* theater. Tradition is this thing presented to people in a museum. I think that if our traditions are kept alive by tourism, then we are on some unstable ground.

Đức's words reveal a certain irony in the processes described above: Cultural producers, who seek to rediscover "Vietnamese" tradition and cultural identity unpolluted by foreign influence, play right back into the hands of global capitalist forces. That is, the revaluation of culture, as Đức points out, has engendered its commodification and its consumption by *foreign* tourists. Much to Đức's regret, Vietnamese culture has become, for international auiences, a globally mediated, mass-consumed "commodity-form of experience" (Chakrabarty 2007, 85).

Đức's quote also reconfirms scholarly insights that engagements with culture and history are often bound up with anxieties about inauthenticity and lack of value or meaning, also demonstrated in the previous chapter on tourism to war sites. This, too, has been the case with martyr temples and traditionalized monuments, which have met with disapproval from Vietnamese cultural critics on account of an alleged lack of authenticity. Though intending to reflect "ancient Vietnamese architecture" [*kiến trúc cổ truyền*], these memorial structures have been disparaged as "imitation" by artists and architects who point to careless craftsmanship, excessive use of vibrant colors, and cement, rather than wood construction (Doãn Đức 2000, 19).

Such critiques demonstrate that the terrain of Vietnamese aesthetics is one of dynamic contestation and revaluation. And while there is little consensus as to what Vietnamese monumental art and architecture might be, there is more agreement on what it is not. Vietnamese aesthetic imaginaries are largely articulated through binary oppositions that inadvertently reinscribe essentialist discourses of difference: us/them; eastern/western; traditional/modern; harmonious/discordant. Yet, despite this binary logic, aestheticization, traditionalization, and a shift to a transnational aesthetics of peace has entailed more a blending or pastiche of aesthetic styles and techniques rather than a rejection of that which is presumed to be not Vietnamese. Even martyr temples exude "foreign" monumentality and index other transnational trends. In conversation, an employee at Bến Dược Martyr Memorial Temple compared the site to the Vietnam Veterans Memorial in Washington, D.C.—both record the names of tens of thousands of war dead. Traditionalization then has not replaced "non-Vietnamese" designs, forms, or aesthetics so much as it has merged with them. At the Củ Chi martyr cemetery, a refurbished marble

FIGURE 4.17. Refurbished Củ Chi district martyr cemetery, Ho Chi Minh City. Photograph by the author.

obelisk with a new temple crown stands behind an unrestored (still cement, though with fresh yellow paint) socialist-realist statue of a mother tending to an injured soldier (Figure 4.17), demonstrating how both "traditional" and "modern" characteristics in Vietnam's memorial landscape signify national, cultural, and aesthetic agency, as well as the enduring visual presence of past imperial histories.

PART 3

Incommensurable Pasts

Contested Truths

Museums and Regimes of Representation and Objectivity

CHAPTER FIVE

The Vietnamese are an incredible example of how to forgive and forget . . . I would like to speak for my country, the United States, and say *I'M SORRY* for all the atrocities that we committed here.

—OREGON, USA, JULY 1998, ARMY MUSEUM, HANOI

An interesting exhibition but please try and learn the difference between propaganda and historical truth.

—UNSIGNED, OCTOBER 1999, ARMY MUSEUM, HANOI

This is my first time at the museum. I feel proud and moved by the exhibits, and inspired to continue working to build my country. I respectfully thank all the heroic mothers, heroic men, and heroic women for everything they have given to my generation.

—VIETNAM, JANUARY 2000, ARMY MUSEUM, HANOI

Is history a big joke? In the past we expelled the colonists and invaders (white people). Now we welcome them again! I hate this.

—CHINA, OCTOBER 2004, MILITARY HISTORY (ARMY) MUSEUM, HANOI

Hang on! Didn't China occupy Vietnam for 1,000 years?!

—UK, OCTOBER 2004, MILITARY HISTORY (ARMY) MUSEUM, HANOI

This chapter looks at museums as transnational sites for co-produced histories and discordant memories. As the above excerpts from *"cảm tưởng"* [comment] books placed at the end of museum exhibits show, museums are spaces of transnational contestation where differing audiences accept, dispute, or rework the messages and meanings of displays. What is propagandistic untruth to one might be inspirational narrative to another. While entries in comment books communicated a diverse range of emotional responses to U.S. violence and its representation—including desires for reconciliation ("I'm sorry Vietnam!"), expressions of U.S.-Vietnamese solidarity ("We are all one—one enemy, one hero"), criticism of exhibits ("Why depict war with photos of young smiling girls?"), and condemnation of a repeated history of empire ("US out of Iraq!")—they also index an important shift in museums that has occurred in Vietnam in tandem with the rapid development of an international tourism industry, namely a marked increase in foreign attendance. Museums are thus increasingly subjected to the critical gaze and scrutiny of international visitors, some of whom praise, while others contest the historical truths and representational practices they encounter.

The increase in numbers of foreign tourists to Vietnamese museums has engendered certain changes to exhibits as museum officials refashion historical narratives with a view toward communicating with more diverse domestic and international audiences. Museums, of course, are not merely repositories for static information or fixed representations of a national past. Rather, museum exhibits, and the stories they narrate, are in continuous flux and under constant curation as artifacts and images are reframed, removed, or repositioned in relation to one another to convey to the viewer new historical truths. The recuration of exhibits, I demonstrate below, cannot be disentangled from larger global economic and political transformations that influence and direct transnational flows of knowledge, capital, images, and material objects. What new, recombinant narratives of history are presented to viewers when U.S. historical knowledge—in the form of photographs, books, and veteran-donated objects—are integrated into Vietnamese exhibits? How have shifts from Soviet to French financial support and expertise impacted the production and presentation of history? What do changes in text and the close of exhibits reveal about desired inclusion in particular global economic networks? When traced over time, museum modifications provide critical insights into the complex ways historical knowledge production shapes and is shaped by the ebbs and flows of international relations and changing configurations of global power. As Daphne Berdahl has argued, "The work and the politics of memory and museums can be a window onto larger political processes and landscapes of nation-building, identity formation, and belonging" in a period of rapid socioeconomic and geopolitical change (2005, 167–168).

It has been suggested that western public museums have become more democratic institutions in recent years as marginalized social groups have exercised increasing control over how their memories and histories are collected, arranged, and presented in exhibits (Simpson 2001; Lavine and Karp 1991). The embrace of multiculturalism has engendered an explosion in the number of ethnic museums and cultural centers, particularly in North America, marking important shifts in the balance of power and in cultural authority over representation and meaning (Clifford 1997). The discourse of museum "democratization" suggests that knowledge produced about the Other is less colonized, less disciplined, and more open to differing cultural systems of value and practices of representation. The inclusion of "alternative perspectives" from oft-silenced voices in disenfranchised spaces has provided new venues for the expression of unofficial and nondominant historical subjectivities in the public sphere. Yet despite such changes, critical questions remain concerning the control of knowledge and ownership of history, as evident in debates over the repatriation of cultural properties that remain on display or housed in museum archives.

Democratization has also meant changes in the meaning and accessibility of museums, from temples of high art for bourgeois elites to mass cultural production and entertainment for broader public consumption (Huyssen 1995, 18; T. Bennett 1995, 25–27). Moreover, as sites for competing knowledge practices and memory, museums have become critical spaces at which visitors assume active roles in questioning cultural-historical truths and claims to objectivity (Lavine and Karp 1991, 7). Democratization thus suggests that museums in western contexts are no longer passive settings for the absorption of information and the contemplation of history, but politicized, multicultural—and, increasingly, transnational—institutions in which power, representation, and ownership of history are contested and negotiated between multiple social actors, including museum directors, sponsors, organizers, staff, experts, and spectators (see Linenthal 1995). In this chapter I am also concerned with diverse audience reception of museums and exhibited history, but I situate my analysis within a larger framework of global political economy to examine the entangled processes of museum democratization and transnationalization. I focus my attention on power struggles that have erupted over historical authority, knowledge, and objectivity in Vietnamese museums in which layered postcolonial and postwar memories produce certain truths for domestic and, more recently, global consumption. How do shifts in audience attendance and response affect the narratives that are communicated in exhibits? What happens when Vietnam's Other—such as the U.S. veteran—speaks out and contests his representation? Attention to both national and international actors, especially U.S. visitors, and their desires and efforts to master the past and lay claim to a particular history reveal certain assumptions regarding the questions: whose war and whose history? (Maier 1988).

Imperial to Postcolonial Knowledge: Shifting Museum Landscapes in Vietnam

In my fieldwork visits to museums in Hanoi and elsewhere, an essential component to the museal setting was often absent: Vietnamese visitors. While urban museums in Hanoi and Ho Chi Minh City consistently attracted international tourists, and at times groups of Vietnamese schoolchildren, provincial and municipal museums away from tourist centers remained largely empty or closed, or at times put to other social uses, such as the afternoon beer garden and badminton court on the grounds of the city museum in Hải Phòng that promptly closed at dusk each evening.[1] Free admission for Vietnamese citizens has not drawn voluntary visitors in large numbers.[2] This suggests that museum patronage in a nonwestern context may be more complicated than Bourdieu (1984) suggested for France, and is not only linked to a specific bourgeois cultivation of cultural appreciation, since museums in Vietnam are no more successful in attracting an emerging middle- and upper-class population than they are at drawing the masses. Rather, the lack of "taste" for museums in Vietnam points not only to the cultural specificity of Bourdieu's analysis, but also to a specific history and legacy of empire.

The story of the empty museum is not unlike that of the vacant memorial site in the previous chapter: both are invented traditions linked to imperial histories and culturally unfamiliar visual and taxonomic practices that involve the production and discipline of particular historical memories. The idea of the museum—as a heterotopic space of western modernity that embodies the "idea of accumulating everything [and] the desire to contain all times, all ages, all forms, all tastes in one place" (Foucault 1998, 182)—is not indigenous to Vietnam, but a product of early-twentieth-century French colonialism. In modernist narratives, the birth of the museum signified a specific relation between the nation and its history marked by the atrophy of tradition and memory, and the destabilization of cultural identity (Huyssen 1995, 26). Museums were spaces in which to counteract the instabilities of modernity and to turn into spectacle state power and its technological and cultural superiority (T. Bennett 1995). Desires to display the lives and histories of Others, in particular, shaped and was shaped by historically specific visual and classificatory regimes of knowledge produced through the accumulation, organization, and exhibition of that which was foreign, exotic, and rare (Cohn 1996; Mitchell 1988; Norindr 1996).

In Vietnam in the years following World War I, as colonial governmentality shifted from strategies of brute conquest and cultural destruction to policies of paternal benevolence and concern for historical antiquity (Anderson 1991[1983], 181), the French constructed four museums to collect, protect, and display Vietnamese cultural patrimony: the Louis Finot Museum in Hanoi (now the National History Museum of Vietnam), the Blanchard de la Brosse Museum in Ho Chi Minh City (now the Museum of History), the Parmentier Museum in Đà Nẵng (now the Museum of Chăm Sculpture), and the Imperial Museum of Emperor Khải Định in Huế, today the Imperial Museum (Doãn Đức 1998, 53; Tai 1998, 188). Built in an era of escalating criticism of French aesthetic universalism, the museums reflected a trend toward incorporating vernacular architectural design into French monumental structures (Doãn Đức 1998, 53; Wright 1991, 200–201). On the other hand, as sites of French political and cultural hegemony, colonial museums were constitutive of a much larger structure of colonial systems of scientific knowledge production that included ethnology, archaeology, and other fields in which colonial domination was manifest in practices of collecting, exhibiting, recording, preserving, and viewing (Salemink 2003; Norindr 1996; see also Cohn 1996). In the postcolony, museums—as political inheritance entangled in new relations of power (Anderson 1991 [1983], 178)—continued to function as spaces for the discipline of knowledge and the management of culture and memory, though they produced very different authoritative accounts of history.[3] In 2000, museum directors I interviewed estimated that there were more than 120 state and provincial museums in Vietnam (all nonprivate), with approximately 22 located in Hanoi, demonstrating that the "government considers museums to be an important pillar of its cultural policy (Sutherland 2005, 157).

Despite their proliferation, the "newness" of museums as sites of cultural and historical memory that evoke "foreign" knowledge and viewing practices contributed to the alienation of the populace from such spaces. Like monuments, museums are a relatively new and modern form of commemoration, one that the population also feels generally disconnected from. Over the course of my research in Hanoi, few expressed an interest in visiting museums. Many cited a lack of time, while most professed a lack of interest on account of what they identified as unaesthetic and uncreative exhibit presentations that are straightforward, didactic, chronological, and noninteractive. One female journalist, who had initiated and then abandoned an ambitious exhibition project, summarized her experience: "Museums stay empty because curators do not put any heart into their work. There are so many great stories to tell, but they don't do a good job of presenting them. There is nothing attractive about the museums; no lights, no sounds, no films. They are basically boring." Involuntary visits to museums while on school, organization, or company field trips to mark commemorative holidays did not inspire visitors to return. "We do not have a tradition of going to museums, like in the West," I was often told. In a large discussion group in Hanoi with lawyers and law faculty from a local university, respondents explained they would rather spend free time with friends and family in parks, cafés, beer halls, or newly built shopping malls, not in pedagogical spaces of history—an argument also made about historical tourist sites in chapter 3.

The alienation of youth, in particular, from museums reflected their increasing ambivalence about the past and a preoccupation with new opportunities in Vietnam's globalizing economy. Private international MBA programs continue to attract record numbers of enrollees, despite the high fees, while students fill the departments of economics, trade, finance, and foreign languages at state universities. The past, it seems, plays little role in, and indeed can only hinder, the attainment of desired prosperous futures. One university student who studied English and international finance at the time of my research talked about using her free time to study Chinese, rather than visiting public sites of memory: "I don't like to go to museums. It's always war history, war history. I'm fed up. I've heard enough. I'm more interested in the development of the economy than in war and politics." However, some students inscribed museums not as sites of history, but as bridges to the future. In the early morning hours on the weekend in Hanoi, students often roamed the grounds of the museums and other tourist sites looking for western tourists with whom they could improve their English-speaking skills.

Museum officials were aware of and deeply concerned about increasing historical distance and disconnect of Vietnam's youth from museums. In an interview, the director of the Museum of the Vietnamese Revolution in Hanoi emphasized to me the critical role that museums play in imparting to postwar generations moral values and revolutionary traditions, such as sacrifice, valor, and gratitude. Knowledge of the past serves as a building block for the future: "It is important to know about history. This museum is about Vietnamese freedom, unification, and independence. If the young people do not learn about this past, they will not have a proper understanding of the present and they will not be able to build and modernize our country for the future." Museums are thus sites of pedagogical power in which the state produces moral and educated citizens through the management and discipline of historical memory (Foucault 1977). Visiting museums and knowing national history affirms social-historical identification and inclusion in a larger civic polity (Maleuvre 1999, 3).

Although museum officials in interviews boasted high attendance rates (the director of the Hồ Chí Minh Museum in Hanoi cited one million visitors in 2000), they were also cognizant of problems attracting a domestic audience, particularly in less touristic areas. Many of my museum visits to peripheral sites in Hanoi or outlying provinces consisted of touring a spectator-less building with staff members who accompanied me to turn on and off the electricity as we moved through dark and unventilated rooms. On January 25, 2000, two articles in the *Hà Nội Mới* [*New Hanoi*] newspaper addressed citizens' apparent lack of museum sensibilities. The first article pondered why field trips to museal institutions do not inspire students to voluntarily return and concluded that museums were not sites of aesthetic and historical appeal. In the second article, on the same page, President Trần Đức Lương appealed to officials to modernize museums and make them more culturally and aesthetically attractive to spectators. Some museums indeed heeded the call, and the adoption of new exhibition practices culminated in one of the best-attended exhibits to date: "Hanoi Life in the Subsidy Period" [*Cuộc Sống ở Hà Nội Thời Bao Cấp*]. This exhibit opened in the summer of 2006 in the Museum of Ethnology in Hanoi, and took a more critical approach to examining the difficulties and the productivities of an impoverished postwar era through interactive, visually stimulating, and textually informed displays (see also MacLean 2008).

National History in Public Museums: Narrating the "American War"

The making of a postcolonial "new history" [*lịch sử mới*]—an unfolding developmental story of resistance, revolution, and victory—played a critical role in building and legitimizing a Vietnamese socialist nation-state (Pelley 2002, 9–10). Historiographical processes in the Democratic Republic of Vietnam, Patricia Pelley (2002) has argued, were fraught with tensions and competing visions and ideas about how to frame history as officials attempted to disentangle the newly founded state from colonial social and historical structures and practices, and establish a Marxist paradigm of history based on the inclusion of new voices, sources, and methodologies.[4] Historians have long argued that historiography is a process not of discovering facts but of manufacturing truth. Hayden White, whose seminal works in the 1970s pointed to the interpretive framework of history, identified the historian as an inventor of truths, one who arranges historical events into a "hierarchy of significance" to produce a coherent chronicle with a selected beginning and end (1973, 7). Not unlike the identification of ethnography as a fictive, literary mode of partial knowledge production (Clifford 1986), White characterized historical narratives as "verbal fictions, the contents of which are as much *invented* as *found,* and the forms of which have more in common with their counterparts in literature than they have with those in the sciences" (1978, 82; emphasis in the original). Likewise, museums are spaces in which such fictions are manufactured and given historical value and meaning through selective representations of the past. The entanglements of remembrance and forgetting that underlie curatorial acts and choices about regarding what to preserve and highlight as history or consign to fading memory index particular relations of institutional power that shape the organization and dissemination of knowledge in regimes of historical truth (Foucault 1980).

National history in Vietnamese museums, displayed in collections of photographic images and historical artifacts (not all of them "real"), is a story of defensive wars fought for self-determination that have spanned nearly two millennia: from one thousand years of Hán domination (111 BCE to 938 CE) and recurring Mongol, Champa, and Ming invasions between the thirteenth and fifteenth centuries to one hundred years of French colonization (1858–1954) and a subsequent U.S. imperial regime, until 1975 when "total victory" was achieved. Emphasis on the nation's two-thousand-year history of continuous uprisings against invaders, and invincibility in the face of powerful enemies, has sustained *new history* discourses of national unity and a timeless tradition of resisting foreign aggression (Pelley 2002, 159). The narrative of indomitable [*bất khuất*] Vietnamese who drew upon their heroic traditions [*truyền thống anh hùng*] to fight against and triumph over foreign invaders [*ngoại xâm*] can be found in most museums, irrespective of the theme and content; for example, it structures historical accounts in the women's museums in Hanoi and Ho Chi Minh City, and of Vietnamese prisoners in Hanoi's Hỏa Lò Prison Museum, among others. Narratives of heroic sacrifices by all citizens, men and women, old and young alike, unite the Vietnamese nation into an imagined moral community of shared historical memories of resistance. The ubiquity and repetition of this narrative reveals "how contemporary national identity is constructed in opposition to empire" (Sutherland 2005, 153), shaped by selective memories of common revolutionary struggle for national autonomy.

The war story presented in museums is not only defensive in action, but also victorious in outcome, and thus elides stories of suffering and defeat. As argued in chapter 2, representations of hardship are typically overshadowed by images of more mundane activities of everyday life in wartime. Likewise, museum narratives highlight military and civilian victories rather than failure and defeat— terms reserved for U.S. forces and their "lackeys." For example, exhibit titles at the Military History Museum in Hanoi regularly employ the term "defeat" in the section on the "Resistance War against the Americans for National Salvation (1954– 1975)": "Defeating the American Policy of New Colonialism (1954–60)," "Defeating the 'Special War' Strategy (1961–65)," and "Defeating the 'Local War' Strategy (1965–68)" all document the successes of Vietnamese forces in thwarting U.S. military might and imperial intent in southern Vietnam. Such discourses and representations often had the effect of turning U.S.-claimed victories and advances into setbacks or even defeats, a pattern that reflects competing analyses of the war's progression. For example, while the Tết offensive is seen as a defeat for Hanoi in U.S. history, its victory in Vietnamese memory is linked to its significance as a crucial turning point, and the beginning of the end of the war.[5] Bombing campaigns over northern Vietnam are also portrayed as a victory for Vietnam on account of the number of aircraft shot down and pilots taken prisoner—statistics that were regularly reported on the front page of newspapers. The B-52 Victory Museum is a case in point, as is the newly renovated Air Defense–Air Force Museum, which exhibits images of citizen militia who "taught the US air force, one of the most powerful in the world, a memorable lesson!"—including one old man who devised an elaborate homemade device that he used to shoot down planes while hidden in a tree. Items on display made from the metal of destroyed U.S. aircraft, such as musical instruments and household utensils, remain a silent testimony to U.S. defeat. As I walked with Ngọc, a museum employee and career professional in the Vietnamese military, through the exhibits, past the posters documenting the number of U.S. bombers shot down over each northern province, past the photographs and objects accumulated from POW arrests, and past images of victorious Vietnamese pilots returning from their missions, I ask her about Vietnamese aircraft: "Oh yes, many were destroyed." And Vietnamese pilots killed? "Yes—there were many martyr pilots." Is there a display with such information? She looked at me curiously. "If you want to learn about the martyr pilots, you can go down the street to the war monument where their names are engraved on memorial stelae." The museum, in other words, was a space to recall and celebrate the nation's victory, not to commemorate the deaths of its heroes.

Vietnam's war story is defensive, victorious, and also continuous. In the revolutionary narrative presented in museums, the French and U.S. wars are closely entangled and presented on a historical continuum, as a three-decade "people's war of liberation" between 1945 and 1975. Uprisings and revolts against the French colonial regime during the late nineteenth and early twentieth centuries culminated in the August Revolution in 1945, when the political void of post-Japanese occupation allowed the Việt Minh front to seize power and declare an independent and free Democratic Republic of Vietnam under the leadership of Hồ Chí Minh. The French soon retaliated and attempted to regain control over its lost colony. Thus began the "First War of Resistance" ["First Indochina War," in the West], a nine-year war (1945–54) and predecessor to the "Second War of Resistance against U.S. Imperialism" that continued until 1975. In Vietnam's historical memory, these two wars are merged into a thirty-year war (1945–75) in which three generations fought and died for "national salvation." However, the year 1955 does not mark the initiation of U.S. activity in Vietnam (which is generally not recognized in U.S. history until much later), but rather a shift from "interference" during the French War to progressive occupation, particularly in the southern areas where an imperial "puppet" regime had been established. In the Museum of the Vietnamese Revolution in Hanoi, the role of the United States in the First War of Resistance against French Colonialism is documented with photographs and statistics on U.S. financial support of the war (80 percent of its total costs according to one display, a figure confirmed in Nguyễn Khắc Viện 2007, 274). Photographs from the early 1950s show Richard Nixon and Dwight D. Eisenhower in Vietnam conferring with French military generals, images that directly implicate U.S. involvement in French colonial efforts. A nearby painting from 1950 shows students in Saigon protesting "American imperialists' intervention in the Indochina War."[6] Thus, in Vietnamese national history, the American War does not begin where the French War ends; rather, the former is a continuation of the latter. As early as 1950, U.S. imperialism had been recognized as a threat to the new socialist state, and the struggle to expel its imperial presence became part and parcel of the fight to defeat French colonialism (Nguyễn Khắc Viện 2007, 236).

Museumization: Post–*Đổi Mới* Modifications

In the previous chapter it was argued that the construction and renovation of war monuments has increased significantly, though unevenly, in the more prosperous years since *Đổi mới* economic reform. The same argument can be made for Vietnamese museums, which have also been the beneficiaries of increased state investment as the result of extensive plans to modernize and further diversify the museum landscape.[7] In the 1990s, museumization saw the construction and opening of numerous museums in and around Hanoi, including the Hồ Chí Minh Museum in 1990; the Vietnamese Women's Museum in 1995; the Museum of Ethnology, the B-52 Victory Museum, and the Hỏa Lò Prison Museum ("Hanoi Hilton") in 1997; and the Ho Chi Minh Trail Museum in 1999, followed by the Museum of Public Security in 2001. More recently, several established museums have undergone large-scale renovation and reorganization, such as the newly restructured Military History Museum (formerly the Army Museum) in 2003. In Hanoi in the summer of 2007, the newly built and merged Air Defense–Air Force Museum (previously two separate institutions) had just opened on the outskirts of the city (Figures 5.1–5.3). The Museum of the Vietnamese Revolution had also finished several phases in its multistage restoration, and sections of the complex that housed the Vietnamese Women's Museum had been demolished as part of the site's extensive renovation and expansion. As stipulated in Decision No. 156/2005/QD-TTg, dated June 23, 2005, on the museumization of Vietnam's landscape through 2020, more than twenty new museum projects have been planned, the themes of which will disrupt the sustained focus on war and revolution to examine, for example, Vietnam's scientific achievements, including a proposed Vietnamese Agriculture Museum and the Vietnam Medicine and Pharmacy Museum; national arts and culture, such as the Traditional Performing Arts Museum and the Applied Fine Arts Museum; and the nation's material production, including a Petrol and Oil Museum, the Vietnam Cement Museum, and the Museum of Vietnamese Textiles and Garments.

Insertions: New Productions of Knowledge

In addition to new construction and renovation, new permanent exhibits have been added to many museums since the 1990s, expanding wartime and postwar narratives to include previously omitted perspectives and actors. In 1995 the Army Museum in Hanoi opened a two-room exhibit entitled "Vietnamese Heroic Mothers" [*Bà Mẹ Việt Nam Anh Hùng*] to pay tribute to over 41,000 mothers who were granted, some posthumously, the state honorific title of heroic mother in recognition of their tremendous sacrifices.[8] Although museum representations depict Vietnamese women as active participants and combatants in the revolution and wars of resistance, albeit often in dualistic roles as devoted mother with a baby in one arm and ardent nationalist with a rifle in the other (see also Enloe 1996), the "Heroic Mothers" exhibit gave voice, agency, and public recognition to a large constituency of less-acknowledged historical actors whose primary contributions to the revolution were made within the capacity of motherhood and in the sacrifice [*hy sinh*] of their children for the cause of national liberation.

During my preliminary research in 1997 and 1998, it was common for museums to end their stories at 1975, as if history had been completed and peace achieved with "total victory" over enemy forces (Figure 5.4). Even the Hồ Chí Minh museums in both Hanoi and Ho Chi Minh City ended not in 1969 with the former president's death, but in 1975 with the defeat of the United States and the Republic of Vietnam. Few narratives of postwar reconstruction and reunification were offered, and rarely was the image of postwar peace shattered by references to subsequent border conflicts with Cambodia and China. When I returned to commence fieldwork in 1999, several changes had taken place and new exhibits had been

FIGURE 5.1, FIGURE 5.2, and FIGURE 5.3. In 2007 the Air Defense (*top*) and Air Force (*bottom*) museums were merged into the newly built Air Defense–Air Force Museum (*next page*) on the grounds of the now-demolished Air Force Museum. Note its use of colonial-style architecture. Photographs by the author.

opened that further broadened the presentation of Vietnamese history to include the postwar years of socialist modernization and globalization.

In 1999 the Museum of the Vietnamese Revolution in Hanoi extended the museum's historical documentation past 1975 with two new successive exhibits that inserted Vietnam into a socialist national and global world order. The first room, entitled "Vietnam on the Road to Building a Wealthy People, a Strong Country, and a Just and Civilized Society, 1976–1999," traced postwar industrializing processes and productivity through material objects, images, and charts, including statistics on state exports, economic growth, and widening industrial sector. Similar traveling exhibitions on socialist modernization opened in 2000 in the Museum of the Revolution in Ho Chi Minh City (now the Ho Chi Minh City Museum) and the Hồ Chí Minh Museum in Hanoi. These exhibits represented postwar Vietnam as twenty-five years of continuous socialist progress and global integration and did not distinguish between pre- and post–*Đổi mới* periods of socialist and market economies, or an era that in the West has been called "post–Cold War."

Vietnam's role as a respected member of the international community of nations—again, no distinctions made here between shifts from socialist to non-socialist economic practices since controlled market reform has been envisioned as constitutive of the larger project of *socialist* nation building—was confirmed in the

FIGURE 5.4. The "Total Victory" room, the last chronological exhibit in the Military History Museum, Hanoi. The quote by Hồ Chí Minh above the tank reads: "There's nothing more precious than independence and freedom." Photograph by the author.

second exhibit to open in 1999 in the Museum of the Vietnamese Revolution. "Collections of Economic Objects in the Period of 1976–1999" displayed lavish gifts bestowed upon highly ranked Vietnamese government officials (including Hồ Chí Minh, despite the exhibit's time frame) by visiting international heads of state from socialist and capitalist countries, demonstrating to museum visitors world recognition of the legitimacy and sovereignty of the newly reunified, postwar Socialist Republic of Vietnam. Such representations counter prevalent images and discourses of Vietnam as having been a "closed" and "isolated" society cut off from the "outside" (read: western capitalist) world. Narratives of global friendship and solidarity, though in the context of the war, were also conveyed to visitors in the permanent exhibit that opened at the Army Museum in Hanoi in 1999, "The World Supported Vietnam's Wars of Resistance," which documents through photographic images, posters, and newspaper articles antiwar protest movements in communist and noncommunist countries, including the United States. This same exhibit (though different images) can now be found in several museums, including the War Remnants Museum in Ho Chi Minh City (which opened the exhibit in April 2000 as part of the twenty-fifth anniversary celebration), the Vietnamese Women's Museum in Hanoi, and the Air Defense–Air Force Museum, among others.

Not unlike trends in monument construction, museumization has also entailed a rethinking of the emphasis on war in museum discourse and representation, and a desire to include more narratives of peace. This was voiced most clearly by Hương, a director at the War Remnants Museum, in 2004 as we discussed an international traveling exhibition at the museum on Vietnamese children's paintings of war and peace:

> In future projects, the emphasis will be on peace. We plan to include more information on antiwar movements and have a room for peace activities. Our goal is to teach the youth about peace, not only war. Down the road I hope to change our name to Museum of Peace, but not yet because there are too many wars in the world right now and the effects of war are still being felt here in Vietnam.[9]

A focus on peace thus did not propose to disregard past violence, as the children's paintings on the legacies of war in peacetime demonstrate (Figure 5.5), but expressed the longing to move away from its glorified and heroic representation in public sites of memory to create more critical knowledge about the past and new practices of representation in the present.

The museumization of Vietnam's landscape indexes larger geopolitical and global economic shifts that have occurred in the post–Cold War era. Whereas museum projects before the collapse of the Soviet Union attracted international support from socialist nation-states, such as the Hồ Chí Minh Museum in Hanoi, which was designed and funded with Russian and Czech assistance, more recent years have seen increased collaboration with western capitalist countries and international institutions. In 1995, a one-month UNESCO "museum development" workshop for Vietnamese curators was held in Huế city and focused on the how-tos of museum organization, maintenance, and display. More recently, the French government has also played an instrumental role in bilateral museum assistance. A three-year transprovincial project on museum architecture and museology was implemented in 2004 with a team of French experts in Hanoi and Ho Chi Minh City in collaboration with the Ministry of Culture and Information. In an interview, the cultural attaché at the Consulate of France in Ho Chi Minh City explained that the goal of the project was not to provide funds (the state and local People's Committees would finance the multimillion-euro overhaul and construction of museums), but to offer expertise on "museum conception and formation," including the practical application of theories of museum design and use of space in relation to object display, preservation, and rotation (as opposed to static and permanent exhibition). The creation of a "global strategy" for a stronger Vietnamese presence in the international field of museums was also stressed. "The Ministry of Culture and Information is very concerned about Vietnam's international image," he explained,

FIGURE 5.5. Submission to the 2004 exhibition "Children's Paintings on the Topic of War and Peace" on display at the War Remnants Museum.

linking Vietnamese interest in the program to a "national identity problem": "They want to modernize museums and develop their cultural function to create a new international identity." Not unlike the regional director of PeaceTrees (chapter 1), the cultural attaché was careful to emphasize an assistance model based not on control and delegation, but enablement and empowerment: "We are only here to offer expertise. The French government is considered a partner and can only make suggestions. The Vietnamese manage the project and they make the final decisions."

Yet at times this model of autonomous decision making and joint collaboration proves more an imagined ideal than a real practice. Museum construction and modification has been a process not wholly disconnected from fluctuations in international diplomacy, as well as global interventions (direct and indirect) in historical narration and representation that index particular geopolitical relations of power. Vietnam is not only a recipient of museum aid, it should be noted. In 2000 it contributed $4 million to help build the Kaysone Phomvihane Museum in Laos (*Việt Nam News,* May 17, 2000), which commemorates the life of the former prime minister and president, highlighting his revolutionary ties to Hanoi and the "special relations" between the two counties (Tappe 2008: 265–267). Museums are thus transnational social fields in which the politics of knowledge, history, and memory are entangled with larger global economic and geopolitical processes. In Vietnam, the creation of a new international image via "museum development" has not only included expansions (new buildings) and insertions (new exhibits) as outlined above, but also the reediting and deletion of certain narratives and representations based on strategic assessments of changes in global diplomacy and economic connectivities.

Deletions: Turning Enemies into Friends

Vietnam's postreunification conflicts with Cambodia and China, as mentioned in chapter 2, are notably absent from most museums. During my research I located two exceptions, both of which were small exhibits on the "Southwest Campaign" in military museums that draw few international and domestic visitors. In Đà Nẵng, the Area 5 Army Museum in 2000 contained a one-room exhibit entitled "Vietnam's Assistance to Cambodia," with images of Pol Pot atrocities and Vietnamese troops "liberating" the Cambodian countryside. In Hanoi, the Air Force Museum had an even smaller display with several photographs of Vietnamese villages devastated by invading "Pol Pot pirates," along with weapons used to protect the border. However, this exhibit has since been dismantled and was not integrated into the newly renovated, merged, and renamed Air Defense–Air Force Museum, which opened in July 2007.

Such historical omissions have not always been the case. In interviews, museum officials pointed to the post–*Đổi mới* removal of exhibits on Cambodia and China. While some claimed that post-1975 episodes of violence did not warrant museum representation since they did not constitute wars, but short-term campaigns [*chiến dịch*] or struggles [*đấu tranh*],[10] others, such as the director of exhibits at the Military History Museum, explicitly linked the rearrangement of museum exhibits to larger diplomatic shifts and concerns: "In 1979 we introduced some exhibits on the border conflict with China, but then closed them after relations with China improved in 1991. Today, there is no longer a need for such displays." In this director's view, the function of the museum is not only to document history, but also to mobilize sentiment, such as anger, suspicion, or pride. The decision to remove representations of "Chinese aggression" signals the displacement of such states of affect as new geopolitical, diplomatic, and economic interests and concerns come to the fore. By the director's own estimate, the museum receives more than a thousand Chinese tourists every week, the majority of foreign visitors to the site and to Vietnam in 2000. Anxiety about Chinese visitor reception of exhibits resonates with the French cultural attaché's claim that Vietnamese museums have become sites for reconsideration of Vietnam's international self-presentation.

Changes in strategies and choices of representation in the context of improved Vietnamese-Chinese diplomacy beg the question of what modifications have been made to museum exhibits as relations with the United States have evolved. When I posed this question to the director at the Military History Museum, he abruptly responded: "We will never change or close exhibits on the American War! It was a long struggle and a great victory. But we will tell the youth to look to the future. We know many people in the United States were against the war and we highly appreciate this." At the Hồ Chí Minh Museum down the street, however, I received a different response. While conducting fieldwork I heard rumors that the U.S. government had discreetly suggested the removal of certain museum displays as a precondition to normalizing relations. Two rooms in particular were reportedly of concern: one on "western decadence" that featured a life-size image of Marilyn Monroe alongside an Edsel car emerging out of the wall, and another room on the misuse of science and technology that juxtaposed images of Hiroshima and the young napalmed girl, Phan Thị Kim Phúc. Neither display had been dismantled during my research, through the latter was closed due to "technical problems." The museum director denied such rumors, but he did describe a careful mediation of historical knowledge in relation to deepening integration in a U.S.-dominated global capitalist economy:

> There were many crimes committed by the United States during the war and we called them American imperialists [đế quốc Mỹ] and enemies [giặc Mỹ]. Today we call them friends [bạn]. In general the language used today in museums and newspapers is softer. Words like "crimes" [tội ác] are too strong for the exhibits and not suitable for foreign relations. We have a tradition of forgiving past enemy offenses in order to make friends for the future. We need to respect history and also not forget the past. But at the same time we are concerned with our nation's economic development.

Deletions and changes to museum exhibits and discourse point to a crisis of representation and a state of knowledge ambiguity: while the director recognizes and links the need for new public narrations of history to particular political and economic concerns, he himself resisted such shifts at the outset of our interview by referring U.S. actions as "crimes." In other words, personal sentiment about U.S. accountability does not always correspond to shifts in national discourse demonstrating ambivalence toward rewriting this history. Much to the chagrin of many Vietnamese citizens, some of whom in press commentaries have also demanded the softening of public language, such a "slip" occurred during President Clinton's historic visit to Vietnam in 2000 when the prime minister called U.S. intent during the war "imperialist," a term that Clinton defiantly rejected. Several of my research respondents winced when this hit the press: what will the United States (and, in particular, investors) think about a government that still seems "stuck in the past"?

Mapping Geopolitical Change: The War Remnants Museum

In chapter 2, I introduced the War Remnants Museum in Ho Chi Minh City as the site of the transnational commemorative exhibit, "Requiem." In the next sections I map out the various modifications made to the museum since its founding in 1975 to provide a more focused case study of the ways in which museum representations in certain touristic contexts have been refashioned for and by international audiences. I say "certain touristic contexts" here because those museums off the beaten tourist path—such as the Area 5 Army Museum in Đà Nẵng that in 2000 still maintained an exhibit on the Cambodian "Southwest Campaign"—have undergone less historical re-presentation. The War Remnants Museum, one of the most popular museums in Vietnam, attracts approximately half a million visitors a year, two-thirds of whom are foreigners, according to museum estimates. It is also a controversial site of knowledge production that attempts to appease, integrate, and at times moderate diverse transnational expressions of memory. Its tendency to engender contestation is, in part, linked to the multiple and ambiguous messages the museum conveys to visitors: while it has selectively modified its language and altered its images to conform to western notions of objectivity, it simultaneously maintains and inscribes a public memory of "US war crimes as 'crimes' that must be redressed and accounted for even in their ultimate irreparability" (Yoneyama 2005, 143).

On September 4, 1975, only months after the fall/liberation of Saigon, the Exhibition House for U.S. and Puppet Crimes [*Nhà Trưng Bày Tội Ác Mỹ Ngụy*] opened its doors in the former U.S. Information Building in central Ho Chi Minh City, where the War Remnants Museum now stands. During the wars with France and the United States, exhibition houses were crucial sites for the public documentation and visual display of atrocities, conveyed through images and objects that served to mobilize memory, sentiment, and action. For example, in Hanoi, an Exhibition House for French War Crimes opened during the revolution in Bà Kiệu temple, on the grounds where the Alexander de Rhodes memorial once stood. The exhibition closed in 1954 with the defeat of France at Điện Biên Phủ and subsequently reopened as the Exhibition House for American War Crimes after the U.S. began to bomb northern targets in 1964. In Đà Nẵng, an American War Crimes Exhibition House, like that in Ho Chi Minh City, opened in 1975, and another one in Sơn Mỹ (Mỹ Lai), Quảng Ngãi province, in 1976.[11] According to museum officials, the exhibition houses in Hanoi and Đà Nẵng were closed in the early 1990s as relations with the United States began to improve and visual documentation of crimes was "no longer needed." "There is peace and cooperation between the two countries now, so it's not a good idea to maintain such exhibits," a staff member at the Đà Nẵng Area 5 Army Museum explained, revealing the ways in which the geopolitics of the present (i.e., renewed diplomatic ties with the United States) affect visual representations of the past in contemporary spaces of historical memory.

In Ho Chi Minh City, the Exhibition House for U.S. and Puppet Crimes remained open, though it underwent significant changes in the postwar era. In the late 1970s, during the Cambodian and Chinese conflicts, curators expanded the exhibits to include displays on border atrocities. In 1990, the name was changed to the Exhibition House for Crimes of War and Aggression [*Nhà Trưng Bày Tội Ác Chiến Tranh Xâm Lược*], dropping the descriptors "U.S." and "Puppet." According to Hương, a director, when relations with China were normalized in 1991, the section on Chinese hostilities was closed (as in the Military History Museum in Hanoi). Displays on the "Southwest Campaign" were also removed, and the exhibition house once again prioritized U.S. violence. Museum pamphlets during this time emphasized the "atrocious crimes committed against the Vietnamese" by U.S. troops and their allies. In July 1995, days before diplomatic ties between Vietnam and the United States were officially normalized, the words "crimes" and "aggression" were dropped when the exhibition house was upgraded to museum status and its name changed once again, to "War Remnants Museum" [*Bảo Tàng Chứng Tích Chiến Tranh*].[12] English- and Vietnamese-language brochures distributed after 1995 also reveal a complete elision of these terms, a practice which has continued through subsequent pamphlet redesigns until the present day. According to Hương, the movement away from a language of "crimes" occurred in the aftermath of the end of the U.S. embargo in 1994, as the numbers of U.S. veterans and U.S. tourists traveling to Vietnam increased and complaints were made to her about the use of this term.[13] The War Remnants Museum thus demonstrates how museal institutions and the historical truths they produce are entangled in webs of global interdependencies and uneven relations of power that affect and shape the representation of knowledge and memory.[14]

Cảm Tưởng: Audience Responses to Museum Representations

Changes to exhibits and the removal of the word "crimes" from the museum's discourse in the aftermath of U.S. criticism indicate an important shift in museum representational practices as officials accommodate and negotiate the discrepant truths of an increasingly international audience. Yet the refashioning of history does not signify changes to the museum's pedagogical aims to teach about the "crimes" of U.S. occupation; rather, their objectives have been broadened to include the education of "uninformed foreigners." Museum curators are privy to a general lack of knowledge about Vietnam in other countries, especially in the United States,[15] and they make concerted efforts to convey particular historical truths and interpretations through practices of self-representation. At the War Remnants Museum, photographs, such as the graphic image of a smiling U.S. soldier proudly displaying a "VC" head as a war trophy, are used to reveal a criminal element to the war. The caption, which was mentioned and objected to by several U.S. tourists with whom I spoke, read: "After decapitating some guerrillas, a GI enjoyed being photographed with their heads in his hands." While the "crime" of the event is not directly stated in the text, it is clearly implied. According to one museum director, "Americans have told me that they do not have a lot of information about Vietnam in the United States. They didn't even know that Vietnam was fighting for independence and that the involvement of their country was not necessary! When they come here and see for themselves the war crimes committed by U.S. troops, they feel ashamed." Yet U.S. and other foreign visitors had strong mixed reactions to the use of such images to stand as representative of the war.

In addition to interviews, one research method I adopted to track the affective responses of domestic and international visitors to museum exhibits on war was to read and record comments left in the thick red "impression" [*cảm tưởng*] books typically placed at the end of exhibits for visitors to share their thoughts and criticisms. A quick browse through of any of these books reveals a transnational cornucopia of historical reflection and commemoration in multiple languages, including Vietnamese, Chinese, Hebrew, Spanish, German, Japanese, Dutch, and French, though English remains the dominant language of commentary.[16] Reading these texts over the past decade, it has been possible to trace larger shifts in Vietnam's international tourism industry and policy, such as the suspension of visa requirements for members of the Association of Southeast Asian Nations (ASEAN) in 2005. At the start of my research, Europeans, North Americans, and, to a lesser extent, Chinese visitors wrote most of the commentaries. More recently, entries have been written by tourists from Thailand, Malaysia, Brazil, Turkey, and South Africa, an indication of broadening international tourist interest in Vietnam. There has also been a marked increase in hostility toward the United States after 2001 as visitors linked an imperial history of U.S. crimes and torture in Vietnam to Afghanistan and Iraq, and in particular to Abu Ghraib. "America is a disaster for mankind," read one remark in the War Remnants Museum impression books in 2006.

U.S. visitors used the comment books in various museums as a tool to express a range of intense and often ambivalent emotions. On the one hand, comment books became a tool for healing and reconciliation; they were often used to apologize for the extraordinary suffering inflicted upon the Vietnamese people, as evidenced in the quote at the beginning of the chapter (see also Laderman 2007, 191). Entries were written in a confessional style, often by veterans, with long sentimental ruminations that at times exceeded one page. In one reflective statement, a veteran wrote extensively about his pacifism and involuntary combat duty in Vietnam. Another shared his personal reconciliation, facilitated by his return to Vietnam: "A lot of pain, quiet now." Other U.S. visitors reflected on their antiwar activism, criticized the U.S. government for learning little from the past, or thanked the Vietnamese people for a warm welcome to their country. And still others used the books to honor the memory of fallen comrades and family members, often with religious connotation: "In memory of my childhood friends, from many years ago. May God bless them all," read one entry at the Khe Sanh Museum, on the grounds of the former marine base. Remembrance and honor were at times extended to fallen former enemies in expressions of masculine solidarity: "For all the warriors who died here, suffered here, fought here, on both sides," a returning veteran wrote at Khe Sanh, inserting a quote from Michael Herr's *Dispatches:* "That's the American flag you are kicking." Such nationalist sentiments appeared in many comments at Khe Sanh in particular, as commemorative and apologetic tones gave way to expressions of regret for *not* winning the war. In one entry a veteran lamented: "I am sorry the U.S. government and its finest young men couldn't protect the Vietnamese people from the lie that is communism. When I see Vietnam today I can't help but feel that we could have done more to help this beautiful country, protect it from corrupt communist officials and people who hide the truth from their own." Likewise, an expression of gratitude similarly invoked the salvation myth that underlay the war, while also remembering and commemorating "the South": "Thank you Americans and South Vietnamese for fighting for freedom."

International visitors, including Americans, at times responded harshly to such comments. When U.S. visitors criticized the presumed lack of freedoms and democracy in Vietnam, others directed that criticism back at the United States. Comment books thus became a place where U.S. foreign policy was discussed and debated. Entries left by Europeans before 2002, for instance, frequently stressed the need to remember Vietnam and not forget the past, lest the United States start another war. Comments before 2001 made specific reference to Kosovo and the Gulf War, situating Vietnam in a continuous history of unjust U.S. military interventions (see also Laderman 2007, 194). Americans often responded defensively to these written attacks. Provoked by denunciations of U.S. global hegemony, one American linked U.S. actions to centuries of European colonial history. Another visitor supported that observation with the example of atrocities committed against Austra-

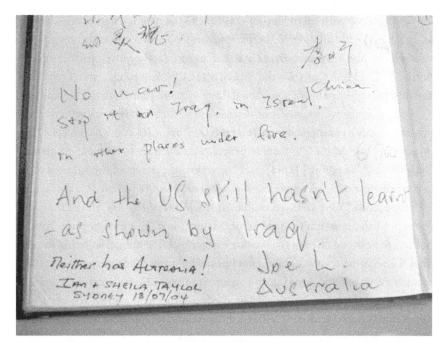

FIGURE 5.6. Comment book discussions of western imperialism, War Remnants Museum, 2004. Photograph by the author.

lian Aborigines. And still another responded: "You're absolutely right. The whole West has a history of oppression." Condemnation of U.S. imperialism, while often direct—"I hate America," wrote a visitor from Istanbul in 2005—was also complicated by visitors who pointed to more complex imperial histories that involved other countries that had also participated in the war in Vietnam (Figure 5.6):

> No war! Stop it in Iraq, in Israel, in other places under fire. China, 6/5/04
> And the US still hasn't learnt—as shown by Iraq. Joe L., Australia, 6/5/04
> Neither has Australia! Ian and Sheila Taylor, Sydney, 18/07/04

Vietnamese visitors did not participate in these transnational exchanges that largely took place in English, nor did they critique U.S. military action and history. Rather, their entries pointed to the inspiration, pride, and knowledge they received from their museum visits. Pupils and university students, who wrote the majority of the Vietnamese-language entries frequently expressed feeling proud [*tự hào*] and moved [*xúc động*] by the tremendous sacrifices and achievements of their country. Patriotic affirmations of love for the nation (according to one entry, "even more now") combined with sentiments of gratitude to the national heroes and the museum for its documentation of "heroic traditions" to reaffirm state legitimacy and validity of its historical memory. As one student wrote at the Museum of the Revolution in Ho Chi Minh City (now the Ho Chi Minh City Museum), "I never really understood though I had heard much about the revolution. Thank you for showing me."

Like the positive responses of Vietnamese visitors, some foreigners used impression books as an opportunity to praise the "beautiful country" and the "impressive history" of the Vietnamese people, who are seen as "brave," "forgiving," "courageous," "peaceful," "kind," and "persevering." Others, however, used them as a means to criticize Vietnamese historiography and representational practices as "propaganda." One German woman at the Military History Museum reacted strongly to the museum's discourse of "victory" and "glorious history: "War is nothing to be proud of, even when you are victorious. The human suffering on both sides is always too severe. It should not be used for propaganda purposes. This museum is a relic of backwards minds and ancient times." Commentators' ostensible concerns with objective "truth" (as opposed to "propaganda") reveal a particular moral high ground in which self-assuming erudite foreigners chide Vietnamese historians for their alleged obsolete ways of thinking and for *not* having learned the true lesson of war: it is *not* about glory. "An otherwise excellent museum spoiled by one-sided distortions of FACTS of the war," read an acerbic remark by a U.S. visitor to the War Remnants Museum, suggesting Vietnamese untruths and the warping of western-confirmed facts. A division between transparent U.S. "truth" and deceptive Vietnamese "propaganda" rendered Vietnamese history invalid: "Thank you Commonwealth of Kentucky," one U.S. citizen wrote in response to the "Requiem" exhibit, "for this marvelous collection of photographs in contrast to the sick communist war propaganda in the other building." Comment books thus became a means to contest what some U.S. (and other) citizens perceived to be communist lies and historical inaccuracies, as seen in one entry that contested the "stupid, biased point of view" presented at historical sites that "always portrays" U.S. and allied Vietnamese forces as "running for their lives." Complaints about the curation and narration of U.S. defeat indicated desires to "save" history (and U.S. memory) from "communist propaganda" that had misrepresented and misconstrued the "facts" of the war.

Creating "Objective" Histories: Reimaging Exhibits

During interviews, museum officials typically stressed the praise they received from foreign visitors, rather than their complaints. Stories of redemption—of the

U.S. veteran on his knee asking for forgiveness, as outlined in chapter 1—tended to overshadow criticism of museums as lacking in historical veracity. At the War Remnants Museum, however, officials were frank about critical international responses to exhibits, especially from U.S. visitors. As argued in chapter 2, exhibits at the War Remnants Museum are unique in that they do not celebrate or glorify war, but reveal its immense trauma and enduring legacies of suffering. This is reinforced through the use of graphic imagery to depict U.S. atrocities and scenes of torture, murder, and rape. U.S. bombs, military vehicles, "tiger cages," and malformed fetuses further convey the means and long-term effects of imperial violence. There is little heroism presented here, just the grim "facts" of war presented in photographs and "biographical objects" (Hoskins 1988) that personalize mass suffering and anchor Vietnamese memory to particular bodies, artifacts and contexts of war.[17]

Museums in the West, it is commonly believed, are modern, democratic institutions that provide objective balanced facts to visitors who are encouraged to draw their own informed historical and analytical conclusions. Historical narratives in Vietnamese museums, on the other hand, were considered by many to be suggestive, outdated, ideologically driven, closed to interpretation, or just plain wrong. There is a long history in the West of fetishizing facts and corresponding discourses of truth and objectivity in the fields of historical as well as scientific inquiry. A "fact" is presumed to fall outside the realm of interpretation. It exists as something simply recorded, experienced, or seen "that has been neither socially constructed nor possesses its own history of construction" (Latour and Woolgar 1986, 105). Yet, as Lorraine Daston (2006) and others have argued, scientific objects, like historical events, are not simply observed in nature, but socially produced and endowed with factual meaning. Entrenched beliefs in the inherent objectivity of western-produced facts (without questioning the process through which objects or events became endowed with such authority) instilled in many western visitors to Vietnam a sense of defiance toward museum exhibits and their counter-interpretations of the war that were thought to produce nonobjective and nonfactual histories and other arbitrary untruths.

Hương, at the War Remnants Museum, is aware of the importance of historical objectivity to western audiences and has made significant efforts to appease foreign criticism that exhibits are "biased" and lack balance. In an interview she explained:

In 1993 we began to use text and photographs from western sources, like U.S. newspapers and *Life* magazine. We had received complaints about the use of Vietnamese images and interpretation, that the exhibits were too one-sided.

> Now we try to use more objective material and to present events as having two sides. We have kept some Vietnamese explanations, but have also diversified the collection with materials from the United States, Europe, and Japan.

Hương pointed out several changes that had been made to "balance" the museum's presentation of history: the display of Ishikawa Bunyo's collection of war photography; the now-permanent exhibition of "Requiem" and other photographs from non-Vietnamese news agencies; the correction of historical inaccuracies pointed out by U.S. veterans and other visitors; and the inclusion of U.S. material objects, such as veteran-donated war and antiwar relics, including patches, clothing, medals, and peace bracelets. In the first room of the museum, "Historical Truths," curators had even included a photograph of a contemplative and withdrawn Robert McNamara with the oft-cited quote from his book, *In Retrospect: The Tragedy and Lessons of Vietnam* (1995), which was also on display: "We were wrong, terribly wrong." Yet reactions to this "balance" were mixed. On the one hand, a few U.S. visitors were disappointed to find that the exhibits had been "toned down" for international tourists, as one U.S. veteran described. Another American man interested in communist pop culture who had traveled extensively in Cuba expressed similar regret that the images and rhetoric were "no longer in your face": "I thought it would be more hard-line anti-USA like the Museum of the Cuban Revolution that pits the revolution against U.S. imperialism."

However, the majority of responses I received from U.S. visitors, predominantly between 1999 and 2001, declared that the War Remnants Museum, like other museums in Vietnam, was "full of propaganda." For these critics, the inclusion of images and artifacts from outside Vietnam did not make the exhibits any more truthful and unbiased, but in fact appropriated and distorted U.S. historical memory by inserting them into Vietnamese spaces of history. When I spoke with three U.S. tourists (two students and their professor) at the Apocalypse Now nightclub in Ho Chi Minh City, one woman criticized the image at the War Remnants Museum of the U.S. soldier posing with his war trophy: "It's one-sided. They should include the North Vietnamese atrocities. A lot of my dad's friends were here during the war and that's not what they were doing. The museum takes all these photos from the war and adds captions to turn them into propaganda." The professor nodded in agreement: "Yes, it's basically propaganda." The use of the term "propaganda" here denies U.S. historical accountability and the veracity of the images and the suffering they represent. The women's comment suggests that U.S. historical truths (communist atrocities) are antithetical to fabricated Vietnamese memory (U.S. soldiers taking pleasure in their kill). In this denial, complex racial ideologies of Vietnamese inferiority that motivated the dehumanizing acts depicted in the images are neglected. At issue here was not the moral accountability of the United States, but that of Vietnamese officials, who borrowed images from the West and inserted them into a "distorted" history. Western press photographs in Vietnamese contexts thus became unruly images and "matter out of place" (M. Douglas 1996 [1966]).

Kim Phúc in Vietnam: An Image "Out of Place"

Photographic images of the war are fundamental to the production and representation of history in Vietnamese museums. Offering insights into the political and historical dynamics of their time, photographs are cultural vehicles of memory, ideology, emotions, and values, and as such, they have the power to evoke polarized meanings and responses (Sontag 1990 [1977]). The photograph is presumed to offer a window onto the past; it freezes a moment in time and space, appearing to capture and transmit particular sensory complexities. The photograph helps the viewer to imagine, feel, and experience history. It materializes the past in the present, transforming the "there-then" to "here-now" (Barthes 1981, 7). The there-ness of the photograph imbues it with an aura of factual objectivity and an "undeniable authority . . . grounded in its temporal and physical presence. It was there" (Edwards 1992, 7). The knowledge produced by the photograph presumedly cannot be contested—the recorded image stands as pure representation, evidence of a "real" event caught on film: The experience happened (Tagg 1988).

The inclusion of U.S. press images in the War Remnants Museum upset many of these fundamental assumptions about photography. Rather than maintain its credibility and objectivity, the traveling image acquired a new register of value and meaning as it traversed borders and entered into new settings (Kuhn and McAllister 2006, 5). Arjun Appadurai's (1986) now-classic text on the social lives of things brought to our attention the cyclical movement of commodities into and out of circulation, and the process through which objects acquire context-specific values and meanings that are contingent upon shifts in historical and cultural use and exchange. With photographs, value and meaning are likewise contingent upon particular contexts of viewing. Western "democratic" images in Vietnamese socialist spaces are reinterpreted as propaganda and devalued as "matter out of place," thus rendering its message historically invalid, as demonstrated in the example of the war trophy image. The irony, of course, is that photographs of the war were taken in Vietnam and thus, it could be argued, have made their long journey "home." Moreover, the insertion of U.S. news images into Vietnamese museum contexts communicates the same moral and antiwar messages. The issue here, then, is ownership and control of history and the sentiment that the "Vietnam War" is a U.S. story that can only be told through particular noncommunist and non-Vietnamese subject positionings. To examine the tensions between resignification and historical invalidation, I examine the politics of display and the transnational movement into and out of circulation of the renowned photograph of the napalmed Phan Thị Kim Phúc taken by Huỳnh Công (Nick) Út in 1972.

Nick Út's photograph of Phan Thị Kim Phúc has long assumed an iconic, if not sacred, status in the United States and in the history of war photography (Hariman and Lucaites 2007, 173). Along with Eddie Adams's photograph of a "VC" execution and Ronald Haeberle's visual documentation of the Mỹ Lai massacre, it has come to constitute the "iconic currency" of the Vietnam War (J. Young 2000, 54), emblematic of its chaos, suffering, and cruelty. The iconicity of this image lies in its affective power, its ability to shock, enrage, and distress the observer. It is rendered sacred insofar as it signifies to the viewer a pure and presumably unmediated representation of the most innocent and vulnerable victims of war: children. The photograph cautions the viewer to rethink military intervention and the scientific impulse to develop advanced technologies of war. But despite its purity of representation, even this image has the power to arouse debate.

There is a dissimilar repertoire of photography used in Vietnam to represent the war, as argued in chapter 2. Through the late 1990s, these discrepant visual histories largely remained in separate contexts of historical memory, until recent collaborative efforts have brought such works into new, often joint, exhibition spaces. At times there have been unenthusiastic and ambivalent responses to border-crossing images of war that travel between both countries. In a 2002 *Los Angeles Times* review of Tim Page's "Another Vietnam: Pictures of the War from the Other Side" (2002), a reporter shows the collection of photographs taken by revolutionary photojournalists to a Vietnamese American (former ARVN) photographer. As he thumbs through the book, the photographer becomes agitated and irate, and evokes the image of Kim Phúc, which is on display in Vietnam, he claims, so that the communist officials can elicit international sympathy for the country. Linking Vietnam to the U.S. war on terror, he queries the reporter: How would he feel if Osama bin Laden were to show a picture of a young female victim of a U.S. bombing attack and claim U.S. responsibility? How would U.S. citizens feel if bin Laden "took advantage" of such an image and attempted to "make it more important" by putting it on display? (Johnson 2002). While the photographer does not deny the "truth" of the image, that Kim Phúc was an accidental victim of U.S. war technology, he does question the specific context of viewing and knowledge production: in Vietnam, the "manipulated" photograph loses its validity and objectivity to become mere propaganda.

The photographer's response was not unique; resistance to Vietnamese "appropriation" of U.S. and, in this case, South Vietnamese historical memory often centered on the image of Kim Phúc, whose napalmed body became the embattled site for political struggles over ownership and control of history. When removed from its "proper" capitalist space of belonging, the purity and sacredness of the image was violated; it became unruly "matter out of place," defiled by communist interpretation and intent that "confuse and contradict cherished classifications" of noncommunist memory (M. Douglas 1996 [1966], 37). When inserted into a contrasting political context and narrative of history (that of U.S. imperialism), the image of Kim Phúc took on a new social life that signified to certain people the exploitation of meaning and loss of authority over memory.

The photograph of Phan Thị Kim Phúc has been intermittently displayed at the War Remnants Museum. During my fieldwork between 1999 and 2001, the image was not on exhibit, though it had been previously, according to museum staff. By 2004, it was back on display, positioned alongside the 1995 portrait of a scarred and partially exposed Kim Phúc as an adult holding her infant child. These images have remained on exhibit through July 2008, the last time I visited the museum. When I spoke with Hương in 2004 about the museum's revolving display of the photograph, her critical tone revealed a strong ambivalence toward another politicized, though less discussed in the United States, aspect of the photograph: Kim Phúc's international celebrityhood. On the one hand, the photograph's symbolic significance and iconic status made its absence conspicuous, as was noted in impression books: Where is the infamous picture of the naked, napalmed girl? On the other hand, in Hương's view, Kim Phúc had been a "privileged victim" who had received significant international attention and aid, and now lived a life of relative comfort in Canada. Indeed the photograph of Kim Phúc embracing her child suggests to the viewer the possibility of postwar serenity, reconciliation, and regeneration, rather than ongoing traumatic suffering (Hariman and Lucaites 2007, 184–186). What about unknown victims who are *not* the recipients of international aid and *not* in the media spotlight, whose suffering remains unknown and unacknowledged? Hương asked me rhetorically. "There are still so many victims, unprivileged victims, and this museum should be a place to tell their stories." Hương then told me about her efforts to curate the new exhibit on former U.S. senator Bob Kerrey and the Thạnh Phong village massacre in which he took part on February 25, 1969. "Thạnh Phong village is so poor. When I went to collect materials for the exhibit, they didn't even have photographs of the victims. I had to take pictures of the graves and the village as it looks today to represent the massacre in our museum." In her passionate commitment to convey new knowledge of wartime atrocities, Hương faces a critical dilemma: how to give representation to grievous acts of violence for which there are no images and few, if any, witnesses?

Drawing upon the work of Zeynep Devrim Gürsel (2007), I suggest that museum directors are brokers of images and mediators of knowledge, not unlike people in the industry of international photojournalism. As Hương attempted to negotiate conflicting demands in her editing and presentation of the war, she faced another impasse: whether or not the museum exhibited the image of Kim Phúc could be considered manipulative propaganda or an act of censorship and selectivity. Conflicts over U.S. press images in Vietnamese spaces of memory thus expose cracks in fundamental beliefs about photography: objectivity and truth are *not* intrinsic to the image, but contingent upon "suitable" contexts of viewing. When taken out of its "democratic" context and used to represent communist (read: nondemocratic) history, the western image no longer signifies truth but propaganda. The image of Kim Phúc, treated as sacred U.S. historical property, thus loses its aura of truthful objectivity when it returns to its original setting, Vietnam. Such frictions over truth, objectivity, and ownership of history, I have argued, not only work to invalidate Vietnamese historical authority and memory (questioning the intent to represent), but also redirect critical attention away from image content—imperial acts of violence—and larger issues of historical accountability.

Museum Democratization?

In the beginning of this chapter I wrote of the "democratization" of western museums that scholars argue has taken place since the 1960s, a process linked to shifts in the power relations of knowledge production, and diversity in representation and consumption practices. The Vietnamese museums discussed above show evidence of change that similarly suggest democratizing processes, albeit partial and situated. The recuration of exhibits, including the addition of postwar narratives of peace, suffering, and productivity, and the inclusion of other historical subjectivities (such as heroic mothers and U.S. veterans) have played a critical role in reshaping and expanding museum representations and narrations, as have international visitor critiques. Democratizing practices, however, are selective, ambiguous, and at times involuntary. On the one hand, there exist global relations of unequal power, the dynamics of which play out in the terrain of historical memory. Vietnam, a poorer and less powerful nation, must consider the possible political and economic repercussions of its public presentation of official history (thus the removal of the word "crimes"). On the other hand, despite diversification in museum participation and representation, significant silences remain—most notably, nonrevolutionary perspectives from southern Vietnam (and even alleged PAVN atrocities, as the student suggested). However, such exclusions are by no means definitive, as demonstrated in the case of "Requiem" in chapter 2.

Comparatively, there are also limitations to the democratization of museums in the United States, as evident in the *Enola Gay* controversy at the Smithsonian

National Air and Space Museum in the mid-1990s. Preparation for the highly anticipated exhibition sparked vigorous debate between veterans, curators, historians, activists, and others about how to remember the atomic bombing of Japan: as excessive force that took lives or as necessary violence to end war and save lives (Linenthal and Engelhardt 1996). Yet, there were significant transnational silences in these discussions and in the scaled-back display that finally opened, namely the perspectives of Japanese victims. As Lisa Yoneyama has argued, efforts to include bombing artifacts from Hiroshima and Nagasaki were perceived as "transnational penetration" of the national borders of historical memory (2001, 332). Representation of Japanese experiences, it was feared, would confer the status of victimhood on Japan (rather than victimizer), which would then suggest that the bombing had been an act of U.S. aggression, rather than one of salvation.

Though different historical contexts, the continuities in U.S. historical memory of Japan and Vietnam are worth noting: U.S. soldiers as saviors, not aggressors; U.S. actions as moral and just (in response to threat), not excessive and unmerited; U.S. intention as benevolent, not imperial. Moreover, there is a similar reluctance to acknowledge the victimhood of both Japanese and Vietnamese persons. As I argued above, a focus on "propaganda" in Vietnamese museums displaced attention away *from* the violence of U.S. empire conveyed in exhibit photographs *to* museum officials accused of producing historical untruths. In an interview, John, a U.S. veteran who has lived several years in Vietnam, described his visit to the War Remnants Museum with a delegation of returning veterans: "There was a lot of anger at the museum." For John, the exhibitions were a harsh, yet accurate, documentation of the cruelty of war, one that "shows the suffering of the Vietnamese people." Yet this shift from Vietnamese as enemy aggressors to suffering victims proved difficult for some veterans in his group to make. "They could only focus on their own loss and pain," John lamented, pointing to resistance toward conferring the status of suffering on non-American Others, a topic to which I now turn.

Tortured Bodies and the
Neoliberal Politics of
Historical Unaccountability

CHAPTER SIX

In 2006 the popular U.S. television show *Amazing Race* traveled to Vietnam. Upon arrival in Nội Bài international airport in Hanoi, contestants, who race around the globe in competition for a one-million-dollar prize, were instructed to find their way to Hỏa Lò prison, the now popular tourist attraction formerly and "infamously known as Hanoi Hilton," the narrator informed viewers as the camera cut to an image of a French guillotine followed by dark and decrepit prison cells. "During the Vietnam war hundreds of American servicemen were held captive in Hoa Lo," the voice continued as black-and-white footage of captured and handcuffed U.S. pilots played. "One of the most notable prisoners," said the narrator, "was John McCain." Next scene: The teams have found their way to the prison-turned-museum. They are instructed to locate McCain's flight suit, on display in one of the exhibits. The prison doors open, and contestants run hurriedly through the grounds in search of the "treasure." At no point did the narrator allude to the history of Hỏa Lò, that it had been built by the French in the late nineteenth century as part of an extensive colonial prison apparatus that housed Vietnamese communist and anticolonial revolutionaries (Zinoman 2001), a history to which most of the museum is devoted. This marginalization of U.S. memory in a space that commemorates the Vietnamese revolution quickly became apparent to viewers and contestants, who raced through a maze of rooms and hallways, unable to locate the POW exhibit. Eventually McCain's flight suit and helmet were found hanging in a glass case in a small, inconspicuous space that presumably housed U.S. POWs during the war (see Figure 6.5). While most couples ran in, grabbed their next "clue" (assignment), and ran out, with but a passing glance at the exhibit, two teams stopped in front of the McCain display case to bow their heads and take a moment of silence out of respect for McCain, his fellow prisoners, and U.S. servicemen "still fighting and sacrificing their lives," one of the team members told the camera, thus linking the historical memory of the Vietnam War to current military intervention in Iraq. What was not shown in *Amazing Race*, however, further complicated this presumably unstaged spectacle of U.S. memory: next to McCain's flight suit were tennis shoes, a bed with a mat, photographs of POWs attending Catholic mass and playing volleyball in the courtyard, and a book on Vietnam's humane policy [*chính sách nhân đạo*], thus presenting an image of tolerable, even comfortable living conditions that sharply contradicts the sinister depictions of the "Hanoi Hilton" that inform U.S. historical imagination.

This chapter addresses competing and ambiguous memories and representations of "humane" and "inhumane" acts carried out against U.S. POWs during the war in Vietnam. I am interested in the reappearance and reexamination of such images and discourses in the current Vietnamese context of global market reform, and the new meanings and force they take when positioned in relation to renewed accusations of POW torture and other human rights violations, as well as in relation to photographs of U.S. abuse of Iraqi prisoners. In triangulating Vietnam, Iraq, and the United States I am not suggesting the similitude and uniformity of U.S. intervention in differing historical and cultural contexts, though there are striking parallels in the underlying ideologies of American moralism and exceptionalism that have motivated and rationalized these and other U.S. imperial interventions. There are, moreover, clear parallels in the escalating tensions between memory and forgetting, redress and unaccountability, that this chapter explores.

Situated in a postwar context, the analysis here demonstrates that unlike Vietnam's reconciliatory gesture toward the United States—a practice commonly referred to as *khép lại quá khứ, hướng về tương lai* (close the past to face the future)—the reverse has occurred in U.S. policy toward Vietnam: that of *recalling* the past to shape the present and the future. In the years following the end of the war, allegations of pernicious human rights violations (also linked to POW/MIA issues) strengthened the pro-embargo agenda and stalled normalized diplomacy until 1995. Thereafter, as bilateral trade and U.S. foreign investment in Vietnam increased (and met many red-tape difficulties), accusations of wartime torture and violence resurfaced, perhaps not uncoincidentally as the U.S. strengthened its efforts toward dismantling "market socialism" and expanding economic liberalization. What is of particular interest to me here are the linkages between discourses of human rights and U.S. practices of neoliberalism, which I use here to refer to the idea that economic growth and "the elimination of poverty (both domestically and worldwide) can best be secured through free markets and free trade" (Harvey 2005, 64–65). As Aihwa Ong has argued, in the wake of the occupation of Iraq, U.S. neoliberalism has come to signify a "radicalized capitalist imperialism that is increasingly tied to lawlessness and military action" (2006, 1). As I demonstrate below, it has also become increasingly tied to moral unaccountability (both in Vietnam and Iraq) as practices of memory that recall, for example, torture and human rights violations in the "Hanoi Hilton" and privilege certain narratives of state violence while silencing others.

The geopolitical and global historical politics that underpin allegations of human rights violations, and the contested claims to truth that ensue, figure prominently here (Bradley and Petro 2002). I am concerned not with the debates over universalism and cultural relativism that have occupied the focus of much academic inquiry, but with human rights as a regulating and disciplinary "global moral project" (Asad 2000, 15). This is not to deny state violence or refute people's claims in Vietnam and elsewhere that their rights have been violated. Rather, following the lead of Jacques Derrida, I aim to call attention to global hierarchies of power that inform the deployment of human rights discourses and accusations of "crimes against humanity," "torture," and "terrorism." Derrida reminds us that it is "often in the name of human rights, and to punish or prevent crimes against humanity that we come to limit or at least imagine limiting the sovereignty of certain Nation-states" (2001, 52). Such limitations, he cautions, are "only imposed where it is 'possible' (physically, militarily, economically), that is to say always imposed on small, relatively weak States by powerful States" (ibid.).[1] In what follows I draw from Derrida's insights to demonstrate how U.S. empire has necessitated its global economic intervention in Vietnam under the pretext of human rights and "neoliberal salvation." As David Harvey (2005) and others have argued, the neoliberal state enacts a language of rights to position itself as a guarantor of individual freedoms, such as freedom of choice, property rights, free market, and the right to prosperity. In the context of socialist Vietnam, proponents of U.S. neoliberalism imagine it as a tool to save the Vietnamese nation and to help it evolve from socialist repression, privation, and suffering into capitalist freedom and plentitude. Free market practices are thus held to be the logical, rational, and indeed inevitable solution to communist moral and economic inadequacies (see Gibson-Graham 1996). This logic, I argue, informs and indeed disrupts ongoing "normalization" processes between Vietnam and the U.S. as a moralizing discourse of rights (and violations thereof) is mobilized in a concerted effort to rescue and reform Vietnam through management and discipline of "proper" global market practices.

There is a long historical relationship between U.S. human rights discourses and challenges to sovereignty, as Derrida's observation foretells. Representations of "savage" communists with no value for human life or respect for freedom justified military intervention and attempts to "save" the country from communism. General Westmoreland's now-infamous quote from Peter Davis's 1974 documentary *Hearts and Minds,* that the "Oriental doesn't put the same high price on life as does a Westerner," furthered unsubstantiated rumors and reports during the war that parents had used their children as human bombs and shields, and as detonators of mines, signifying the ultimate violation of human rights, trust, and innocence. This chapter examines the lingering legacies of dehumanizing discourses thirty years after the end of the war, and ongoing struggles in Vietnam to rehumanize the nation and its history in the face of U.S. unaccountability and challenges to its historical memory. Despite recent accounts that praise the "good relations" that have unfolded between Vietnam and the United States in the decade since diplomatic relations were restored (see Burghardt 2006), reconciliation remains contentious and fraught with suspicions and recurring accusations. In what follows I analyze representations of Vietnam's "inhumanity" in U.S. memory, including congressional documents and POW narratives, and Vietnamese efforts to counter such claims by professing a tradition of humanitarianism in ideology and action. The tensions between valuation and devaluation of Vietnamese wartime acts raise critical questions about subject position, power, agency, and suffering: What constitutes torture and what is its ambiguous relationship to compassion? How is the naming of torture itself an act of symbolic violence that silences the suffering of others? What do accusations of torture and human rights violations "do" in the context of emerging neoliberalism in Vietnam?

Victim or Victimizer: Abu Ghraib and Memory in Vietnam

On April 30, 2004, the twenty-ninth anniversary of the end of the war, I arrived in Ho Chi Minh City. Within days of my arrival, news of torture and abuse at Abu Ghraib prison broke in the international press. Almost immediately, images began to circulate in cybercafés in various locations in the city. The scandal was covered in the Vietnamese media in abridged reports from foreign press sources, such as Reuters or the BBC, found on the back page of newspapers in the international section accompanied by one or two small photographs. Friends, some of whom had sent notes of condolence after September 11, 2001, were silent on the matter in my presence, not wanting to somehow offend my presumed American sensitivities. The presence of a tragic and now repeated past was palpable in the air.

Days later a commentary by Phạm Hồng Phước, "Connections and Heart-Wrenching Contrasts," appeared in the popular *Công An Thành Phố* [Ho Chi Minh City Police] daily newspaper. At the bottom of the article were two graphic photographs placed alongside one another to illustrate his cases of comparison: the murder of 504 civilians in Sơn Mỹ village (Mỹ Lai) and the abuse of Iraqi prisoners.[2] Drawing parallels between the Mỹ Lai massacre and the Abu Ghraib scandal, the author lambasted the recurring misconduct and crimes of U.S. soldiers during wartime and suggested that their actions reflect a dehumanizing ideology that "puts little worth on the lives of people who are not American citizens" (2004, 13). His exposure of the racist inequalities that underpin the differential valuation of lives concluded with a rhetorical question: "Wherever U.S. soldiers are at war, will they engage in acts that violate the human rights of others?" (ibid.).[3]

Critiques such as Phạm Hồng Phước's that used images of violence to mobilize memory and to suggest a visual trajectory of inhumane U.S. imperial acts did not go unnoticed by U.S. officials. Two weeks later on May 29, 2004, Voice of America (VOA), the international broadcasting service of the U.S. government, aired a story in Vietnam called "Prisoners of War" that effectively shifted the subject position from tortured *Iraqis* to tortured *Americans* who themselves have suffered a long history of mistreatment at the hands of their enemies in wartime. The devaluation of Iraqi bodies and the disavowal of their suffering demonstrates what Judith Butler has called a "differential allocation of grievability," which "operates to produce and maintain certain exclusionary conceptions of who is normatively human" (2004, xiv–xv). Such a system differentiates between lives that are livable and grievable and lives that are not; lives that in Fassin's terms are sacred and lives that are sacrificeable (2007, 508). The VOA report, adopted from U.S. media sources, such as the *Washington Post,* and broadcast in Vietnamese, was quick to dismiss the grievability of tortured and humiliated Iraqi prisoners by conferring the moral status of suffering upon U.S. servicemen only:

> The recent abuse of Iraqi prisoners by American soldiers in Abu Ghraib prison in Baghdad, denounced in international public opinion, has disturbed and sickened every American citizen. In reality, very few people remember that American POWs also had to endure shame and manifold suffering in past wars, including the war in Vietnam. ("Prisoners of War," VOA, May 29, 2004)

The broadcast detailed the violence inflicted upon U.S. soldiers, agents of international betterment, at the hands of their "uncivilized" enemies: they were blindfolded and tortured in the Gulf War, buried alive by the Japanese during World War II, and unjustly executed in Korea. The remainder of the report concerned a highly sensitive and controversial topic in Vietnam: the alleged abuse of U.S. prisoners during the war who were reportedly kept in a state of perpetual hunger and regularly beaten in Hỏa Lò prison, the "Hanoi Hilton." VOA implicated not only prison guards in the cruel treatment of U.S. POWs, but also the residents of Hanoi.

Its description of the infamous "Hanoi March" in 1966, when captured U.S. pilots were paraded through the streets in front of angry residents, detailed the intimidation and ridicule to which the soldiers were subjected as irate Hanoians threw excrement, stones, water, and bricks at the prisoners in a deliberate attempt to humiliate them.[4]

This attempt by VOA to position Americans as victims rather than perpetrators of inhumane wartime acts and, conversely, Vietnamese as victimizers instead of victims of U.S. bomb attacks was not well received in the Vietnamese press. Only days after the broadcast, the website for Voice of Vietnam (VOV) radio posted a response that accused VOA of fabricating a story that misrepresented Vietnam's tradition of generosity and tolerance [*truyền thống bao dung nhân ái*], with the intent to divert international attention away from U.S. troops and their cruelty toward Iraqi prisoners ("An Unconvincing Comparison," VOV News, June 4, 2004). A few weeks later, the popular and widely circulated tabloid *An Ninh Thế Giới* [World Security] published a two-part report by journalist Đặng Vương Hưng, "American Prisoners at Hỏa Lò: A Story Told Just Now." Like VOV, the author accused VOA of attempting to mollify and deceive current public opinion concerning the abuse of Abu Ghraib prisoners by broadcasting a commentary on the torture of U.S. pilots over thirty years ago in Hỏa Lò prison. Đặng Vương Hưng meticulously examined—and rejected—accusations of mistreatment leveled by VOA. What did the U.S. pilots eat? he asked his readers. Quoting a general from the People's Army of Vietnam (PAVN), he reported that POWs received good care and special meals; they were fed three times a day and provided with foodstuffs such as meat, fruit, bread, and other provisions for a western diet, including milk and potatoes. An accompanying photograph showed pilots in dark prison uniforms washing vegetables together in preparation for a meal. The article further documented holiday and other leisure activities that presumably took place in the prisons—claims that are also recorded in the Hỏa Lò museum with photographs of inmates playing volleyball or attending Christmas mass. The author pondered: Why did U.S. prisoners receive such treatment despite their war crimes and why did they eat better than the average Vietnamese person, who went hungry during the war? Because on the foreign relations front, he concluded, the prisoners were "special guests" and "precious capital" whose lives were valued and given meaning despite their disregard for the lives of the Vietnamese people they had bombed (Đặng Vương Hưng 2004, 29). Contrary to representations in the VOA broadcast of inhumane acts conducted by Vietnamese, the treatment of American POWs in Hỏa Lò prison, the journalist argued, was representative of the "humane policy" [*chính sách nhân đạo*] of the Party, the people, and the state: "There is probably no country in the world that would have treated U.S. prisoners as well as Vietnam. This is because of a thousand-year tradition of leniency and humanitarianism as practiced by our people" (ibid.), a view similarly expressed in the VOV report and in the Hỏa Lò prison exhibit.

The purpose of my extensive citations here is neither to refute the substantive content of the VOA broadcast nor to deny individual claims of abuse. The hunger, illness, beatings, and other suffering endured by POWs in Hanoi prisons has been well documented in postwar memoirs.[5] Yet even in these accounts one finds ambiguity concerning intent: John McCain, for instance, is unclear if the lack of proper medical treatment for his injuries is due to a scarcity of resources or to cruel and deliberate punishment (1999, 192). In an interview in Hanoi, a former POW who "has the wounds to prove torture" recalled the constant hunger that gripped him during his five years of imprisonment, though he also surmised that POWs conceivably received more food to eat than the local population, particularly after 1970, when prison care suddenly improved. But again, my concern lies neither in affirming nor in denying the veracity of these stories, but in the ambiguities that surface in competing memories and representations of cruelty and compassion. Following Talal Asad (2000), my intention is to explore what it means to enact a moralizing discourse of human rights and their violation in the context of U.S.-Vietnam postwar reconciliation and neoliberalization.

Human Rights and Historical Unaccountability in U.S. Policy toward Vietnam

Human rights have long been linked to U.S. international policy and criteria for the allocation of foreign aid. As Michael Ignatieff has argued, "Across the political spectrum since 1945, American presidents have articulated a strongly messianic vision of the American role in promoting rights abroad" (2005, 13), an assumed position as global protector that has allowed the United States to justify military action as humanitarian intervention. Human rights, Talal Asad also suggests, have been "integral to the universalizing moral project of the American nation-state—the project of humanizing the world—and an important part of the way many Americans see themselves in contrast to their 'evil' opponents" (1993, 147). The construction of the uncivilized and barbaric communist Other, in particular, reinscribes essentialist binaries that celebrate the humanitarian and economic achievements of "modern" capitalist civilizations while berating the presumed moral failures and deficiencies of noncapitalist ones. Such constructions were instrumental to prolonging U.S. military intervention in Vietnam, and they continued to shape postwar relations as the United States strove to politically and economically discipline Vietnam for its unsatisfactory human rights practices. Not unlike the VOA broadcast, a focus on Hanoi's accountability for U.S. POWs and MIAs allowed U.S. government officials to elide critical discussion of its own moral failures and economic responsibilities toward Vietnam.

During the war, emotionally charged reports in the United States of abused POWs served as proof of the inhumanity and callousness of the enemy regime. Accusations of cruel and indecent treatment that violated the Geneva Conventions, including "physical torture, psychological terror, public display, insufficient medical care and treatment, neglect of health, dietary, and sanitary necessities . . ." (U.S. House of Representatives 1969, 3, 10), not only served to rally support for the war, but also justified and prolonged U.S. intervention (Gruner 1993, 19).[6] Allegations that the "air pirates," as U.S. pilots were called in Vietnam, would be tried for their war crimes against humanity and perhaps even executed (as reported in the Soviet press) were met with threats of retaliation by U.S. military advisers, who called for a rapid and intense escalation of bombing and mining campaigns in northern areas.

As the war drew to a close for the United States in 1973 following the Paris Peace Accords, and POWs returned home, preoccupation with U.S. troops believed to remain in captivity intensified and eventually came to dominate public policy toward Vietnam, including the continuation of economic sanctions and a trade embargo, in the postwar years (Stern 2005, 9; Martini 2007, 21–24).[7] The POW/MIA issue further displaced war responsibility from the United States to Vietnam, as Washington pressured Hanoi to provide a full accounting of missing U.S. troops, the absent bodies of whom, Thomas M. Hawley argues, have stood for Communist deceit and U.S. defeat, "an ever-present reminder of the catastrophe that continues to afflict the American body politic" (2005, 4). In congressional documents, Hanoi is frequently accused of uncooperative behavior, such as withholding strategic information and hiding POWs and MIA remains for use as bargaining chips to secure pledged aid (U.S. Senate 1977, 18–19; U.S. House of Representatives 1982, 19, 27).[8] Postwar reports of "live sightings" and images of enslaved U.S. bodies in captivity, further entrenched in U.S. social imagination with films such as *Deer Hunter* (1978) and *Rambo: First Blood, Part 2* (1985), fueled conflict between Vietnam and the United States, who used the POW/MIA issue to stall diplomatic and economic normalization and deny reconstruction aid.[9]

The question of war reparations, in particular, brought to the fore issues of moral and historical accountability that further exacerbated postwar tensions. Monetary compensation, Richard A. Wilson has argued in the context of post-apartheid South Africa, is key to reconciliation processes (2001, 22), though as John Borneman points out, it is "not in itself sufficient for settling accounts," which also requires moral accountability and acknowledgment of wrongdoing (1997, 103). It was precisely the entanglements of moral and financial culpability that became a

grave concern for U.S. officials, who opted to discuss the payment not of reparations, but of "reconstruction aid," a more neutral term that avoided any implicit
moral confession of guilt, and positioned the United States as a provider of humanitarian assistance alongside the aid initiatives of other nation-states. In Chapter VIII of the 1973 Paris Peace Accords, the U.S. government initially agreed to
contribute to Vietnam's postwar reconstruction (Asselin 2002, 85). An amount of
$3.25 billion was proposed in a letter from U.S. president Richard Nixon, contin-
gent upon congressional approval, but was later reneged on as the POW/MIA issue
intensified around allegations that U.S. personnel remained in captivity (Martini
2007, 29–30; H. B. Franklin 1993, 183–184). The ambiguous line between aid and
redress, with its moral connotations of wrongdoing and responsibility, was further
cause for its rejection by the U.S. administration (M. Young 1991, 303).

Throughout the process of normalization—initiated in 1977 and formally established in 2005—"progress" on the POW/MIA front remained a key precondition for normalizing relations, and for ending the U.S. trade embargo (Stern 2005,
27). Hanoi's cooperation was to be rewarded with U.S. diplomatic recognition and
global capitalist integration.[10] Vietnamese preoccupation with locating the remains
of an estimated 300,000 of their own MIAs (on the side of the revolution) remained
largely unacknowledged in these discussions, as a concern for 1,500 U.S. bodies
trumped one third of a million Vietnamese. Responsibility for "imperial debris"
such as Agent Orange (Stoler 2008, 206–207) was also shirked as the U.S. government accused Hanoi of using lethal chemical weapons against H'mong ethnic minorities in Laos and Vietnam (U.S. House of Representatives 1979).[11] So effective
and profound was the displacement of U.S. moral and financial responsibility that
Vietnam, having received no war reparations or U.S. assistance with postwar reconstruction, was required to pay $145 million—the debt incurred during the war
by the Republic of Vietnam—and other financial claims to the United States as part
of normalization agreements (Martini 2007, 202).

In the postnormalization years, allegations of deceitful practices and human
rights violations have continued to inform U.S. policy. In congressional hearings in
1995 and 1997, for example, the Vietnamese administration was again accused of
withholding records and POW remains, presumably for ransom or revenge.[12] The
Vietnamese state was also referred to as "totalitarian," "not civilized," and a "dic-
tatorial regime," and even compared in several instances with Nazi Germany and
Stalinist Russia (U.S. House of Representatives 1995, 1997). References were repeatedly made to political and religious repression, to the absence of democratic freedoms and other "core values" of the United States, and to the suffering inflicted by
the Vietnamese government on countless numbers of people (House of Representatives 2005, 2–3, 41).[13] I do not refute these accusations. Clearly state violence and

repression in Vietnam are present, though the extent of human rights violations is a controversial, much debated topic. Rather, I am interested in what such representations of Vietnam do and the responses they engender from a population that commonly sees the United States as meddling in the internal affairs of other less powerful sovereign states.

Representations of Vietnam in U.S. congressional discourse not only suggest a naturalized connection between communism and human rights violations, but also resurrect the myth of oriental despotic power—an earlier orientalist rendition of the clash of civilizations where "the West" is founded on humane liberal and democratic models of governance, while governmentality in "the East" is rooted in repressive regimes of power that wield total control over the masses (Wittfogel 1957). There is a long history of debate concerning whether or not "Asian values" and human rights are fundamentally different, if not totally incompatible. From Burmese militarism and Singaporean authoritarianism to Vietnamese communism, Southeast Asia is consistently thought to be not quite civilized. Pointing to prevalent historical and culturally specific conceptions of freedom across the Asian continent, scholars have complicated such views and the belief that liberal "rights" and "freedom" emanated out from the capitalist West to other, less civilized corners of the world (Ta Van Tai 1988; Kelly 1998). Yet, self-declarations of an "Asian way," as a response to western global hegemony (Ong 1999, 81), risk reaffirming western perceptions of Asia as morally inferior—not yet modern and not yet humanized.[14] While Vietnam has not argued for the particularity of an "Asian" approach to human rights (unlike Singapore or Malaysia), its positioning by the United States as a communist Asian country devoid of rights and freedoms works to deny its populace the status of global and moral "citizens of humanity" (Malkki 1994).

In the next section I return to the controversial issue of POW torture and examine the ways Hanoians debated and disputed such accusations by drawing upon an essentialized history that places much emphasis on Vietnam's "strong tradition of respect for human rights" (Ta Van Tai 1988, 233).

From Friend to Foe: John McCain and the Un/Naming of Violence

In April 2000, during the twenty-fifth anniversary celebration of the end of the war, U.S. Senator John McCain returned to Vietnam for his seventh visit. Because McCain had been a strong proponent of reconciliation and normalized relations between the two countries, he had long been identified in Vietnamese public discourse as a "friend of Vietnam." McCain had visited several times Trúc Bạch Lake in central Hanoi, where his plane was shot down on October 26, 1967, reportedly during his twenty-third bombing mission. Both the Vietnamese and international press have extensively covered McCain's return visits, especially his reunions with the now elderly man, Mai Văn Ổn, who reportedly saved McCain's life by pulling him from the water and protecting him from angry villagers who attempted to beat him for dropping bombs on their homes.[15] With McCain's ascendancy in politics, Ổn became somewhat of a celebrity for his actions, and photographs often showed both men in a jovial pose, embracing one another for the cameras—images, I was told, that demonstrate Vietnam's "tradition of making friends out of enemies."[16] A stone monument to honor the People's Defense Forces who shot down the A-4 Sky-hawk marks the site with an engraved image of McCain ejecting from his exploded aircraft (Figure 6.1).[17]

In April 2000, however, McCain was not welcomed back. Rather, his visit was met with anger by many residents of Hanoi after the U.S. media released an interview in which McCain employed the racial epithet "gooks" to refer to the prison guards he claimed had tortured him during his incarceration at Hỏa Lò. Hanoians were disturbed by his racist remarks and his slanderous portrayal of their nation. In everyday conversations they reminded me that only a few years back, in 1994, McCain had publicly thanked the government and the people of Vietnam for their benevolent treatment and kindness.[18] In the press and in interviews, citizens pondered how McCain could employ dehumanizing and racist characterizations to refer to people who had valued and respected his life enough to rescue him from death. Moreover, how could their good deeds and compassionate wartime acts now be revalued and reinscribed as inhumane?

McCain's reference to torture, in particular, incensed my research respondents, who angrily called attention to the everyday violence experienced by the general population during the war, suffering rendered mute in the narratives of POWs. Voicing their own histories of suffering, they pointed to the manifold hardships and sacrifices endured to keep U.S. servicemen alive with food that famished civilians could have eaten. Such gestures, in their view, demonstrated to the world a humanitarian tradition of forgiveness, rather than one of revenge and retribution. This is reflected in the following excerpt from an interview with a museum employee from Hanoi:

> We have no hatred for Americans. We always knew that it wasn't the American people who were behind the war, but their government. But that McCain. I don't understand him. When he first came to Vietnam he thanked the people for saving his life. Now he returns to say bad things about us. I was born in 1965 and I remember the war. I remember the bombs and having to wear a straw hat to protect my head from shrapnel. McCain doesn't understand how

FIGURE 6.1. "On October 26, 1967, at Trúc Bạch Lake, the People's Defense Forces of Hà Nội capital captured alive John Sidney McCain, American Air Force Major whose A4 airplane was shot down over Yên Phụ electric plant, one of ten planes shot down that day." Photograph by the author.

angry people were after their families and children were killed by his bombs. He doesn't understand how people suffered from hunger. This is why I am angry with McCain for what he said. People couldn't eat because of him. First they saved his life and then they had to feed him! American prisoners could not eat rice soup like us; they had to have potatoes. They had food to eat when we went hungry. People sacrificed a lot for those prisoners.

In addition to an emphasis on shared food provisions, respondents also pointed to benevolent care and protection that McCain and other pilots received after they ejected from their aircraft into lakes and rice fields. Though official policy prohibited villagers from subjecting the downed servicemen to violence, POW narratives recount harsh beatings and taunts, in addition to acts of compassion, blurring the lines between humane and inhumane treatment (see, for example, McCain 1999, 190). It was hard to contain the anger of the crowds who had witnessed death and devastation from the bombs, I was told. The renowned photographer Văn Bảo captured an image of one POW taunted by a farmer who pulled the injured pilot's hair as he was transported past the agitated crowd on an oxcart. "The villagers did not hurt him, despite raised emotions," the photo caption at the Air Defense–Air Force Museum reads.

While respondents contemplated and debated whether or not pilots had been treated harshly by furious villagers before police arrived (or before someone stepped in to defend the pilots), and whether or not abuse had taken place in prisons behind closed doors, there was less ambiguity regarding the issue of torture: it did not happen. When it came to the matter of POW abuse, lines were unambiguously drawn between probable misconduct by individuals in positions of power (i.e., guards) and an official policy of humane treatment that prohibited torture—a term more clearly associated in my respondents' minds with French colonial and Saigon regime penal practices as encountered in official historiography and published memoirs by Vietnamese revolutionaries. What constitutes torture? I was asked by a female journalist from Hanoi, who also acknowledged the probability of POW mistreatment but challenged the intentionality of cruelty:

> I think that torture is too strong a word for what happened. During the war years, life was very hard for us. We never had enough food while the Americans had a certain lifestyle they were used to, so they were sometimes given meat and potatoes. For them torture was having little food, even though we had even less to eat—just some rice and no meat. Or if we had meat it was very old with insects inside. They don't understand that we didn't have any shoes to wear, so they think that when they must go barefoot then it is torture. It isn't a problem if I walk across the street with no shoes. But for you, you are not used to it, so you might think it is torture. Or sleeping on a board. That's all we had, but because Americans weren't used to it and were sore in the morning, they called it torture.

These debates reveal tremendous stakes in the naming of violence—such as the use of the word "torture"—for, as Veena Das has argued, "the struggle over naming reflects serious political and legal struggles" in both national and, in this case, transnational contexts (2006, 206). There are equally significant consequences when violence remains unnamed as pain and suffering are silenced, denied, naturalized, and made invisible (Scarry 1985). In the differential valuation of suffering (Dickson-Gómez 2004, 146), the violence of everyday life for Vietnamese during the war—hungry stomachs, bare feet, bomb shrapnel—escapes the naming of violence as their bodies were reduced to "bare life" (Agamben 1998), devalued and dehumanized, no longer seen as livable lives, to invoke Butler's model of grievability. While Butler's analysis speaks explicitly to the dehumanization of tortured Iraqi bodies, the parallels are striking: the silencing in POW narratives of the everyday violence enacted upon Vietnamese bodies is not unlike the dismissal in the Voice of America broadcast of violence against Iraqi prisoners.[19] In both cases, "[a]t stake here are no longer processes of memorialization or forgetfulness but rather the normalization on the Other's dehumanization and the creation of a moral complicity that destabilizes public discussion . . ." (Biehl, Good, and Kleinman 2007, 4–5).

The reluctance of my Vietnamese respondents to name torture should not be seen as a total disavowal of violence experienced by POWs, nor uncritical adherence to state discourses and claims to humanitarianism. As mentioned, some respondents surmised that despite public commitment to a "humane policy," certain individuals most likely did violate regulations. Rather, their refusal to identify torture should be read as a claim to what Achille Mbembe has called "the status of suffering in history—the various ways in which historical forces inflict psychic harm on collective bodies and the ways in which violence shapes subjectivity" (quoted in Das 2006, 212–213, see also Morris 1997, 40). Ethnography, in particular, has shown subjectivity to be "the ground on which a long series of historical changes and moral apparatuses coalesce" (Biehl, Good, and Kleinman 2007, 3). By refusing to name torture my respondents attempted to humanize their devalued wartime acts and to express their subjectivity as shaped by broader social and historical conditions of suffering and sacrifice. In so doing, they recast the self as both victim of violence and moral agent of compassion (Asad 2003, 79), subject positions denied in U.S. historical memory and in current reconciliation processes. In asserting dynamic and shifting subjectivities, they strove to recuperate their humanity and their own historical memory, thus engaging a "politics of global recognition" that calls attention to unacknowledged and unaccounted for "historical wounds" (Chakrabarty 2007, 84).

Visualizing Humanity: Photographic and Material Representations of Compassion

Vietnamese responses to John McCain's allegations of torture demonstrate the contentious interplay between competing claims to historical truth and the displacement of both U.S. and Vietnamese state violence. At issue here is not which voice in fact represents "truth." As Hayden White reminds us, history is itself a mode of fiction making in which knowledge producers arrange and fuse fragments of the past—"facts"—into a comprehensive and ordered whole (1978, 124–125). Rather, I am interested in how historical truths come to be known, communicated, represented and refuted. To my respondents, Vietnam's moral response (good treatment of POWs) to an immoral transgression (U.S. invasion) signified a just and humane history that confirmed Vietnam's membership in a "global humanity" and the "community of civilized nations" from which the U.S. has long attempted to exclude it.

This moral history was not only voiced by respondents in conversation and interviews, but was also given visual and material representation in public spaces of memory, such as museums.

As argued in chapter 5, the national history presented to viewers in Vietnamese museums outlines the historical recurrence of defensive war and just military victory. Integral to this war story are narratives of humanitarianism that find representation in compassionate wartime acts caught on film or embodied in particular historical artifacts. In Hanoi, institutions of military memory such as the B-52 Victory Museum and the recently renovated Air Defense–Air Force Museum exhibit visual "facts" that attest to such truths. Both museums, which fall under the jurisdiction of the Ministry of Defense, document the successful efforts of the military and local militia groups, that include "young girls," "old men," and "ethnic minorities," to defend Hanoi and other targets of U.S. bomb strikes. Exhibits on the number of aircraft shot down by citizen and military defense units over northern Vietnam (4,181 according to the Air Defense–Air Force Museum), invoke wartime journalistic practices that tallied such statistics on the front page of the daily press, often providing readers with images of captured pilots and their downed airplanes. "Every village is a fortress to fight the Americans," one caption reads in the Air Defense–Air Force Museum under an image of a middle-aged man with a rifle, who signals the approach of U.S. planes by beating a large drum. Aircraft wreckage and recovered objects from pilots, including their uniforms, weapons, and communication equipment, visually narrate what in Vietnam is called "Điện Biên Phủ in the air," a reference to France's humiliating defeat in 1954.[20]

Inserted into these victory narratives are representations of Vietnam's humanity and benevolence toward captured U.S. pilots shot down over enemy territory. As argued in chapter 2, museum photographs tend to emphasize the agency rather than the victimhood of citizens during the war. Photographs that document the rescue, care, and protection of downed U.S. servicemen show this moral agency to be a specific gendered positioning, that of women engaged in humane and feminine acts of compassion and fortitude. This is seen, for example, in photographs of female volunteers and members of defense forces who have captured downed pilots and lead them in an authoritative yet protective manner to authorities. The most iconic of these images shows a petite, young, barefoot, and armed Vietnamese woman, Nguyễn Thị Kim Lai apprehending a disarmed, larger and older U.S. pilot, William Robinson, who hangs his head in defeat as she maintains a confident and commanding pose (Figure 6.2). The set of contrasts embodied in the image symbolically suggests the resolve of a feminized, diminutive, yet determined nation up against—and defeating—a powerful, now emasculated, enemy.[21] In museum pho-

FIGURE 6.2. Nguyễn Thị Kim Lai leading captured U.S. pilot William
Robinson in present-day Hà Tĩnh province, 1965. Photograph by Phan Thoan.
© Vietnam News Agency.

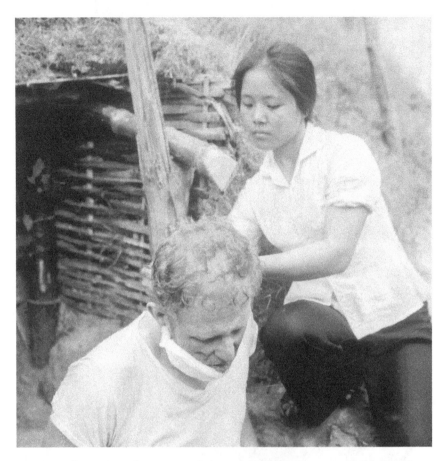

FIGURE 6.3. "American pilot Major Nichols moved by a Vietnamese girl's kindness." Photograph displayed in the Air Defense–Air Force Museum. Photograph by Phan Huy. © Vietnam News Agency.

tographs, women are also represented as sympathetic caretakers and healers who dutifully tended to the wounds of injured U.S. pilots (Figure 6.3), thus tempering images of militarized femininity with those of women as nurturing caregivers and peacemakers. These visual displays of an essentialized humanity present to viewing audiences carefully crafted images of Vietnam as a moral and civilized nation that responded to unwarranted enemy aggression with dignity and even compassion.

One of the most contentious historical sites for competing claims of humane and inhumane wartime acts is Hỏa Lò prison, dubbed the "Hanoi Hilton" by U.S. POWs. Opened as a "historical vestige" in 1997, the remains of the French colonial prison complex occupy a central place in both U.S. and Vietnamese historical memory, but for very different reasons, as suggested in the case of the reality show

Amazing Race. In Vietnamese historiography, the large numbers of political prisoners incarcerated by the French colonial regime, many of whom occupied important positions in the Communist Party, contributed to the rapid organization and expansion of communist cells and revolutionary activity (Zinoman 2001, 212–215). Today Hỏa Lò is celebrated and commemorated, to paraphrase the museum brochure, for the vital contributions made to the revolution by thousands of imprisoned patriots who sacrificed their lives and endured years of suffering to help achieve the nation's freedom and independence from French colonialism. This dominant historical narrative largely displaces U.S. memory of the site as the "Hanoi Hilton," which occupied a comparatively brief nine years (1964–1973) of the prison's century-long history.[22]

A sensory history of French colonial inhumanity and abuse of Vietnamese revolutionaries contrasts sharply with visual evidence of Vietnamese generosity and humanity toward U.S. prisoners during the war. The exhibits on the imprisonment of Vietnamese patriots, which dominate the focus of the site, demonstrate the "complete absence of modern ideas of rehabilitation and behavioral modification in French colonial prisons" (Zinoman 2001, 97). Corporal punishment, the museum shows, was institutionalized as the norm to structure everyday lives; for example, emaciated and at times unclothed mannequin prisoners are shown shackled to communal wooden beds in what were overcrowded and cramped dormitory conditions (Figure 6.4). The disciplinary apparatus of "French colonial crimes" [*tội ác của thực dân Pháp*] is put on full display for the viewer: confinement rooms (referred to as dungeons), the guillotine, and instruments used to inflict great pain all contributed to the "physical and spiritual torture" of prisoners, according to museum explanations.

By contrast, the U.S. POW exhibit, which occupied but one room (and recently expanded to two), exemplifies Vietnam's "history of humanitarianism" through the juxtaposition of text, images, and objects that attest to more humane living conditions for U.S. servicemen.[23] Compared to the bare life of Vietnamese prisoners under French colonial rule, the exhibit on U.S. POWs suggests a more comfortable spiritual and physical existence with individual beds and mats, shoes and clothing, cigarettes, books and writing materials (Figure 6.5). Images that accompany the display show communal sport, religious, and other social activities, alongside portraits of celebrity POWs, including John McCain. Outside the exhibit, a sign reminds visitors of the historical context of violence in which their imprisonment occurred: "Though having committed untold crimes on our people, American pilots suffered no revenge once they were captured and detained. Instead they were well treated with adequate food, clothing and shelter." The museum's contrasting exhibits on French cruelty and Vietnamese humanity serves to invert modernist

FIGURE 6.4. Exhibit on Vietnamese revolutionaries imprisoned at Hỏa Lò.
Photograph by the author.

logic that ascribes cruel and degrading punishment to less developed, "barbaric"
societies and civilized treatment to more advanced "democracies" (see Rejali 2007).
By calling attention to both French and U.S. "crimes" (and note how this historical site has *not* abandoned a discourse of war crimes), and naming the violence enacted upon Vietnamese bodies, museum exhibits, like my research respondents, challenged an entrenched, racialized history of cruelty that sees inhumane
and immoral acts as something "savage races" do to modern peoples (such as the
torture of U.S. POWs), while the violence and suffering inflicted on the Other
by "the expanding United States" (such as the bombing of Vietnamese villages
or the abuse of Abu Ghraib prisoners) have no place or role in this history (Asad
2003, 103).

Neoliberal Salvation and Suspicions

There are high geopolitical and global economic stakes in the naming and unnam-
ing of violence for both Vietnam and the United States as struggles over memory
and history shape and are shaped by uneasy and ambivalent postwar economic relations. U.S. accusations of torture and human rights violations take on new meaning and purpose when reinvoked in the context of Vietnam's emerging neoliberal

FIGURE 6.5. Exhibit on U.S. prisoners of war in the "Hanoi Hilton." John McCain's flight suit hangs to the left. Photograph by the author.

economy. John McCain's multiple trips to Vietnam, it should be noted, were made primarily out of concern for U.S. business interests and desires to acquire a strong economic foothold in Vietnam's rapidly expanding market. Moreover, his comments on torture came at the threshold of signing the much debated U.S.-Vietnam Bilateral Trade Agreement (BTA), which was seen by many in Hanoi as a challenge to the country's economic sovereignty and its commitment to "market socialism."[24]

Vietnamese responses to accusations of torture—grappling with the possibility of cruelty, yet ultimately professing a "thousand year tradition of leniency and humanitarianism" (Đặng Vương Hưng 2004, 29)—reflect larger anxieties and suspicions of U.S. desires to "fix" Vietnamese society and its economy through further liberalization, as stipulated in the BTA. Fears about U.S. economic domination surfaced in interviews and everyday conversations, as Hanoians weighed the advantages of economic "progress" ("We must allow Americans to come back if we want our economy to develop") against a perceived threat to Vietnam's autonomy and growth ("The BTA benefits the United States, not Vietnam. It would force us to become dependent on the United States. Why do strong countries always try to dominate the weak?"). Respondents identified in the BTA what they felt to be broader U.S. imperial ambitions to "do away with socialism and impose U.S. capitalism" on Vietnam and the larger world.[25] Vinh, a student in Saigon during the war, who lived in Hanoi at the time of our interviews (and had worked on the peace projects), linked suspicions of the BTA to postwar animosity: "There was a lot of hatred toward the United States during the war and afterwards because of the embargo. The embargo was horrible and kept us very poor. Life was extremely hard; it was like a second war, but without weapons. And now this trade agreement—why should we trust the U.S. government when we have no reason to?" Both anxieties about future sovereignty and memories of past violence and hostility shaped and informed ambivalences and reservations about the expansion of political and economic relations with the United States.

From a conventional U.S. perspective, the shift toward global capitalism and the increasing visibility of U.S. transnational corporations in Vietnam were interpreted as a defeat of socialism—"an irrational disruption of the 'normal' progression of history toward capitalism" (Anagnost 1997, 7)—and a delayed victory for the United States. As the common catchphrase goes: "Vietnam won the war, the United States won the peace." Many of my Vietnamese interlocutors familiar with this argument offhandedly dismissed it. In pointing to Vietnam's "market socialist" economy, their rejection of U.S. triumphalism resonated with economic transformations in Asia, Eastern Europe, and elsewhere that have similarly reconfigured hegemonic capitalism by only "partially subordinating themselves to the demands of major corporations and global regulatory agencies" (Ong 2006, 75; see also Stark and Bruszt 1998; Burawoy and Verdery 1999). As was clear in the provisions of the BTA, the United States perceived Vietnam's cautious, too slow approach to privatization as inhibiting the growth of the market and U.S. investment opportunities ("Vietnam Reforms" 2003). The BTA thus attempted to naturalize the hegemony of global neoliberal capitalism as a necessary and inevitable course away from "unfree," unproductive, noncapitalist economic practices that have obstructed the pace of Vietnam's integration into the global market economy.

Vietnam's "insufficient progress" in human rights has also been identified as having constrained its global integration and its diplomatic and commercial ties with the United States (Daley 2004). As Talal Asad has suggested, "the historical convergence between human rights and neoliberalism may not be purely accidental" (2003, 157). More attention needs to be paid, he maintains, to the *political and economic practices* by which attempts are made to regulate 'desirable conduct' in the world" (ibid.; emphasis in the original). In U.S. public and official discourse, neoliberal capitalism is presented as a "gospel of salvation" (Comaroff and Comaroff 2001, 2), a mode of humanitarian intervention imagined to rescue the Vietnamese nation from economic, social, political, and moral privation. With its humanist promises of freedom, rights, and progress, the message is clear: one needs "free" market capitalism to be fully human. Desires to forge a new capitalist moral and economic order in Vietnam that embraces liberalist qualities of freedom, choice, rights, and individuality often surfaced in U.S. congressional hearings. In a 1997 examination of U.S.-Vietnam relations, for example, a House committee member proposed free market capitalism *as practiced in the United States* as a solution to political, religious, and social repression: "Increasing US economic and political interaction with Vietnam will encourage market development [and] foster respect for human rights and political liberalization" (U.S. House of Representatives 1997, 4). Neoliberalism as a means to humanize and moralize the Vietnamese nation also reverberates in U.S. media. In a *Los Angeles Times* article on President Bush's trip to Hanoi in 2006 to attend an Asia-Pacific Economic Cooperation (APEC) trade summit, Vietnamese American residents of California, in an area colloquially referred to as "Little Saigon," expressed their hopes that Bush could save Vietnam from poverty and instill the importance of democratic rights: "Bush comes from a country that represents freedom and democracy; he needs to remind Vietnam that if they want to benefit from the free market trade then they have to abide by the human rights laws" (Tran 2006). The conflation of free trade and the global market with humanity, morality, democracy, and prosperity serves to reinforce its inverse: noncapitalist practices as insufficiency, lack (of freedom and rights), scarcity, and anti-democracy (Gibson-Graham 1996, 8, 44).

What emerges here, yet again, is the bifurcation of the world into "good" democratic and lawful capitalist nations that support international human rights (including the "right" to have open markets) and unfree, not-quite-capitalist countries that violate civil and economic rights, including limiting access to the free market. In the years following the signing of the BTA in 2000, the United States continued to accuse Vietnam of intent to deceive, and in particular, of engaging in unfair and illegal trade practices. The controversial Vietnam Human Rights Act of 2004 (HR 1587), "To Promote Freedom and Democracy in Vietnam," that passed in the House of Representatives in July 2004, only months after the Abu Ghraib scandal became public, coincided with several trade lawsuits aimed at Vietnamese small-scale producers for allegedly dumping shrimp and catfish on the U.S. market, thus further strengthening claims to both "uncivilized" social and economic conduct. These allegations and the subsequent increase in tariffs have had devastating consequences for Vietnamese fishermen and shrimp farmers. Contrary to neoliberal theory, the adoption of free market institutions did not result in economic progress and the elimination of poverty for these novice entrepreneurs who thought they were playing by the global rules. As Vietnam embraced global market practices and assumed a competitive edge, the United States, looking out for its own business interests, revived and redirected its dehumanizing discourses, questioning the economic ethos of farmers, as if citizens of a socialist country could not possibly engage in honest or legitimate forms of capitalism.[26] Once a threat to the "free world," a rapidly globalizing Vietnam, with its unruly yet productive fusion of socialist and capitalist practices, has now emerged as an economic threat to the United States and its neoliberal "free" practices.[27]

Conclusion

Empires of Memory and Knowledge Production

We're an empire now, and when we act, we create our own reality.
—UNNAMED OFFICIAL IN THE BUSH ADMINISTRATION, OCTOBER 2004

What makes the United States an empire? U.S. historiography and studies of American culture and society have long expressed ambivalence about identifying the United States as a global imperial polity, though such positions have begun to shift since the international events following September 11, 2001 (Stoler 2006, 8; Coronil 2007, 262–263; Ong 2006, 143). As anthropologists have made clear, however, discussions of U.S. empire transcend territorial annexations or military occupation to more broadly address the "interlaced forms of economic and cultural impositions and holdings that such an unsubtle macropolity allows" (Stoler 2006, 9). This book has explored these interlaced impositions of U.S. empire in the intersecting spheres of historical memory and a globalizing economy in postnormalization Vietnam. It has attempted to bring more ethnographic nuance to analyses of the "topography of U.S. power—its exercise, effects, negotiation, protest, and limits" (Lutz 2006, 593), by taking into account international state and non-state actors who do the work of empire on the ground through their efforts to contest and tame unruly, "non-objective" socialist histories and "improper" economic practices. U.S. neoliberalism has thus been shown to be an economic and historical-cultural mode of intervention rooted in a specific moral regime of objectivity that aims to discipline historical and economic subjects, who in turn refute and rework global modes of regulation by calling empire, with its self-created realities and lack of historical accountability, into question.

With the expansion of U.S. corporations into Vietnamese spaces of capitalist opportunity, the endurance and resurgence of U.S. empire has become increasingly and unsettlingly ironic. In July 2007, as I sat with Liên in a government office in Hải Phòng in front of a map of the city and its surrounding areas, she pointed to a rural district on the outskirts of the city's rapidly expanding suburbs. "Here," she said, fingering the township that had been infamously and "accidentally" bombed by U.S. pilots in 1972. Liên recalled that day with great sadness. She had walked over ten kilometers with her father, who was evacuating her and her siblings from their home in the city center. To avoid the heavily bombed road connecting Hải Phòng and Hanoi, her father had decided to head south to a presumably safer area. They eventually came upon the bombed village in Kiến Thụy district, not long after its destruction: "It was terrifying. I was only twelve. I saw trucks loaded with dead bodies. I will never forget that day." When I asked her why she thought the village had been bombed, she told me a rumor that circulated at that time: U.S. pilots wanted to lighten the load of their planes before heading back to the carrier ship so they released their bombs, irrespective of the civilian populations below. One week after this conversation, following a brief excursion to Ho Chi Minh City, I boarded a flight back to Hải Phòng. As the plane took off and the elderly woman next to me thumbed through the glossy in-flight magazine, gazing upon the wealthy urban lifestyle sold in its pages, the pilot's voice came over the loudspeaker: Low winds, clear visibility, *thanks* for flying with us. I froze. I looked around. No one else seemed to notice; most continued to sleep. Did anyone understand the pilot's native English? Was I the only one who realized that the captain flying this Vietnam Airlines Airbus 320, soon to descend upon Cát Bi airport, Hải Phòng, only miles from Kiến Thụy, was a U.S. pilot?

Gayatri Chakravorty Spivak has argued that subaltern historiography offers a theory of change that focuses not on transitions (for instance, in modes of production), but on confrontations that are positioned "in relation to histories of domination and exploitation" (1988, 3). This book has explored both concessions and confrontations with U.S. empire in postwar Vietnam, for this has not been a wholly uncontested story of reconciliation and global reintegration. Ambivalences and suspicions toward U.S. intentions run deep in Vietnamese society (deeper in some areas than others), challenging at times the scope and the reach of U.S. neoliberal economic practices. "Hồ Chí Minh once said that the United States would forever try to invade Vietnam, so now we watch very carefully. America thinks it is powerful and can impose its ways on the world. So we try to be prepared because we know your government wants to influence our economy," a male university student once said to me in a hushed voice, explaining what people "really say" about current U.S. civilian and corporate presence in Vietnam.

In their endeavors to create and dominate new markets, U.S. corporate actors have found that the unredressed suffering that underlies and fuels such suspicions may potentially be an economic liability. During my visits to Vinh City, Nghệ An province, in 2000 and 2001, hostility toward the United States was palpable and American presence was minimal (with the exception of occasional U.S. MIA teams). The impoverished provincial capital and its surrounding areas were devastated during the war by heavy U.S. bombing that left few buildings standing. By 2006, the city had changed significantly, and signs of increasing prosperity and involvement in the market economy were more visible in sections of the urban landscape. Though such changes have had an uneven impact on local residents, they have meant an improved life for Vũ, a key research respondent: Vũ's income had recently increased tenfold when he left his state job for employment in a newly arrived U.S. insurance company. His duties were to train staff and to support the sales of life insurance policies, a novel concept in Vinh and other provincial areas of Vietnam.

When we last met in August 2007, I asked Vũ about the challenges he faced creating a new commodity need and selling a U.S. product to a largely impoverished consumer base. He laughed and agreed it was a difficult task. Yes, the residents of Vinh think about the war and the bombs, and yes, they are skeptical of buying life insurance policies, especially from a U.S. company. They still harbor hatred, he told me quietly. More upbeat, Vũ explained the strategy he had been taught to counter such "bad" memories and suspicions: "I tell them about the humanitarian work that [the company] carries out in Vietnam. It's on their website—you can go there and see for yourself." Yet in its attempt to forge a benevolent image of responsible U.S. capitalism though humanitarian generosity, the company elides the issue of moral-historical accountability by avoiding any direct mention of the war on its website, referring instead to its postwar social and economic legacies (poor disabled children) without any suggestion of possible war-related cause (such as dioxin exposure). As Lisa Yoneyama has argued, effective redress "would consist of a critical remembering in which past memories are recalled to become urgently relevant to present efforts to seek social and cultural transformations" (2003, 61). Clearly in its silences, the insurance company has assumed a stance akin to that of the U.S. government, which disentangles and dissociates reconciliation from redress (humanitarian acts are to fix Communist Party, not U.S. policy, wrongs). In the end, with some anxiety, Vũ relayed that customers often decline to buy his company's policies, unconvinced of the need for the product or opting for those of a non-U.S. competitor. Linked in their minds to a history of unprovoked and unreparated violence and suffering (after all, it was the East Germans, not the Americans, who rebuilt their city), the U.S. life insurance company appears to have few long-term prospects in Vinh.

Many U.S. citizens would read the story of the U.S. pilot flying into Hải Phòng or the presence of a U.S. life insurance company in Vinh through the same lens that they read the opening of Nike-contracted factories outside of Ho Chi Minh City: as a sign of victory, that the United States, in the end, won the war through capitalism. Indeed, this book has documented how U.S. triumphalism, and its revival in Vietnamese spaces of memory, is a motivating force behind efforts to "fix" or "rescue" Vietnam from presumed historical inaccuracy, a backwards economy, undemocratic policies, or inhumane practices. Confrontation with U.S. defeat in historical narratives and images that brought U.S. hegemonic historiography to crisis was unsettling to many (Spivak 1988, 4). "But we were so trained," one returning veteran still grappling with U.S. defeat pondered in a beer garden in Hanoi. "We never lost one battle. It was down to an exact military science," he insisted, still imagining U.S. triumph as an objective and rational inevitability.

This book has also shown how resistance to Vietnamese celebratory representations of U.S. defeat, and the impassioned responses it engendered—"I'm not a patriotic person, but when they rubbed their victory in my face, I felt a sense of patriotism I never knew I had"—are deeply rooted in conventional U.S. scripts of history that resist decentering U.S. trauma and memory. Desires to bring "objective democratic truth" (U.S. history) to "one-sided communist propaganda" (Vietnamese memory) reflect a moral struggle to frame and control historical knowledge and memory of the war as a fight against communism (the "Vietnam War") and not U.S. imperialism (the "American War"). Thomas C. Wolfe has examined the operations of power and the role of western knowledge interventions in the downfall of socialism: "In fact, we might think of the entire Western project to bring socialism to an end and to bring the freedoms of market and democracy . . . as a vast knowledge project that continues to operate after the achievement of the proximate goal of destroying socialism" (2000, 211). Likewise, this book has traced how a capitalist knowledge project in Vietnam has battled Vietnamese socialism in transnational spaces of intersecting memories, operating through historically specific, western epistemic and moral virtues of truth and objectivity and their corresponding knowledge practices (see Daston and Galison 2007, 39–41). U.S. knowledge interventions that privilege certain memories of Vietnamese state violence (POW torture) while silencing others (U.S. bombing of civilians) signify a Foucauldian "order of historical things" based on the arrangement of empirical "fact" and "truth" into particular taxonomic configurations of differentiated knowledge that constitute and validate empire (Foucault 1994 [1966], 57–58). U.S. empire in postnormalization Vietnam exercises power not through overt acts of domination and subjugation, as attempted during the Cold War years, but through a "new notion of right, or rather, a new inscription of authority and a new design of the production of norms" (Hardt and Negri 2000, 9). The enactments of power and a moral historical authority that manages, advocates, and normalizes particular forms of knowledge and memory (new forged realities) are thus key to U.S. operations and its expanding sphere of influence in Vietnam.

Transnational Histories and the Co-production of Memory

In addition to examining memories of empire and empires of memory, this book has also attempted to map out and discern some of the broader changes that have taken place in Vietnam's *transnational* landscape of memory since *Đổi mới* economic reforms were implemented in the late 1980s. With global capitalist reintegration, increasing numbers of foreigners have brought to Vietnam their mass-mediated memories and knowledge of the war, and a curiosity (or sometimes apprehension) about what had become of the defiant communist country that had twice defeated international superpowers in recent history. This is not to argue that the current transnationalization of memoryscapes in Vietnam is somehow new. Beyond the story of U.S. imperial designs to shape and discipline historical knowledge and representation are other histories of Chinese, French and Soviet regimes, that similarly maintained and reproduced authority through interventions in memory; for example, through the construction (or destruction) of temples, museums, and monuments. As I argued above, some of these memory projects were imposed upon Vietnam (such as public commemoration of French heroes), while others were collaborative acts, as in the case of Soviet and Czech technical and financial assistance to museums. Likewise, with the United States, many memorial projects have also been cooperative and reconciliatory, though not completely devoid of U.S.-centric historical imaginaries. So this is not a case of controlled and directed practices of memory as a device to rule, as with French colonialism. Rather, this book has traced the more subtle operations of power that underlie transnational history making and the instrumental role of U.S. citizens, many of whom resisted the "provincialization" of U.S. historical memory in Vietnamese public spaces of history, and sought through various means to recenter it (Chakrabarty 2000).

Modifications to representations of Vietnamese historical memory have not unequivocally been an outcome of external global forces. Just as central, if not more so, to the refashioning of history in the public sphere have been Vietnamese social and historical actors who have actively disparaged monuments, rejected museums, criticized government spending on the memory industry, reinvented historical sites as spaces of love or capitalist production, and sent letters to the press objecting to "outdated" political discourse. Cosmopolitan cultural producers and other diverse groups of globally connected Vietnamese, including employees in the international tourism industry, workers in multinational corporations, students and professionals who have trained abroad (both in socialist and in capitalist countries), families with overseas kin networks, etc., constitute an historically shifting and patchy transnational landscape shaped by the legacies of war, colonialism, nationalism, socialist internationalism, and global capitalism. In this book I have shown how "other transnationals" (Hannerz 1998a), such as ARVN veterans who work as tour guides, street vendors who sell Zippo lighters and other war paraphernalia, and Vietnamese men and women involved in reconciliation projects, contributed to the diversification of historical knowledge in public, and often capitalist, spaces for the expression and communication of their oft-silenced transnational memories. There are no clear distinctions here between what might be configured as "local" (of the people), "national" (of the state), and "global" (beyond the nation) memory, as the boundaries are ambiguous and the alignments unclear. The same citizens who decried the unaesthetic designs of official monument production reaffirmed national declarations of humane POW treatment when it came to the silencing of Vietnamese suffering in U.S. historical memory. Likewise, artists and architects reworked but did not reject foreign and national memorial practices when they "Vietnamized" state sites of memory. ARVN veterans most clearly aligned their historical memory with that of the U.S. forces, although some of these men also spoke about the importance of the legacy of "Uncle Hồ." Movement between multiply intertwined realms of official and unofficial memory that extend beyond the nation to encompass global historical experiences, perspectives, and imaginaries prompts the question of the extent to which it is possible or even useful to speak of an autonomous "national" history.

Ernest Renan once wrote that "the possession in common of a rich legacy of memories" is essential to constituting the nation and national history (1990 [1882], 19). Forged around notions of mutual suffering and communal forgetting, national history acts as a "technology of territoriality" that, like cartography, produces a particular self-image of the nation as a united and spatially delimited geo-body (Thongchai 1994, 16). But it is precisely the assumption that experiences of suffering can be shared, geographically contained, and evenly mapped onto various cultural and economic spheres of the nation that are troubling and require the transcendence of national borders in the study of history (Thongchai 2002). In his work on ethnic absolutism, Paul Gilroy (1990) has cautioned that "national history" is a problematic and elusive term that assumes a continuous and homogeneous history and identity that is neatly delimited and contained within the political-territorial borders of the nation. In linking national history to the exclusionary and nationalist politics of ethnic and cultural belonging, Gilroy cautions against adopting a language of "the nation" that homogenizes historical experience, denies internal differentiation, and elides historically dynamic transnational interconnection. "The borders of the nation may represent a rather arbitrary point at which to pause in our efforts to comprehend the past," he argues (Gilroy 1990, 118).

This study has taken up such calls to transcend the national borders of history to examine historical knowledge production in Vietnam as a *transnational* process that involves variously situated institutions and actors and their global engagements with memory. As Andreas Huyssen has observed, "The form in which we think of the past is increasingly memory without borders rather than national history within borders" (2003, 4). This book has argued for more attention to be paid to border-crossing memories and their entanglements to produce what I have called recombinant history, a term that attempts an ethnographic understanding of the complexities involved in the reorganization and diversification of knowledge and memory of the war. By transcending the nation, recombinant history foregrounds the mobility of memory and resulting frictions in historical knowledge production. When applied to changes occurring at Vietnamese public sites of memory, it provides a framework for addressing the reconstitution of knowledge and history, based not on displacement (the memories expressed by ARVN veterans as tour guides do not trump Vietnamese official memory) but on processes of encounter, contestation, and rearticulation. In signifying the diversification and uneasy coexistence of competing historical truths and logics of representation, recombinant history demands the decentering of modernist celebratory metanarratives of the nation-state (Chakrabarty 2000, 41) to allow for memory practices that exceed the frame of autonomous and bounded "national" histories.

The cases presented here demonstrate that history making in Vietnamese public spaces is a relational and uneven process of historical *co-production* that involves multiple overlapping and intersecting representations of the war. I say "relational" because there are considerable disparities in the force and directionality of traveling memories, images, and knowledge. This book has shown, for example, how the United States continues to police and maintain its borders of historical memory, while U.S. penetration of Vietnam's memorial landscape has been more profound. One would be hard pressed to find "VC" relics for sale outside the Vietnam Veterans Memorial Wall in Washington, D.C., or a museum exhibit in an American city in which U.S. troops are referred to as "enemies." Indeed, Vietnamese historical and cultural production that has managed to access museums, galleries, or performance spaces in the United States, such as the photography exhibits I discussed, has frequently been targeted by anticommunist protesters who disparage such work as "propaganda." Vietnamese expressions of solidarity—that war occurs between governments and not people—do not always resonate with U.S. postwar memory. Clearly there are deep historical wounds among multiple U.S. populations that have yet to heal. Yet historical wounds in Vietnam often have little choice but to heal (at least publicly). As U.S. empire expands its cultural and economic presence—flying the country's national aircraft, employing sons and daughters in U.S. offices and factories, inserting U.S. memories into museum displays and tourist scripts—the uneven transnational co-production of history cannot be dissociated from gross inequities in global power and wealth that continue to differentiate these countries.

This study of remembrance and representation has revealed particular global configurations of power that underlie and influence transnational memory work. Historical co-productions are not utopic, but highly ambivalent projects marked by shifting ambiguities and lingering silences. They are neither desirable nor unfavorable; they accommodate and resist multiplicity, retain and relinquish historical authority. They expand and constrain projects of memory corresponding to changes in representational practices. While Foucault (1980) identified the mechanics of power in relation to knowledge production and the management of truth, this book suggests a *global* politics involved in the entanglements of power and knowledge as a disciplinary regime of U.S. truth and memory is confronted by Vietnamese efforts to manage and contain U.S. economic and geopolitical hegemony. Vietnamese actions to maintain sovereignty over its own operations and representations of historical memory are not unlike its current "market socialist" approach to the economy. The merging of capitalist and noncapitalist economic logics and knowledge practices demonstrate not a definitive "defeat" of socialism—a claim denied by many in Vietnam—but its recombination as a strategy to delimit and control the reach and penetration of U.S. capitalism and its empire of memory into Vietnam's growing economy and its still-scarred landscape of history.

NOTES

Introduction

1. The text of this interview can be found at http://vietnam.usembassy.gov/pv11192000e.html. President Clinton's speech at the National University, as well as other briefings and remarks made during his visit, can be found at http://vietnam.usembassy.gov/speech_briefing.html.

2. The text of Lê Khả Phiêu's remarks was printed in *Lao Động* [Labor] newspaper on November 20, 2000. On November 18, 2000, the *Nhân Dân* [People] newspaper printed on the front page a Vietnamese translation of Clinton's speech and a speech by President Trần Đức Lương.

3. This tension between explaining the war through the lens of "communism" or "imperialism" was not new in 2000. It had also emerged as a key point of discussion at the historic 1997 conference in Hanoi, "Missed Opportunities? Former U.S. and Vietnamese Leaders and Scholars Reexamine the Vietnam War, 1961–1968," which former U.S. secretary of defense Robert McNamara attended. Reporting on the conference, Shipler writes: "The Vietnamese listened closely, but they seemed truly puzzled by the American obsession with the spread of Communism and sought more explanation. 'If the reason was to fight Communism,' they asked in a list of questions submitted beforehand, 'why did the U.S. not help China in 1949, or why did the U.S. not help the Batista regime in Cuba in 1959?' They never got an answer, only a litany of conflicts, including two that nearly took the superpowers to war: the Berlin and Cuban missile crises of 1961 and 1962" (1997, 35).

4. For scholarly literature on Vietnam that supports such claims, see in particular Giebel (2004), Kwon (2006), Pelley (2002), Malarney (2002), Werner (2006), Leshkowich (2008), and the volumes edited by Tai (2001a) and Taylor and Whitmore (1995).

5. For a broad and cogent theoretical overview of scholarship on memory, see Klein (2000). For anthropological studies of memory in relation to histories of violence and/or colonial encounters, see, for example, Malkki (1995); Handler and Gable (1997); Yoneyama (1999); J. Cole (2001); Spyer (2000); Mueggler (2001); Trouillot (1995).

6. For this reason, scholars of postsocialism in Eastern Europe view social change in former East Bloc nations "not as transition from one order to another but as transforma-

tion—rearrangements, reconfigurations and recombinations that yield new interweavings of the multiple social logics that are a modern society" (Stark and Bruszt 1998, 7; see also Verdery 1996; Burawoy and Verdery 1999).

1. Return to Vietnam

1. On Hồ Chí Minh in the United States, see Quinn-Judge (2002, 20–21) and Duiker (2000, 50–51). According to Marilyn Young, the U.S. provided France with $160 million in aid in 1946 to fight the war in Vietnam (1991, 22). Nguyễn Khắc Viện estimates that U.S. economic support increased to $385 million—covering 60% of the total costs of the war—by 1953, and by 1954, 80% of the costs (2007, 274). On Norman Morrison's life and death, and the impact of his act on Vietnam, see Morrison-Welsh (2006).

2. All quotes are paraphrased and translated from detailed field notes written in Vietnamese and English at the time of interviews and conversations.

3. See A. Young (1995) on traumatic memory as a modern, nineteenth-century invention, and its reformulation in 1980 as PTSD (post-traumatic stress disorder).

4. In her conclusion, Curtis notes that certain veterans feared she would represent them as "a group of maladjusted, hand-wringing Vietnam vets who were here [in Vietnam] for emotional closure" (2003, 251). Instead, she claims her interlocutors were on a historical mission only: "[T]he tours I accompanied were squarely focused on the discussion of operational level battle histories and on understanding veterans' roles in those histories" (2003, 12). While many of my interviewees spoke of returning to "find closure," they were in no way disinterested in history or representative of "maladjusted vets." Curtis seems correct to be wary of the predominance of stereotypical images of alienated and unstable veterans, though an emphasis on healing or closure need not imply such a condition. Veterans can be "well adjusted" citizens and still be concerned with closure (as well as with their place in history).

5. Tours of Peace, a nonprofit veteran humanitarian organization, offers trips back to Vietnam to "help veterans and families heal and recover from the trauma" of war. Programs integrate "emotional and humanitarian components," such as the recovery of U.S. war relics and participation in charitable projects (see also Bleakney 2006, 151–152). The name "Tours of Peace" plays with the double entendre of the word "tour" and its slippage between military and leisure metaphors.

6. The Vietnamese government has often reminded international audiences, particularly in the context of tourism, that Vietnam is "a country and not a war." For example, in 1999 and 2000, this phrase could be found on the homepage of the website of the Vietnamese Embassy in Washington, D.C.

7. Early-twentieth-century theorization of war trauma drew upon studies of female hysteria and sexual trauma to better understand the neuroses of soldiers (Kaplan 2005, 28), thus contributing another historical dimension to the emasculation of the Vietnam veteran's suffering body. World War I veterans who experienced combat trauma or "shell shock" were "regarded as cowards and, very much as hysterical women, morally corrupt" (Suárez-Orozco and Robben 2000, 13).

8. See, for example, the "Explosive Remnants of War Civilian Accident Report" for January 1, 2006–September 1, 2006, in which seventy-three incidents in central Vietnam (thirty-two of which resulted in death) were reported by Clear Path International. Posted online at http://clearpathinternational.org/cpiblog/archives/Jan_Sep_06_incident_reports.pdf.

9. Viet Thanh Nguyen makes a similar observation about U.S. veterans, who through cultural and intellectual production in the United States "see in the recovery of Vietnam and the resurrection of Vietnamese voices the potential for their own recuperation" (2002, 111).

10. On the ways in which popular culture, especially film and literature, has reinforced national myths and capitalist ideologies of the United States as a nation of saviors, see Engelhardt (2007 [1995]), and, in relation to the Vietnam War, Hellman (1986) and Jeffords (1989).

11. In recent years, such approaches to "local empowerment" have increasingly structured international GO (government organization) and NGO programs, some of which have moved away from discourses of "development." For example, the GTZ (German Technical Cooperation) uses the term *Zusammenarbeit* (literally "working together") to define itself as an "international cooperation enterprise."

12. The depth of UXO and mine clearance is contingent upon the projected use of the land. For instance, in areas of housing construction a "deep search" of two and three meters underground is required. The clearance project I visited was slated for agricultural use and only required probing to thirty centimeters underground based on estimated tilling and planting practices of local farmers.

13. As one deminer explained: "Anytime you encounter resistance you have to excavate. To do this you start approximately ten centimeters before your point, excavate down ten centimeters, and then slowly begin to probe until you locate [the ordnance]. You can imagine probing the grid only three centimeters—about one inch—at a time: probe, find something, excavate; probe, find something, excavate. Imagine how long it takes to do that . . . One of the smallest land mines is an M-14, which is larger than one inch. So no matter how it's placed in the ground, if you're probing every inch, you're going to hit a portion of it. There's not a chance to miss it."

14. According to a UXB representative, grids are only confirmed free of munitions after they have been rechecked three times, following the deminer, by a team leader and "quality assurance" specialists.

15. Steven Sampson has also argued that the term "reconciliation," as used in the context of postconflict settings, is a specifically western construct, not unlike "human rights," "truth-telling," "accountability," and "transparency" (2003, 181). Borneman rebuffs this idea, pointing to the existence of reconciliatory processes and mechanisms "in some form across time and space" (2003, 200).

16. In recent years an increasing number of Vietnamese veterans and others have returned to former battlefields in search of MIAs, of which the government estimates there to be approximately 300,000—a number that does not include MIAs from the Republic of Vietnam. Many families, and even the military, have turned to spirit mediums

to aid in locating remains, a phenomenon often covered in the mass media. Tài, who had returned several times to the battlefield to search for the remains of his brother (and ultimately found them with the help of a clairvoyant), suggested that like U.S. veterans, Vietnamese veterans would also like to revisit former battle sites, but face certain obstacles:

> Here in Vietnam, veterans also want to return to the battlefields, but for them it is a problem of money. Most live in the countryside and cannot afford to make a trip back . . . Returning is also not so simple. The Americans had large, permanent bases that are easy to find. But not with us. We moved around through the jungle—we never had just one camp. So unlike U.S. veterans, we are not sure where to return to.

17. Reactions to the visit of Nguyễn Cao Kỳ, the former prime minister and vice president of the Republic of Vietnam, to Hanoi in December 2004 exemplifies this tension. Kỳ, who reportedly traveled to Hanoi to pursue an investment plan for a new golf resort outside of Hải Phòng, was eating lunch at a restaurant at which I also happened to be. The staff was on edge—excited, yet critical of his role in Vietnam's turbulent history. As I mingled with a group of employees who eyed Kỳ as he ate with representatives from the U.S. Embassy and discussed the legacy of Hồ Chí Minh, I inquired how they felt about his visit. The manager of the restaurant gave me a standard line in English: "This is a new era. The war ended a long time ago. People now accept and welcome his return to Vietnam." A young employee, however, soon called me over and, with a scowl on his face, told me in Vietnamese: "Nguyễn Cao Kỳ held office in the Saigon regime. For some people, it is not a problem that he is in Hanoi. But many veterans, in particular, hate him and do not want him here."

18. This is also seen in U.S. cultural production, particularly female-produced documentary films that address reconciliation. For example, in *From Hollywood to Hanoi* (1993) the wife of Võ Nguyên Giáp stresses the compassion shared by all mothers who lost sons in the war, a sentiment echoed in the award-winning documentary *Regret to Inform* (1998), which brought together U.S. and Vietnamese widows through shared experiences of loss and grief.

19. Like Vietnamese officials at the "Missed Opportunities?" conference (see Introduction), respondents expressed bewilderment at the idea that U.S. anxieties concerning communist expansion were a driving cause of the war in Vietnam. Some even expressed amusement that the United States feared a small and comparatively less powerful nation. For the vast majority of my respondents in Hanoi, the war did not revolve around communism, but was fought against U.S. imperialism and foreign occupation.

20. Vietnamese respondents in Hanoi referred to cultural and historical practices to explain their politics of forgiveness: while some pointed to Buddhist doctrine ("to forgive is to accept suffering and to believe in a better next life"), others identified an extensive history of postconflict reconciliatory gestures, such as tributary payment and the symbolic offering of Vietnamese princesses to foreign kings.

21. The title of "Vietnamese Heroic Mother" is extended to women who either "sacrificed" three or more children in the war, two children and a husband, an only child, or

one of two children. For details on the legal criteria for the conferment of the title, see the October 20, 1994, Decree No. 176-CP on the implementation of the Ordinance on the State Honorific Title "Vietnamese Heroic Mother" (passed on August 29, 1994) in *Vietnam Law and Legal Forum* (*Công Báo,* December 17, 1994).

22. See Hirschman, Preston, and Loi (1995) on variable data for Vietnamese war casualties. Though reports vary, the number I quote includes an estimated 1.1 million revolutionary forces and a quarter-million RVN soldiers (ibid., 784). The Vietnamese government estimates 4 million casualties for the entire country, both civilian and military deaths.

2. Exhibiting War, Reconciling Pasts

1. See, for example Vasavakul (1997), N. Taylor (2001; 2004, 42–62), Bradley (2001), and Werner (2006).

2. For research on music, films, video games, novels, and comic strips about the war, see edited volumes by Rowe and Berg (1991), Dittmar and Michaud (2000), and Louvre and Walsh (1988). On cultural memory and the Vietnam Veterans Memorial, see Sturken (1997a); on the trope of "friendly fire" in diverse literary and cinematic expressions of the war, see Kinney (2000); on the gendered dynamics of popular cultural representations of the Vietnam War, see Jeffords (1989).

3. This literature is largely concerned with degrees of censorship and the effects of the press and media images on public opinion. See Hallin (1986), Hammond (1998), Wyatt (1993), and A. Hoskins (2004). Some scholars have attempted to include other journalist voices, namely those of western female reporters. See Elwood-Akers (1988) and Bartimus et al. (2002).

4. This spark in interest had much to do with Horst Faas and Tim Page's (1997) book *Requiem: By the Photographers Who Died in Vietnam and Indochina*, from which the photography exhibit draws. A few years later the National Geographic film *Vietnam's Unseen War: Pictures from the Other Side* (2002) was released in conjunction with the book *Another Vietnam: Pictures of the War from the Other Side* (Page 2002).

5. See Đoàn Công Tính (2002), Mai Nam (2001), Hoàng Kim Đáng (2007), and Dương Thanh Phong (Cu Chi Tunnels Historical Remains 2002). For a compilation of renowned photographers that includes Văn Bảo, Võ An Khánh, Nguyễn Đình Ưu, and Vũ Ba, among others, see the volume by the Newspaper of the Veterans of Vietnam [*Báo Cựu Chiến Binh Việt Nam*] (2003).

6. For example, over twenty memoirs of the war were published in 2004 to mark the fiftieth anniversary of Điện Biên Phủ and the then-approaching thirtieth anniversary of the reunification of Vietnam (Việt Hà 2004). This trend continued into 2005 with the immensely popular war diaries of Đặng Thùy Trâm (2005) and Nguyễn Văn Thạc (2005).

7. On memory and photographic representations of the Holocaust, see also Liss 1998), Struk (2004), Milton (1984), Hirsch (1999, 2001), Zelizer (2001), and Brink (2000).

8. For example, CNN sent its former Vietnam War correspondent, Richard Blystone, back to Vietnam to cover the anniversary and subsequent changes in Vietnamese

society since 1975. Reporting live from Ho Chi Minh City, Blystone commented, "This is most likely the last trip to Vietnam for most of us who covered the war. It's nice to see this country at peace"—the implication being that war makes for better news than peace. CNN, news broadcast, April 30, 2000.

9. Ulf Hannerz has called this focus on war "[being] on the trouble trail," to suggest that foreign correspondents "mostly show up at times of wars, upheavals, and disasters, and are already long gone when things begin to return to normal" (1998a, 116).

10. Alter goes on to cite Trinh T. Minh-ha: "For general western spectatorship, Vietnam does not exist outside the war. And she no longer exists since the war has ended." Alter (1997, 45), quoting Trinh T. Minh-ha (1991, 100).

11. During the war, the German-born Horst Faas worked for the Associated Press. The British photojournalist Tim Page worked for United Press International and other western news agencies. Because of their close connections to the U.S. press, the book and the exhibit reflect many common U.S. historical understandings and interpretations of the war.

12. There were originally three sets of "Requiem" photographs in circulation, each of which constituted a separate exhibit. The first set, "Requiem: By the Photographers Who Died in Vietnam and Indochina," began touring U.S. cities in 1997 under the auspices of Gannett Publishing. The second set was displayed in a small exhibition in Japan before being sent to Kentucky, where the images were mounted and prepared for viewing in 1999. A third set later toured select cities in Europe, where it remains today in a private collection in London. The exhibit under discussion here, "Requiem—the Vietnam Collection," is based on the same set of images, but it should not be confused or conflated with the other exhibitions, which were assembled differently, displayed in dissimilar contexts, and motivated by differing interests.

13. Six weeks earlier, at the opening ceremony in Hanoi, Richard Lennon had offered the collection "on behalf of the people of Kentucky . . . as a permanent gift to the people of the Socialist Republic of Vietnam . . . with a sincere sense of hope, of healing and of history. May this gift begin a new and strong relationship between the peoples of Kentucky and Vietnam."

14. Despite its limitations, I maintain this method of ordering names and nationalities to analyze the kinds of historical knowledge produced at the exhibit. Thus, *Vietnamese* correspondents, as they are referred to in the exhibit, do not include nonrevolutionary photographers from the Republic of Vietnam.

15. Yet, for all the images of combat that make up historical memory, there is also the issue of *absent* images (Sturken 1997b) and erased bodies (Feldman 1994), since wars have never been photographed entirely free of media restrictions.

16. However, Hallin cites numerous studies, including his own, that "reject the idea that the living-room war meant graphic portrayals of violence on a daily basis, or that television . . . led public opinion in turning against the war" (1986, xi).

17. Iconic images of the Vietnam War have taken on renewed currency in the recent context of the Abu Ghraib prison scandal. For an analysis of the political cartoon "Abu

Ghraib Nam," in which the now iconic hooded figure from Abu Ghraib lurks behind Kim Phúc as she runs down the street, see Hariman and Lucaites (2007, 202).

18. Ultimately, Nick Út agreed to "do the humane thing" and take Kim Phúc and another severely burned woman to the nearest hospital. On the journey, the narrative shifts between concern for the victims and his rolls of film (later referred to as his "good pictures of napalm"), thus demonstrating Nick Út's wavering position between moral responsibility and professional commitment (Chong 2000, 69–71). For a point of comparison, see a discussion of the "moral failures" of photographer Kevin Carter and his subsequent suicide only months after his Pulitzer Prize–winning photograph of the starving child in Sudan stalked by a vulture was published in the *New York Times* (Kleinman and Kleinman 1997, 3–7).

19. On objectivity as ritual practice in U.S. journalism, see Tuchman (1972). See also Schudson (1978), Pedelty (1995), and Peterson (2001), for critical analyses of the ways journalistic practices in the United States have historically grounded its authority in assumptions of objectivity and truth.

20. Initially, the U.S. military attempted to ban female correspondents, deemed a distraction to troops, from remaining overnight on the battlefield (Hoffman 1998). On the difficulties and discrimination faced by female journalists covering the war in Vietnam, see Bartimus et al. (2002) and Elwood-Akers (1988). Edith Lederer, who in 1972 became the first woman to receive a full-time assignment to the AP in Saigon, reported a common sentiment at the time that "women could not stand up to the demands of the world's backwaters and battle zones" (2002, 157).

21. This visual subculture extends to other socialist cultural production on the war as well. See, for example, *Hanoi, Martes 13* [Hanoi, Tuesday the Thirteenth], by the Cuban director Santiago Álvarez (1967), a film that shows Hanoi residents, especially schoolchildren, as they attempted to go about their daily life activities on December 13, 1966, until U.S. bombers attacked. See also Alter (1997) on the collection of films produced during and after the war in northern Vietnam by the prominent East German filmmakers Walter Heynowski and Gerhard Scheumann.

22. Notable exceptions include the War Remnants Museum (the site of the "Requiem" exhibit in Ho Chi Minh City) and the Mỹ Lai Museum in Quảng Ngãi province, both of which rely heavily on photographs of graphic violence produced by western news agencies to document abuse, murder, and mutilation.

23. On the discourse of optimistic futures during the war, see Susan Sontag's essay *Trip to Hanoi* (1968). Likewise, the photographer of Figures 2.1 and 2.2, a battlefield reporter who traveled with the People's Army of Vietnam, explained to me in an interview that his images of war captured widespread sentiments of hope and optimism: "Despite the hardships of war, the bombings and the deaths, we always kept our eye on victory. Though many people died, we remained hopeful, happy, and focused on the future." Benedict J. Tria Kerkvliet has similarly observed that newspaper images during the war depicted "village life [as] serene and filled with people happy and smiling even while they planted paddy, hoed weeds, and spread manure" (2005, 108).

24. This is not to argue that Vietnamese journalists did not in any way photograph civilian and combatant casualties. At times they did, though such images were generally not published in the press, but were displayed during and immediately after the war in the Exhibition Houses for U.S. Crimes [*Nhà Trừng Bày Tội Ác Mỹ*] with the intent of documenting atrocities and fueling the revolution (see also chapter 5).

25. Although the representational practices of Vietnamese photojournalists contrast with wartime photographs produced in the western press, they are in no way unique to Vietnam. Even in the United States the focus on suffering and death in photojournalism is relatively recent, as Lewinski (1978) and Roeder (1993) have shown in their work on heroic (and censored) images from World War I and World War II respectively. In postwar U.S. popular culture, John Wayne assumed the role of the celebrated male hero who further romanticized warfare by associating it with bravery, love, and hypermasculinity—images that initially shaped the subjectivities of many U.S. soldiers who served in Vietnam (Kinney 2000, 17; Hellmann 1986, 93).

26. Captions for Figures 2.3, 2.4, 2.5, and 2.6 are taken from the exhibit and are direct quotations from the book.

27. The expression "Viet Cong"—generally held to be a truncated form of *Việt Nam Cộng Sản* [Vietnamese communist]—has its roots in the post-1954 Ngô Đình Diệm period, when it was used as an ideological weapon to identify opponents of the southern regime as communists or as communist sympathizers and to justify their incarceration and, at times, their execution. The fact that "Viet Cong" and "VC" remain in use today by many people in the United States and beyond exemplifies the long-term effects of wartime misinformation about the NLF as a purely communist institution. On the diverse noncommunist and communist factions, motives, and power struggles within the NLF, see Truong Nhu Tang with David Chanoff and Doan Van Toai (1986).

28. According to an exhibit organizer in Kentucky, the English captions had been adapted from the book and then translated into Vietnamese in the United States. All descriptions, both in Vietnamese and English, were numbered and sent with the mounted photographs to Hanoi. Vietnamese officials never commented on the captions, I was told.

29. This is not to argue that all historical actors are given representation in the museum, nor are all voices equally or uniformly presented. In one room, U.S. forces may be "enemies," while in the next room they are "friends." Veterans of the ARVN do not find their experiences represented in the museum in an official capacity, although those who serve as tour guides may informally share their memories on-site.

30. This act did not violate the signed agreement between the Exhibitor (VNA and the Vietnam Association of Photographic Artists), the Lender (Indochina Photo Requiem Project, Ltd.), and the Donor (Kentucky Requiem Project Steering Committee). The second item of the agreement, signed November 12, 1999, states: "The Exhibitor agrees to present the complete photo collection which consists of approximately 300 (three hundred) pictures and text material. In case the Exhibitor wishes not to present some of the pictures, it has to inform the Lender."

31. In e-mail communication, an exhibit organizer from the Kentucky Historical Society explained the practicalities of the design of the memorial tablets: "The original intent of the layout was to alphabetize the order of the countries. South Vietnam was separate from Vietnam due to the fact that we were dealing with persons from the South and the North, with the number from the North being exceptionally large . . . As for the placement of South Vietnam with the foreign countries . . . [i]t helped to illustrate the political delineation of the conflict, and the overall design just seemed to balance better."

3. Commodified Memories and Embodied Experiences of War

1. Tourism in Vietnam is a rapidly developing industry and important income-generating resource for the national economy. According to the website of the Vietnam National Administration of Tourism (VNAT), in 1990 (the first year for which statistics are offered) an estimated 250,000 foreigners visited Vietnam, a number that had quadrupled to one million by 1994. In the year 2000, VNAT launched its first National Tourism Action Plan, "Vietnam: A Destination for a New Millennium," which succeeded in attracting 2.14 million international visitors, including tourists, business professionals, and overseas Vietnamese. By 2005, this number had increased over 18%, to 3.46 million, the majority of whom are visitors from China and other Asian countries (www .vietnamtourism.gov.vn). For an historical overview of the development of Vietnam's tourism industry, see Kennedy and Williams (2001, 138–142).

2. On French colonial imaginaries and placated tourist representations of Vietnam's past, see Biles, Lloyd, and Logan (1999, 209–214) and Kennedy and Williams (2001). See also Norindr (1996, 155–158) on the marketing and consumption of phantasmatic memories of French Indochina in Southeast Asian tourism.

3. On tourism to World War I sites, see Mosse (1990); to World War II sites, see G. White (1997) on Pearl Harbor, and Diller and Scofidio (1994) on Normandy. On tourist observations of American Civil War battle reenactments, see L. Hart (2007). See also the edited volume on battlefield tourism by Ryan (2007).

4. See, for example, T. Cole (1999) on Holocaust tourism; Ebron (2000) and Bruner (2005) on tourism to slave trade memorial sites in West Africa; Gu, Ryan, and Zhang (2007) and Babb (2004) on "red tourism" and consumption of socialist revolutionary histories.

5. See, for example, *We Were Soldiers* (2002), starring Mel Gibson and Đơn Dương, one of the few Vietnamese actors to play a leading role in a Hollywood production about the war. The film sparked a controversy and was banned in Vietnam for its representation of the Ia Đrang battle as a heroic U.S. victory. Đơn Dương, who plays a commander in the People's Army of Vietnam, was harshly criticized in the Vietnamese mass media and threatened with disciplinary action from the Association of Cinematography in Ho Chi Minh City and the Ministry of Culture and Information (*Người Lao Động* [The Worker], September 5, 2002).

6. Some tour agencies in Ho Chi Minh City customized war tours for particular nationalities, mapping them onto differing historical experiences and memories. In the words of one tour operator: "If you are French we will suggest Điện Biên Phủ, if you are Australian, we will recommend Long Tân and Núi Dất, and if you are American, we will arrange DMZ, Quảng Trị, Khe Sanh, Đông Hà, Hiền Lương Bridge . . . and so on." Tours for the domestic market were also configured differently and formed around sites important to Vietnamese memory, as explained below.

7. "Isn't it dangerous over there?" was a common response I received in everyday conversations in the United States prior to commencing fieldwork in 1999. An April 25, 2000, poll in the *Orange County Register* reported that 71% of respondents (19,540 people) would not consider vacationing in Vietnam.

8. For an analysis of the visual regime of the Khmer Rouge and the "devastated vision" of Tuol Sleng prisoners, see Ly (2003). Ledgerwood (1997) provides a detailed description of the museum compound and its use of visual evidence to document genocide.

9. Desmond's performative approach to tourism builds upon Urry's (2002 [1990]) notion of the "tourist gaze" to include other sensory stimulation involved in crafting tourist environments and pleasures.

10. Benjamin has identified the desire to view up close and possess objects as characteristic of modernity. The modern subject, he argued, endeavors to "bring things 'closer' spatially and humanly. . . . Every day the urge grows stronger to get a hold of an object at very close range by way of its likeness, its reproduction" (1969a, 223).

11. See Lê Thị Quý (1995), Barry (1996), and Nguyễn-võ (2008) on the rapid growth of the sex industry under conditions of economic reform and neoliberalization.

12. For example, on the grounds of the former Khe Sanh (Tà Cơn) combat base, souvenirs of death have been sold as unearthed objects by a local vendor since the mid-1990s. During visits with tour groups to Khe Sanh, many foreigners expressed their discomfort with this commodification.

13. They also index particular global pathways of production and consumption. According to vendors, imitation Zippos are produced in China and then shipped to Vietnam where scripts and images are engraved using original U.S. war-era models before they are sold on the market to international tourists.

14. My use of the term "Viet Cong" here draws from advertisements and brochures in tour agencies in Ho Chi Minh City.

15. MacCannell (1999) has argued that tourist demands for authenticity and attempts to relocate historical truth are consequences of the discontinuities of modernity. For a counterargument, see Bruner's findings that tourists in Bali were less concerned with authenticity than they were with the aesthetic qualities and standards of staged performances, leading him to conclude that "the issue of authenticity has been overdone in the tourism literature" (2005, 209). See also Urry (2002 [1990], 91) on postmodern, "posttourist" ambivalence toward the authentic.

16. This is not to argue that a domestic market for tourism to war sites is nonexistent.

In recognition of the twenty-fifth anniversary of the liberation of Saigon, one domestic tourism agency organized a three-day excursion up the Ho Chi Minh Trail. According to the tour operator, the tour would be narrated with stories about the exploits of Unit 559, which built the extensive supply routes, with nights around campfires listening to the wartime tales of local veteran heroes. Twenty-three people signed up for the trip.

17. It may also not be exoticized to the same degree for returning U.S. veterans. For the navy veteran mentioned earlier in this article, Củ Chi was a "fascinating, yet difficult experience," not least because of the random rifle shots in the background that repeatedly started him.

18. My reference to "antimemory" here differs from James E. Young's (1993, 2000) usage of "countermonuments" and "countermemory" to identify alternative expressions and aesthetic representations of memory that challenge conventional modes of monumentalization. Rather, antimemory in this context implies a lack of attention and the refusal to directly engage with historical memory. It is not about the erasure of memory, but about its disregard.

19. According to Article 23 of the Tourism Ordinance approved by the National Assembly on February 8, 1999, "The person working as a tour guide for international tourists must have a tour guide certificate." This can be obtained only if the applicant is a Vietnamese citizen with "good ethical conduct," is in good health, speaks a foreign language, and either has a bachelor's degree with specialized training in the field of tourism or has completed a tourism training course at a designated institution. Most veteran ARVN guides do not have such certification and therefore work unofficially in the tourism industry. As one guide explained: "All the men you meet at my tour agency, we are Saigon military. But we are not allowed to be guides. If I go somewhere with you, I am your friend, not a tour guide."

20. Following national reunification, RVN military cemeteries were closed, partially dismantled, and often vandalized by locals seeking to extract valuable stone and other materials from the sites. In 1999 I traveled with Trung and another ARVN veteran to the grounds of a former RVN military cemetery at Biên Hòa, where we found incense burning on the perimeters of the site to appease the wandering souls who have not been properly cared for in the afterlife. As we wandered through the overgrown landscape dotted with leaning gravestones and empty tombs, Trung recollected his last visit to the cemetery: After the war, government officials informed his family, and others with fallen soldiers, of the cemetery's impending destruction to provide space for new industry (a water plant that now occupies part of the site) and gave notice to evacuate bodies for reburial in family plots. Trung removed his brother's remains from Biên Hòa in 1979 and had not returned until our trip together twenty years later. On our way back to Ho Chi Minh City, we attempted to stop at another RVN military cemetery, but could find no signs of its previous existence. The grounds are now occupied by Isuzu and Mercedes-Benz factories. See Jones (2005), who reports that in January 2005 numerous graves at Biên Hòa had been rebuilt and freshly painted, and the grounds recently tended.

4. Monumentalizing War

1. Gillis links this shift in Europe to the influence of U.S. memorial practices in which officers and soldiers of all ranks were placed alongside one another in military cemeteries dating back to the Civil War (1994, 10–11). Despite this presumed democratization of death in the United States, selectivity in memorial processes effectively effaced female and non-white contributions to U.S. war efforts (see Savage 1994).

2. The term "martyr" is not applied to civilians killed in the war or to troops who died from other causes, such as illness (Malarney 2001, 52). In postwar years there has been a broadening of the conferral of *liệt sĩ* to include sacrifices for the nation outside the context of war; for example, young students who lost their lives in the floods of 1999 in central Vietnam while trying to rescue others were referred to as "martyrs" in the press.

3. This contrasts with official military commemoration in the former Republic of Vietnam (see Figure 3.5). In the spatial configuration of the (now empty) graves at the RVN military cemetery I visited at Biên Hòa, men of rank were separated from common soldiers and placed in closer proximity to the towering central memorial. As stated, this practice is generally not found in war cemeteries in contemporary Vietnam, with two important exceptions: Hanoi's Mai Dịch Cemetery, which contains the hierarchically arranged graves of government leaders and other famous revolutionaries, including Phạm Văn Đồng, Lê Duẩn, and Tôn Đức Thắng. A separate section of the cemetery is reserved for common martyrs who died in the French War, many of whom are without name. Though not exclusively for war dead, the Ho Chi Minh City cemetery also has a separate section for highly ranked Communist Party members.

4. Like commemoration, sculpture in Vietnam has also been linked historically to religious iconography and practice (Nguyễn Hồng Kiên 1996, 40). In pagodas, precolonial sculpture often consisted of the production of gilded or lacquered wooden statues, predominantly of Buddha or other Buddhist figures, deities (such as the three Holy Mothers), bonzes, and occasionally historical personages. Wooden or stone sculptures of sacred animals were also common. Temples occasionally contained statues, such as at the Ngọc Sơn and the Hai Bà Trưng temples in Hanoi. In both temples and pagodas, figurative sculptures were rarely monumental [*hoành tráng*].

5. This monument, according to Nguyễn Vinh Phúc, was "mocked and disparaged" [*chế nhạo chê bai*] by journalists, prompting its removal in 1925 (2000, 11; see also Jennings 2003, 22). The shift in designs between pre– and post–World War I colonial architecture and monumentalization is significant here. According to Wright, the postwar era saw increasing critiques of French aesthetic and political universalism, and efforts were increasingly made to fold vernacular architectural styles into urban development projects (1991, 200–201).

6. These cultural policies also engendered selective iconoclastic and vandalistic acts in the 1950s as officials desecrated and transformed certain historical and religious sites, such as temples and pagodas, into secular spaces to be used, for example, as paddy storage or as schools (Kleinen 1999, 163; Logan 2000, 190).

7. Truthful depictions of the masses, he maintained, necessitated the immersion of cultural producers in the lives of their subjects, not unlike ethnographers: "[O]ne must live with the peasants, live the life of the masses, live with their thoughts, sentiments, and feelings, live with their struggle" (Phạm Văn Đồng 1975, 60).

8. Despite having a prominent role in rites of ancestral veneration, lighting incense and offering flowers to the war dead has been considered acceptable and respectful memorial practice, as evidenced by government participation in such activities during state commemorative ceremonies (see also Giebel 2001). Research respondents emphasized, however, that such acts were gestures of remembrance, not worship, demonstrating how spiritual practices have become secularized and given new meaning. P. Taylor also writes of his respondents' discomfort with using the word "worship" when referring to national historical heroes, with preference given to the term "respect" (2004, 204).

9. Both Malarney (2002, 179–180) and Kwon (2006, 24–27) discuss the dilemma that souls of military and civilian war dead posed for a Vietnamese ontological order that distinguishes between "good" and "bad" deaths. In this symbolically hierarchical division, "good" death refers to a normalized and expected passing that occurs within the proper genealogical and temporal order, allowing for one's transformation to an individuated, commemorated ancestor; while a "bad" death signifies an untimely or tragic loss of life, which in turn denies the spirit a moral identity as an ancestor and suspends it in a liminal state as a ghost [con ma]. Because martyrs were predominantly young people without children who experienced a violent (i.e., "bad") death far from home, in theory they fall outside the ancestral order and remain as ghosts or wandering souls. As Malarney proclaims, "[d]eath on the battlefield was the quintessential bad death" (2002, 179). Yet because such ghosts are associated with danger, bad luck, and malevolence, my research respondents in Hanoi were hesitant to categorize martyrs as such, and some consequently reinscribed them as "good" deaths on account of their noble and dutiful (and not quite unexpected) sacrifice for the nation.

10. Socialist nations, including Cuba, East Germany, Russia, Romania, Bulgaria, Czechoslovaka, and Poland, each assumed a city or provincial area to rebuild in northern Vietnam. For a comprehensive history of the socialist reconstruction of Hanoi in collaboration with Soviet and other socialist architects and engineers, see Logan (2000, 183–219).

11. Boi Tran Huynh claims that the 1967 figurative monument in Thanh Hóa province, *Victory at Nam Ngạn,* by the Soviet-trained sculptor Nguyễn Phước Sanh, was one of the first revolutionary sculptures to depict "soldiers in challenging poses holding rifles skyward and raising arms with determination, their faces alert," and thereafter became a template for future monuments (2005, 170–171).

12. Cement during this era was noted to be new and technologically progressive aesthetic material for Vietnamese sculpture, one that was modern and versatile in its ability to imitate stone (Nguyễn Quân 1982, 103–104).

13. Central-level projects also include large-scale monument designs at the provincial level that are situated in cultural or political centers, or historical sites registered with the state. MCI is also responsible for all foreign monument projects, regardless of their in-

tended placement, as well as all projects to construct statues of President Hồ Chí Minh (Article 13).

14. Monument competitions attract a wide range of submissions, depending on the scope and location of the project. A call for designs in Hanoi for a Hồ Chí Minh statue drew fifty submissions in 2000, while a much larger memorial proposal at Ba Đình square across from the Hồ Chí Minh mausoleum drew twenty-nine submissions in 1992.

15. Comparatively, articles published in *Kiến Trúc* [Architecture] in the 1960s focused on rebuilding the nation and constructing socialist housing for workers and others. From 1984 until the mid-1990s (few issues were published in the 1970s, and no volumes came out in the postwar years until 1984), articles on monuments focused largely on form and design, and on reaffirming the need for their construction within socialist aesthetic frameworks. It was not until the later 1990s that architects placed considerable emphasis on the "national character" [*bản sắc dân tộc*] in architecture and voiced critiques about the "foreignness" and compromised aesthetic and artistic quality of monuments.

16. Ba Đình Square is a large open space for national ceremonies and public events that contains several important political, cultural, and historical sites that are collectively referred to in tourist discourse as the "Hồ Chí Minh Relic Area," and attest to Vietnam's patchwork of architectural legacies. The National Assembly [Quốc Hội], another example of Soviet-inspired architecture, is located on the far side of the square, facing the mausoleum. Stage left of the mausoleum is a stately French colonial building—formerly the headquarters of the governor-general of Indochina (now the Presidential Palace), behind which Hồ Chí Minh's modest stilt house still stands (he refused to live in the palace). Stage right and to the rear of the mausoleum is the Hồ Chí Minh Museum, opened in 1990 on Hồ Chí Minh's hundredth birthday, and designed in collaboration with Russian and Czech architects. Stage left of the museum, directly behind the mausoleum, one finds the One Pillar Pagoda, built in 1049 in "classical Vietnamese" architectural style. A 1994 national war memorial by the Hanoi architect Lê Hiệp, the design of which fuses Vietnamese and non-Vietnamese aesthetics, is located across from the mausoleum, stage left of the National Assembly.

17. Constructed between 1975 and 1977, the Trường Sơn National Cemetery, located in Quảng Trị province in the former DMZ, contains more than 10,000 graves, many of which are marked *vô danh* for unknown soldiers. According to provincial statistics, Trường Sơn is one of seventy-two martyr cemeteries in Quảng Trị province alone.

18. Malarney, for example, explains that the commune in which he conducted research outside of Hanoi does not have a martyr cemetery since remains of the war dead were not found and returned (2001, 63). A key research respondent of mine from Đồng Nai province, north of Ho Chi Minh City, also comes from a village without a martyr cemetery as most of the war dead were RVN troops who fought alongside the United States and are thus excluded from national sites of memory.

19. Some of the most well-known historical stelae in Vietnam are the eighty-two "doctorate stelae" [*bia tiến sĩ*] at the Temple of Literature, location of Vietnam's first university, established in 1076. These stone slabs, which stand on the back of stone tor-

toises, record the names of 1,306 doctoral graduates from 1442 to 1779 (Do Lai Thuy 1993, 3–5).

20. Analyses of conflicting historical accounts of the Hai Bà Trưng rebellion dating back to the fourteenth century can be found in K. Taylor (1983, 334–339).

21. The postreform effects of capitalism on the revival of votive practices is most evident on Hàng Mã Street in Hanoi, where paper objects for sale include motorbikes, cell phones, multistoried homes, kitchen appliances, and cars for ancestors to use in the afterlife, indexing new trends in material aspirations and capitalist consumption practices.

22. See H. Kim (2001, 623–627) and Kwon (2006, 137–153) on struggles over historical meaning and memory in a transnational memorial project that involved Korean veterans and Vietnamese victims of their violence during the war.

5. Contested Truths

1. One notable exception is the Hồ Chí Minh Museum in Hanoi. After paying their respects at the mausoleum, groups of domestic tourists bused in from outlying provinces proceed to the museum, moving quickly through the exhibits in large numbers, often in the "wrong direction" and paying more attention to foreigners than to the presentations of history, thus breaking with a museum's disciplinary order and self-regulating, civilizing strategies (T. Bennett 1995, 62–63).

2. Foreigners typically pay between 10,000 and 20,000 Vietnamese đồng (approximately $0.60 to $1.20).

3. On the postcolonial transfer of museum administration and the founding the Department of Preservation and Museums under the Ministry of Culture in the Democratic Republic of Vietnam, see Tai (1998, 188–190).

4. Pelley also makes the important point that postcolonial *new history* set in motion the creation of dominant narrations and representations "based on the denial of the South and the propagation of a Hanoi-centered vision of history" (2002, 13).

5. Unlike Vietnam, the U.S. typically used body counts to evaluate and determine victory (see Gibson 1986, 165–166).

6. A twelfth-grade history textbook from 1994 also identifies the role of the United States in the French War with a section entitled "Nationwide Resistance against France and U.S. Interference 1946–1954."

7. Like the proliferation of monuments, museumization has also been met with growing citizen disapproval on account of high public expenditures. In 1999, as a bus carrying international tourists drove past a former Vietnamese military base outside of Ho Chi Minh City, a tour guide criticized the construction of a new museum on site: "The war ended twenty-five years ago. We want to forget the past, but they continue to build museums. This is not good. We should put money into schools, not war museums."

8. For the 1994 Ordinance on the State Honorific Title "Vietnamese Heroic Mother" see chapter 1, note 21. The opening of the heroic mothers exhibits in Hanoi and elsewhere (see Tai 2001c, 178–179) came at a time of escalating public criticism of the state for overlooking the contributions of mothers to the war.

9. Tai (2001c, 186) quotes an employee at the Vietnamese Women's Museum in Hanoi who professes a similar desire to represent peace in the museum and not only war.

10. This was also a common public sentiment in Hanoi. For example, one night as I watched a television movie on the French War with a veteran of the American War and his younger brother, the brother turned to me and explained: "First we had a long war with France, then with the United States. Now we have peace." And what about the border conflict with China? I asked. He shook his head: "No, that was quick and only lasted three months." The veteran, still watching the film, nodded in agreement. What about Cambodia? I continued. "That wasn't a war. We went there to help them," the veteran replied.

11. According to Tai (1994, 6), the exhibit in Đà Nẵng was housed in the former U.S. Consulate building.

12. An exhibition house differs from a museum in that the function of the former is only to document and exhibit, while the latter is an institutional site for research, collection, conservation, and education. For example, while the exhibition house documented and displayed war crimes, the War Remnants Museum has expanded its scope and aims to educate visitors on the long-term effects of war, including the potential threats of modern war technologies.

13. Kennedy and Williams refer briefly to attempts to shut down exhibits on U.S. atrocities (2001, 145–146), though they do not clarify who made these efforts and in what capacity.

14. Not all museums have changed their discourse to accommodate improved diplomatic relations with the United States. The Mỹ Lai Museum, across from the peace park described in chapter 4, has kept its red, block-lettered sign positioned atop the entry: "Hatred for American Enemy Invaders Is Forever Engraved" [*Mãi Mãi Khắc Sâu Lòng Căm Thù Giặc Mỹ Xâm Lược*]. According to Vinh, who worked on the peace park and grew up in a village not far from the massacre site: "This is a very controversial sign. Some people have suggested changing it since relations with America have improved, but for what? It marks a particular moment in history and we should keep it."

15. Tour guides also commented specifically on the need to educate U.S. tourists, who they felt were ignorant of Vietnamese history. In the words of one male tour guide in his midthirties from Hanoi: "U.S. tourists who come here know nothing about Vietnam. They have told me this. But they do not seem to care about the information I try to give them. They just talk and talk and talk, even when I am speaking. There are still not many U.S. tourists here. I have heard that they think Vietnam is a miserable, dangerous place."

16. See also Scott Laderman (2007), who has made similar observations in his analysis of impression books at the War Remnants Museum.

17. The presentation of biographical objects in museum spaces is a common representational practice in Vietnam that individualizes the war and encourages the viewer to identify with the victim. For example, the Mỹ Lai Museum displays biographical objects such as forks, bowls, toys, cooking pots, and schoolbooks that had been used by victims. One display reads: "The plastic crab toy of a one-year-old boy, Dó Cu, murdered by U.S. soldiers." The act of identifying whom the object belonged to, the age of the owner, and

the purpose the object served in wartime creates a specific cultural biography that connects the viewer to its particular life history (Kopytoff 1986).

6. Tortured Bodies and the Neoliberal Politics of Historical Unaccountability

1. It was thus a significant and symbolic move on the part of China when it shifted from being a usual target of U.S. criticism for its poor human rights record to officially and publicly denouncing the United States to the international press as a gross violator of human rights in its war against terrorism, thereby asserting China's place as a key global power.

2. The Mỹ Lai and Mỹ Khê massacre took place in central Vietnam on March 16, 1968, when U.S. soldiers killed 504 villagers, mostly women and children. Referred to in Vietnam as the Sơn Mỹ massacre (the village to which the hamlets Mỹ Lai and Mỹ Khê belong), it does not have the same historical resonance as in the United States mainly because, as several respondents explained, Sơn Mỹ was just one of many massacres during the war (see, for example, Kwon [2006] on the Hà Mỹ massacre by South Korean troops). What makes Sơn Mỹ unique is the fact that it was recorded with the camera, though images were not circulated in the international press until 1969. See Oliver (2006) on the ambiguous response to the massacre in the United States.

3. Fassin has referred to this differential valuation as a "politics of life" in which "unequal value [is] accorded to lives on the battlefield: the sacred life of the Western armies of intervention, in which each life lost is counted and honored, versus the expendable life of not only the enemy troops but also their civilian populations, whose losses are only roughly numbered and whose corpses end up in mass graves" (Fassin 2007, 519).

4. The U.S. House of Representatives referred to such treatment in congressional hearings as "public curiosity abuse" (1969, 5).

5. The systematic torture of alleged Vietnamese communists in "tiger cages" in southern Vietnam at the hands of the RVN and U.S. military has also been well documented (see Rejali 2007, 172–178), though Saigon, like Hanoi, officially denied that torture of enemy troops in captivity occurred. Not all accounts of captivity revolve around cruelty and abuse, however. For an alternative perspective that discusses the humane actions of Vietnamese captors toward a female journalist, and the metaphorical kin relations that evolved over the course of her month as a prisoner, see Webb (1972).

6. Conflicting interpretations of film and photographic material released by Hanoi to illustrate its "humane and generous policy" toward POWs contributed to such conclusions. Where Hanoi saw evidence of its humanitarian conditions and treatment, the United States saw worrying signs of "isolation, physical abuse, and serious loss of weight" (U.S. House of Representatives 1969, 15).

7. According to H. Bruce Franklin, 2,255 troops were classified as "unaccounted for" after the war (about half of whom are known to have been killed in action, yet their remains have yet to be recovered), the smallest known number in modern history (1993, 11).

8. In 1977 Vietnam initially refused to cooperate on the POW/MIA front until reconstruction aid was paid, a position that it subsequently abandoned. Thereafter, the bodies and remains of missing military personnel became a tool of Washington's manipulation in its effort to manage and discipline Hanoi. In 1995 MIA remains were explicitly referred to as "the last bargaining chips" for making Hanoi accountable (U.S. House of Representatives 1995, 1).

9. An "Analysis of Live Sightings" in Congress that presented witness testimony and information on the more than 1,500 live sightings took place as late as 1992, only three years before U.S.-Vietnam relations were normalized (see U.S. Senate 1992).

10. It was assumed that "[i]n the modern world, for a regime that has been denied recognition by the United States of America, to be granted such recognition is an important symbol of full admission to the community of civilized nations" (U.S. House of Representatives 1995, 1).

11. In a congressional hearing entitled "Use of Chemical Agents in Southeast Asia since the Vietnam War," it was alleged that the Vietnamese government had sprayed lethal chemicals on the H'mong people after 1976 (U.S. House of Representatives 1979). The brutality of the "chemical attacks" is described in great detail and draws from refugee witness testimonies. While Agent Orange and use of toxic chemicals by the United States during the war is not fully absent, it is quickly dismissed as irrelevant on account of temporal inconsistencies (the hearing examined chemical use *after* the war and denial of its capacity to kill or incapacitate (ibid., 11). With no sense of historical irony, the chairman of the subcommittee boldly stated at the outset of the hearing: "[I]t is Vietnam which must bear the issue of responsibility for using lethal chemical agents in Southeast Asia" (ibid., 2).

12. Even when cooperation was noted, it was tinged with accusations of corruption and deceit. In 1996 the U.S. press alleged that Vietnam had fraudulently used MIA operations for financial gain by charging high fees for transportation services, farmer compensation packages, and wages to laborers who assisted MIA crews in excavation work (Stern 2005, 103). At the same time, in conversations in Vietnam, U.S. MIA personnel discussed the problems they faced spending their daily allowances and other budgeted project funds.

13. Such accusations have propelled human rights legislation "to promote freedom and democracy in Vietnam," such as the House Concurrent Resolution 295 in 2000, HR 1587 in 2004, and more recently HR 3096 in 2007, all of which passed in the House of Representatives (the former two died in the Senate, while HR 3096, which passed on September 18, 2007, is currently awaiting Senate vote).

14. Ong explains that self-orientalizing constructions of Asian modernity draw upon western essentialisms "because they are informed by and are continually produced by negotiating against Western domination in the world" (1999, 81).

15. Curiously, in his autobiography, McCain does not mention Ôn or any specific person as having saved him from the waters (he was unconscious). Contrary to press stories about Ôn protecting McCain from angry villagers, McCain writes of a woman who

rescued him from a brutal beating and then tended to his wounds (1999, 190). In an interview with Diane Fox (1997) Ổn also mentions a nurse who bandaged McCain and splinted his injuries.

16. Mai Văn Ổn's celebrity brought one U.S. veteran to search him out in Hanoi in 1998, as reported by the *Los Angeles Times*. Intrigued by his story (and apparently moved by his impoverished life), the veteran attempted to secure U.S. humanitarian funding for Ổn. When this failed, he reportedly provided Ổn with a monthly pension from his own funds (Lamb 1998, 2).

17. The monument is located on Youth Street [Đường Thanh Niên] on a stretch where courting couples congregate. As with the Củ Chi Tunnels, Vietnamese youth have transformed the immediate area into a space of love and romance. The monument is often surrounded by young lovers who hold hands or sit intimately on benches adjacent to the cement marker and face the small lake, seemingly oblivious to its presence.

18. On April 29, 2000, the newspaper *Tuổi Trẻ* [Youth], quoted McCain during a return visit to Hỏa Lò prison in 1994, *"Rất cảm ơn Chính phủ và nhân dân Việt Nam đối xử tốt với tôi"* [Thank you very much to the government and the people of Vietnam for their good treatment of me]. A photograph of McCain and Mai Văn Ổn smiling and embracing accompanied the text (X. Trung 2000).

19. In his memoirs, McCain displays an unreflexive disconnect from the violent, on-the-ground effects of U.S. bomb strikes. "Combat for a naval aviator is fought in short, violent bursts. Our missions last but an hour or two before we are clear of danger and back on the carrier playing poker with our buddies" (1999, 180).

20. In Vietnam, "Điện Biên Phủ in the air" is a significant historical marker of victory over the United States and its twelve-day Christmas bombing campaign in 1972. The "defeat" is seen as having compelled the U.S. administration to halt bombing, sign the Paris Peace Accords, and exit the war (Asselin 2002, 152). In December 2007, the thirty-fifth anniversary of "Điện Biên Phủ in the air" was celebrated in Hanoi with numerous events and large posters that depicted U.S. bombers falling from the sky.

21. This is one of the most important and iconic photographs in Vietnamese historical memory of the war, and one that was often invoked by my respondents as an example of the nation's humanity and benevolence. A poem written about the photograph by the national poet Tố Hữu, "O Du Kích Nhỏ" [O Young Guerrilla], is commonly memorized by schoolchildren.

22. The prison remained in use after the war. In 1993, two-thirds of the site was demolished to allow for the construction of Hanoi Tower, a modern office/apartment/shopping complex that attracts and houses foreigners.

23. For filmic representations of U.S. prisoners in Hỏa Lò, see the four-part documentary series by Walter Heynowski and Gerhard Scheumann, *Piloten im Pyjama* (Pilots in Pajamas) released in the German Democratic Republic in 1968. Nora Alter (1997) provides an insightful analysis of *Piloten im Pyjama* in relation to other East German cinematic productions of Vietnam and the war.

24. After the BTA was signed in July 2000, import and export flows between the two

countries increased from $1.5 billion in 2001 to more than $11.4 billion in 2007. See Foreign Trade Statistics for the U.S. Census Bureau: http://www.census.gov/foreign-trade/balance/c5520.html.

25. The U.S. ambassador to Vietnam during the time of my field research, Pete Peterson, defended such accusations in a *Los Angeles Times* article: "We are not trying to force anything western on Vietnam. Everything in the trade agreement reflects normal business practices in the world today" (Lamb 1999).

26. That the quality of Vietnamese seafood products for U.S. consumers was also questioned suggests that racialized ideologies also underlie such allegations. As reported in the *New York Times,* Congressman Marion Berry even suggested that Vietnamese catfish was "not good enough for American diners because they came from a place contaminated by so much Agent Orange" ("Great Catfish War" 2003).

27. As reported in the Vietnamese press, Vietnam has since found new and more lucrative markets for its shrimp and catfish products in Europe and Russia, thus decentering the United States from its presumed global market hegemony in Vietnam.

WORKS CITED

Adorno, Theodor W. 1991. *The Culture Industry: Selected Essays on Mass Culture*. New York: Routledge.

Agamben, Giorgio. 1998. *Homo Sacer: Sovereign Power and Bare Life*. Translated by Daniel Heller-Roazen. Stanford, Calif.: Stanford University Press.

Alneng, Victor. 2002. "'What the Fuck Is a Vietnam?': Touristic Phantasms and the Popcolonization of (the) Vietnam (War)." *Critique of Anthropology* 22, no. 4: 495–523.

Alter, Nora M. 1997. "Excessive Pre/Requisites: Vietnam through the East German Lens." *Cultural Critique* 35, no. 1: 39–79.

"An Unconvincing Comparison" [*Một sự so sánh không có sức thuyết phục*]. 2004. Voice of Vietnam. June 4.

Anagnost, Ann. 1997. *National Past-Times: Narrative, Representation, and Power in Modern China*. Durham, N.C.: Duke University Press.

Anderson, Benedict. 1991 [1983]. *Imagined Communities: Reflections on the Origin and Spread of Nationalism*. New York: Verso.

Anh Quang. 1985. "Lăng Chủ tịch Hồ Chí Minh" [Mausoleum of President Ho Chi Minh]. *Kiến Trúc* [Architecture] 2: 29–30.

Antze, Paul, and Michael Lambek, eds. 1996. *Tense Past: Cultural Essays in Trauma and Memory*. New York: Routledge.

Appadurai, Arjun. 1986. "Introduction: Commodities and the Politics of Value." In *The Social Life of Things: Commodities in Cultural Perspective*, edited by Arjun Appadurai, 3–63. Cambridge: Cambridge University Press.

———. 1996. *Modernity at Large: Cultural Dimensions of Globalization*. Minneapolis: University of Minnesota Press.

Asad, Talal. 1993. *Genealogies of Religion: Discipline and Reasons of Power in Christianity and Islam*. Baltimore: John Hopkins University Press.

———. 2000. "What Do Human Rights Do? An Anthropological Enquiry." *Theory and Event* 4, no. 4: 1–33.

———. 2003. *Formations of the Secular: Christianity, Islam, Modernity*. Stanford, Calif.: Stanford University Press.

Asselin, Pierre. 2002. *A Bitter Peace: Washington, Hanoi, and the Making of the Paris Agreement*. Chapel Hill: University of North Carolina Press.

Babb, Florence E. 2004. "Recycled *Sandalistas*: From Revolution to Resorts in the New Nicaragua." *American Ethnologist* 106, no. 3: 541–555.

Balaban, John. 1991. *Remembering Heaven's Face: A Moral Witness in Vietnam*. New York: Poseidon Press.

Ban Hán Nôm. 1978. *Tuyển tập văn bia Hà Nội* [Hanoi Stelae: Selected Works]. Hanoi: Khoa Học Xã Hội.

Báo Cựu Chiến Binh Việt Nam [Newspaper of the Veterans of Vietnam]. 2003. *Ký ức thời oanh liệt: ảnh phóng sự về chiến tranh Việt Nam* [Memories of a Glorious Time: Photographic Material on the Vietnam War]. Ho Chi Minh City: Tổng Hợp Thành Phố Hồ Chí Minh.

Bảo Ninh. 1993. *The Sorrow of War*. New York: Riverhead Books.

Barrelon, Pierre. 1999 [1893]. "Saigon." In *Cities of Nineteeth Century Colonial Vietnam: Hanoi, Saigon, Hue and the Champa Ruins*, translated by Walter E. J. Tips, 33–95. Bangkok: White Lotus Press.

Barry, Kathleen. 1996. "Industrialization and Economic Development: The Costs to Women." In *Vietnam's Women in Transition*, edited by Kathleen Barry, 144–156. New York: St. Martin's Press.

Barthes, Roland. 1981. *Camera Lucida: Reflections on Photography*. Translated by Richard Howard. New York: Hill and Wang.

Bartimus, Tad, Edith Lederer, Tracy Wood, Kate Webb, Laura Palmer, Denby Fawcett, Jurate Kazickas, Ann Bryan Mariano, and Anne Morrissy Merick. 2002. *War Torn: Stories of War from the Women Reporters Who Covered Vietnam*. New York: Random House.

Baudrillard, Jean. 1994. *Simulacra and Simulation*. Translated by Sheila Faria Glaser. Ann Arbor: University of Michigan Press.

Benjamin, Walter. 1969a. "Work of Art in the Age of Mechanical Reproduction." In *Illuminations*, edited by Hannah Arendt, translated by H. Zohn, 217–252. New York: Schocken Books.

———. 1969b. "Theses on the Philosophy of History," In *Illuminations*, edited by Hannah Arendt, translated by H. Zohn, 253–264. New York: Schocken Books.

Bennett, Tony. 1995. *The Birth of the Museum: History, Theory, Politics*. New York: Routledge.

Berdahl, Daphne. 2005. "Expressions of Experience and Experiences of Expression: Museum Re-Presentations of GDR History." *Anthropology and Humanism* 30, no. 2: 156–170.

Biehl, Joao, Byron Good, and Arthur Kleinman. 2007. "Introduction: Rethinking Subjectivity." In *Subjectivity: Ethnographic Investigations*, edited by Joao Biehl, Byron Good, and Arthur Kleinman, 1–23. Berkeley: University of California Press.

Biles, Annabel, Kate Lloyd, and William S. Logan. 1999. "Romancing Vietnam: The Formation and Function of Tourist Images in Vietnam." In *Converging Interests: Traders, Travelers, and Tourists in Southeast Asia*, edited by Jill Forshee, Christina Fink, and Sandra Cate, 207–233. Berkeley, Calif.: Center for Southeast Asia Studies.

Bleakney, Julia. 2006. *Revisiting Vietnam: Memoirs, Memorials, Museums.* New York: Routledge.

Bodnar, John. 1992. *Remaking America: Public Memory, Commemoration, and Patriotism in the Twentieth Century.* Princeton, N.J.: Princeton University Press.

Boi Tran Huynh. 2005. "Vietnamese Aesthetics from 1925 Onwards." Ph.D. diss., University of Sydney.

Boltanski, Luc. 1999. *Distant Suffering: Morality, Media and Politics.* Translated by Graham Burchell. Cambridge: Cambridge University Press.

Borneman, John. 1997. *Settling Accounts: Violence, Justice and Accountability in Postsocialist Europe.* Princeton, N.J.: Princeton University Press.

———. 2002. "Reconciliation after Ethnic Cleansing: Listening, Retribution, Affiliation." *Public Culture* 14, no. 2: 281–304.

———. 2003. "Why Reconciliation? A Response to Critics." *Public Culture* 15, no. 1: 199–208.

Bornstein, Erica. 2005. *The Spirit of Development: Protestant NGOs, Morality, and Economics in Zimbabwe.* Stanford, Calif.: Stanford University Press.

———. 2007. "Sacred Philanthropy: Between Impulse and Obligation." Paper presented at the annual meetings of the American Anthropological Association, Washington, D.C.

Bourdieu, Pierre. 1984. *Distinction: A Social Critique of the Judgment of Taste.* Translated by Richard Nice. Cambridge, Mass.: Harvard University Press.

Boym, Svetlana. 2001. *The Future of Nostalgia.* New York: Basic Books.

Bradley, Mark Philip. 2001. "Contests of Memory: Remembering and Forgetting War in the Contemporary Vietnamese Cinema." In *The Country of Memory,* edited by Hue-Tam Ho Tai, 196–226. Berkeley: University of California Press.

Bradley, Mark Philip, and Patrice Petro, eds. 2002. *Truth Claims: Representation and Human Rights.* New Brunswick, N.J.: Rutgers University Press.

Brink, Cornelia. 2000. "Secular Icons: Looking at Photographs from Nazi Concentration Camps." *History and Memory* 12, no. 1: 135–150.

Bruner, Edward M. 2005. *Culture on Tour: Ethnographies of Travel.* Chicago: University of Chicago Press.

Bùi Đình Phong. 1998. "Cách mạng trên lĩnh vực văn hóa để xây dựng nền văn hóa mới Việt Nam" [Revolution in the Realm of Culture in Order to Build New Vietnamese Culture]. In *Tư tưởng Hồ Chí Minh về xây dựng văn hóa Việt Nam* [Hồ Chí Minh's Ideology of Building Vietnamese Culture], 208–221. Hanoi: Chính Trị Quốc Gia.

Burawoy, Michael, and Katherine Verdery, eds. 1999. *Uncertain Transition: Ethnographies of Change in the Postsocialist World.* New York: Rowman and Littlefield.

Burghardt, Raymond. 2006. "Old Enemies Become Friends: U.S. and Vietnam." November 1. Brookings Northeast Asia Commentary. http://www.brookings.edu/opinions/2006/11southeastasia_burghardt.aspx.

Butler, Judith. 2004. *Precarious Life: The Power of Mourning and Violence.* New York: Verso.

Caruth, Cathy. 1995. "Introduction." In *Trauma: Explorations in Memory*, edited by Cathy Caruth, 3–12. Baltimore: Johns Hopkins University Press.

Cerwonka, Allaine, and Liisa H. Malkki. 2007. *Improvising Theory: Process and Temporality in Ethnographic Fieldwork*. Chicago: University of Chicago Press.

Chakrabarty, Dipesh. 2000. *Provincializing Europe: Postcolonial Thought and Historical Difference*. Princeton, N.J.: Princeton University Press.

———. 2007. "History and the Politics of Recognition." In *Manifestos for History*, edited by Keith Jenkins, Sue Morgan, and Alun Munslow, 77–87. New York: Routledge.

Chong, Denise. 2000. *The Girl in the Picture: The Story of Kim Phuc, the Photograph, and the Vietnam War*. New York: Viking.

Clark, Laurie Beth. 2006. "Placed and Displaced: Trauma Memorials." In *Place and Performance*, edited by Leslie Hill and Helen Paris, 129–138. New York: Palgrave Macmillan.

Clifford, James. 1986. "Introduction: Partial Truths." In *Writing Culture: The Poetics and Politics of Ethnography*, edited by James Clifford and George E. Marcus, 1–26. Berkeley: University of California Press.

———. 1988. *Predicament of Culture: Twentieth-Century Ethnography, Literature, and Art*. Cambridge, Mass.: Harvard University Press.

———. 1997. *Routes: Travel and Translation in the Late Twentieth Century*. Cambridge, Mass.: Harvard University Press.

Cohen, David William. 1994. *The Combing of History*. Chicago: University of Chicago Press.

Cohn, Bernard S. 1996. *Colonialism and Its Forms of Knowledge: The British in India*. Princeton, N.J.: Princeton University Press.

Cole, Jennifer. 2001. *Forget Colonialism? Sacrifice and the Art of Memory in Madagascar*. Berkeley: University of California Press.

Cole, Tim. 1999. *Selling the Holocaust: From Auschwitz to Schindler; How History Is Bought, Packaged, and Sold*. New York: Routledge.

Comaroff, Jean, and John L. Comaroff. 2001. "Millennial Capitalism: First Thoughts on a Second Coming." In *Millennial Capitalism and the Culture of Neoliberalism*, edited by Jean Comaroff and John L. Comaroff, 1–57. Durham, N.C.: Duke University Press.

Connerton, Paul. 1989. *How Societies Remember*. Cambridge: Cambridge University Press.

Coronil, Fernando. 2007. "After Empire: Reflections on Imperialism from the Américas." In *Imperial Formations*, edited by Ann Laura Stoler, Carole McGranahan, and Peter C. Perdue, 241–271. Santa Fe, N.M.: SAR Press.

Coutin, Susan Bibler. 1993. *The Culture of Protest: Religious Activism and the U.S. Sanctuary Movement*. San Francisco: Westview Press.

Cu Chi Tunnels Historical Remains [Khu Di Tích Lịch Sử Địa Đạo Củ Chi]. 2002. *The Documentary Album of Cu Chi, 1960–1975, Album no.2*. Ho Chi Minh City: Mũi Cà Mau.

Curtis, Paulette Gueno. 2003. "Locating History: Vietnam Veterans and Their Return to the Battlefield, 1998–1999." Ph.D. diss., Harvard University.

Daley, Matthew P. 2004. "Trade and Human Rights: The Future of U.S.-Vietnamese Relations." Testimony before the Senate Foreign Relations Committee Subcommittee on East Asian and Pacific Affairs. February 12. http://foreign.senate.gov/testimony/2004/DaleyTestimony040212.pdf.

Đặng Thùy Trâm. 2005. *Nhật ký Đặng Thùy Trâm* [The Diary of Đặng Thùy Trâm]. Hanoi: Hội Nhà Văn.

Đặng Vương Hưng. 2004. "Tù binh Mỹ ở Hỏa Lò . . . Chuyện bây giờ mới kể" [American Prisoners at Hoa Lo: A Story Told Just Now]. *An Ninh Thế Giới*, 28–29. July 1.

Das, Veena. 2006. *Life and Words: Violence and the Descent into the Ordinary*. Berkeley: University of California Press.

Das, Veena, and Arthur Kleinman. 2001. "Introduction." In *Remaking a World: Violence, Social Suffering, and Recovery*, edited by Veena Das, Arthur Kleinman, Margaret Lock, Mamphela Ramphele, and Pamela Reynolds, 1–31. Berkeley: University of California Press.

Daston, Lorraine. 2006. "The Coming into Being of Scientific Objects." In *Biographies of Scientific Objects*, edited by Lorraine Daston, 1–14. Chicago: University of Chicago Press.

Daston, Lorraine, and Peter Galison. 2007. *Objectivity*. Cambridge, Mass.: MIT Press.

Derrida, Jacques. 2001. *On Cosmopolitanism and Forgiveness*. New York: Routledge.

Desmond, Jane C. 1999. *Staging Tourism: Bodies on Display from Waikiki to Sea World*. Chicago: University of Chicago Press.

Dickson-Gomez, Julia. 2004. "One Who Doesn't Know War, Doesn't Know Anything": The Problem of Comprehending Suffering in Postwar El Salvador." *Anthropology and Humanism* 29, no. 2: 145–158.

Diller, Elizabeth, and Ricardo Scofidio, eds. 1994. *Back to the Front: Tourisms of War*. Basse-Normandie: FRAC.

Dittmar, Linda, and Gene Michaud, eds. 2000. *From Hanoi to Hollywood: The Vietnam War in American Film*. New Brunswick, N.J.: Rutgers University Press.

Do Lai Thuy. 1993. *The Stone Stelae at the Temple of Literature*. Hanoi: Thế Giới.

Đoàn Công Tính. 2002. *Khoảnh khắc: ảnh phóng sự về chiến tranh Việt Nam* [Moments: Photographs of the Vietnam War]. Ho Chi Minh City: Thành Phố Hồ Chí Minh.

Doãn Đức. 1998. "Kiến trúc Bảo tàng Việt Nam thế kỷ XX." [20th Century Vietnamese Museum Architecture]. *Kiến Trúc Việt Nam* [Vietnamese Architecture] 2: 53–55.

———. 2000. "Nệ cổ và nhại cổ trong kiến trúc—một hiện tượng tiêu cực, đáng phê phán ở nước ta" [Concerns about the Imitation of Ancient Architecture: A Negative Phenomenon Worthy of Criticism in Our Nation]. *Kiến Trúc Việt Nam* [Vietnamese Architecture] 1: 19–20.

Douglas, John Michael. 1998. "PeaceTrees in Vietnam." Electronic document. November 1. http://www.thingsasian.com/goto_article/article.827.html.

Douglas, Mary. 1996 [1966]. *Purity and Danger: An Analysis of the Concepts of Pollution and Taboo*. New York: Routledge.

Douglass, Ana, and Thomas A. Vogler, eds. 2003. *Witness and Memory: The Discourse of Trauma*. New York: Routledge.

Drummond, Lisa B. W., and Mandy Thomas, eds. 2003. *Consuming Urban Culture in Contemporary Vietnam*. New York: Routledge.

Duiker, William J. 2000. *Ho Chi Minh: A Life*. New York: THEIA.

Dương Thu Hương. 1996. *Novel without a Name*. Translated by Phan Huy Đường and Nina McPherson. New York: Penguin.

Dương Trung Quốc. 1998. "Nghĩ về tượng đài ở Thủ đô" [Thoughts on Monuments in the Capital]. *Kiến Trúc Việt Nam* [Vietnamese Architecture] 1: 37–38.

Duy Thanh. 2007. "Bắt giam phó giám đốc Sở VHTT tỉnh Điện Biên" [Vice Director of the Department of Culture and Information in Điện Biên Province Detained]. Lao Động [Labor], June 14, 7.

Ebron, Paulla A. 2000. "Tourists as Pilgrims: Commercial Fashioning of Transatlantic Politics." *American Ethnologist* 26, no. 4: 910–932.

Eco, Umberto. 1983. *Travels in Hyperreality*. Translated by William Weaver. New York: Harcourt.

Edwards, Elizabeth, ed. 1992. *Anthropology and Photography, 1860–1920*. New Haven, Conn.: Yale University Press.

Ehrhart, W.D. 1987. *Going Back: An Ex-Marine Returns to Vietnam*. Jefferson, N.C.: McFarland, 1987.

Elwood-Akers, Virginia. 1988. *Women War Correspondents in the Vietnam War*. Lanham, Md.: Scarecrow Press.

Endres, Kirsten W. 1999. "Culturalizing Politics: *Doi moi* and the Restructuring of Ritual in Contemporary Rural Vietnam." In *Vietnamese Villages in Transition*, edited by Bernhard Dahm and Vincent J. Houben, 197–221. Passau, Germany: Rothe.

Engelhardt, Tom. 2007 [1995]. *The End of Victory: Cold War America and the Disillusioning of a Generation*. Amherst: University of Massachusetts Press.

Englund, Harri. 2006. *Prisoners of Freedom: Human Rights and the African Poor*. Berkeley: University of California Press.

Enloe, Cynthia. 1996. "Women after Wars: Puzzles and Warnings." In *Vietnam's Women in Transition*, edited by Kathleen Barry, 299–315. New York: St. Martin's Press.

Erikson, Kai. 1995. "Notes on Trauma and Community." In *Explorations in Memory*, edited by Cathy Caruth, 183–200. Baltimore: Johns Hopkins University Press.

Errington, Shelly. 1998. *The Death of Authentic Primitive Art and Other Tales of Progress*. Berkeley: University of California Press.

Espiritu, Yến Lê. 2005. "Vietnamese Women in the United States: A Critical Transnational Perspective." In *Le Việt Nam au feminine, Việt Nam: Women's Realities*, edited by Gisèle Bousquet and Nora Taylor, 307–321. Paris: Les Indes Savantes.

Faas, Horst, and Tim Page, eds. 1997. *Requiem: By the Photographers Who Died in Vietnam and Indochina*. New York: Random House.

Fassin, Didier. 2007. "Humanitarianism as a Politics of Life." *Public Culture* 19, no. 3: 499–520.

Favero, Paolo. 2003. "Phantasms in a 'Starry' Place: Space and the Identification in a Central New Delhi Market." *Cultural Anthropology* 18, no. 4: 551–584.

Feldman, Allen. 1994. "On Cultural Anesthesia: From Desert Storm to Rodney King" *American Ethnologist* 21, no. 2: 404–418.

Ferguson, James. 1994. *The Anti-Politics Machine: Development, Depoliticization, and Bureaucratic Power in Lesotho*. Cambridge: Cambridge University Press.

———. 2006. *Global Shadows: Africa in the Neoliberal World Order*. Durham, N.C.: Duke University Press.

Fife, Wayne. 2005. *Doing Fieldwork: Ethnographic Methods for Research in Developing Countries and Beyond*. New York: Palgrave Macmillan.

Forty, Adrian. "Introduction." 1999. In *The Art of Forgetting*, edited by Adrian Forty and Susanne Kuchler, 1–18. New York: Berg.

Foucault, Michel. 1977. *Discipline and Punish: The Birth of the Prison*. New York: Vintage Books, 1977.

———. 1980. *Power/Knowledge: Selected Interviews and Other Writings, 1972–1977*. Edited and translated by Colin Gordon. New York: Pantheon Books.

———. 1994 [1966]. *The Order of Things: An Archaeology of the Human Sciences*. New York: Random House.

———. 1998. "Different Spaces." In *Aesthetics, Method, and Epistemology,* translated by R. Hurley and others, edited by James D. Faubion, 175–185. New York: New Press.

Fox, Diane [Niblack]. 1997. "The Rescuer Remembers." *Việt Nam News*, May 25.

———. 2005. "Speaking with Vietnamese Women on the Consequences of War: Writing against Silence and Forgetting." In *Le Việt Nam au féminin, Việt Nam: Women's Realities,* edited by Gisèle Bousquet and Nora Taylor, 107–124. Paris: Les Indes Savantes.

Franklin, H. Bruce. 1993. *M.I.A. or Mythmaking in America: How and Why Belief in Live POWs Has Possessed a Nation*. New Brunswick, N.J.: Rutgers University Press.

Franklin, Sarah. 1996. "Making Transparencies: Seeing through the Science Wars." *Social Text* 46/47, nos. 1 and 2: 141–155.

Gibson, James William. 1986. *The Perfect War: Technowar in Vietnam*. New York: Random House.

Gibson-Graham, J. K. 1996. *The End of Capitalism (As We Knew It): A Feminist Critique of Political Economy*. Cambridge, U.K.: Blackwell Publishers.

Giebel, Christoph. 2001. "Museum-Shrine: Revolution and Its Tutelary Spirit in the Village of My Hoa Hung." In *The Country of Memory: Remaking the Past in Late Socialist Vietnam*, edited by Hue-Tam Ho Tai, 77–105. Berkeley: University of California Press.

———. 2004. *Imagined Ancestries of Vietnamese Communism: Ton Duc Thang and the Politics of History and Memory*. Seattle: University of Washington Press.

Gillis, John R. 1994. "Memory and Identity: The History of a Relationship." In *Com-*

memorations: The Politics of National Identity, edited by John R. Gillis, 3–24. Princeton, N.J.: Princeton University Press.

Gilroy, Paul. 1990. "Nationalism, History and Ethnic Absolutism." *History Workshop* 30: 114–119.

Gluckman, Ron. 1997. "Back to China Beach." Electronic document. http://www .gluckman.com/ChinaBeachVietnam.html.

Grant, Bruce. 2001. "New Moscow Monuments, or, States of Innocence." *American Ethnologist* 28, no. 2: 332–362.

"The Great Catfish War." 2003. *New York Times.* July 22, A18.

Gruner, Elliott. 1993. *Prisoners of Culture: Representing the Vietnam POW.* New Brunswick, N.J.: Rutgers University Press.

Gu Huimin, Chris Ryan, and Zhang Wei. 2007. "Jinggangshan Mountain: A Paradigm of China's Red Tourism." In *Battlefield Tourism: History, Place and Interpretation*, edited by Chris Ryan, 59–69. Oxford, U.K.: Linacre.

Gupta, Akhil, and James Ferguson. 1992. "Beyond 'Culture': Space, Identity, and the Politics of Difference." *Cultural Anthropology* 7, no. 1: 6–23.

———. 1997. "Discipline and Practice: 'The Field' as Site, Method and Location in Anthropology." In *Anthropological Locations: Boundaries and Grounds of a Field Science*, edited by Akhil Gupta and James Ferguson, 1–46. Berkeley: University of California Press.

Gürsel, Zeynep Devrim. 2007. *The Image Industry: The Work of International News Photographs in the Age of Digital Reproduction.* Ph.D. dissertation, University of California, Berkeley.

Gusterson, Hugh. 1997. "Studying Up Revisited." *Polar* 20, no. 1: 114–119.

Ha Huy Giap. 1978. "Fostering New Socialist Men and Women." *Vietnamese Studies* 52: 16–22.

Habermas, Jürgen. 1987. *The Philosophical Discourse of Modernity: Twelve Lectures.* Translated by Frederick Lawrence. Cambridge, Mass.: MIT Press.

Hagopian, Patrick. 2006. "Vietnam War Photography as a Locus of Memory." In *Locating Memory: Photographic Acts*, edited by Annette Kuhn and Kirsten Emiko McAllister, 201–222. New York: Berghahn Books.

Halbwachs, Maurice. 1992 [1952]. *On Collective Memory.* Translated by Lewis A. Coser. Chicago: University of Chicago Press.

Hallin, Daniel C. 1986. *The "Uncensored War": The Media and Vietnam.* Berkeley: University of California Press.

Hammond, William M. 1998. *Reporting Vietnam: Media and Military at War.* Lawrence: University Press of Kansas.

Handler, Richard, and Eric Gable. 1997. *The New History in an Old Museum: Creating the Past in Colonial Williamsburg.* Durham, N.C.: Duke University Press.

Hannerz, Ulf. 1998a. "Other Transnationals: Perspectives Gained from Studying Sideways." *Paideuma* 44: 109–123.

———. 1998b. "Transnational Research." In *Handbook of Methods in Cultural Anthropology*, edited by H. Russell Bernard, 235–256. Walnut Creek, Calif.: Altamira Press.

———. 2003. "Being There . . . and There . . . and There! Reflections on Multi-Site Ethnography." *Ethnography* 4, no. 2: 201–216.

Haraway, Donna. 1988. "Situated Knowledges: The Science Question in Feminism and the Privilege of Partial Perspective." *Feminist Studies* 14, no. 4: 575–599.

Harding, Sandra. 1991. *Whose Science? Whose Knowledge? Thinking from Women's Lives*. Ithaca, N.Y.: Cornell University Press.

Hardt, Michael, and Antonio Negri. 2000. *Empire*. Cambridge, Mass.: Harvard University Press.

Hariman, Robert, and John Louis Lucaites. 2007. *No Caption Needed: Iconic Photographs, Public Culture, and Liberal Democracy*. Chicago: University of Chicago Press.

Hart, Gillian. 2002. *Disabling Globalization: Places of Power in Post-Apartheid South Africa*. Berkeley: University of California Press.

Hart, Lain. 2007. "Authentic Recreation: Living History and Leisure." *Museum and Society* 5, no. 2: 103–124.

Harvey, David. 2005. *A Brief History of Neoliberalism*. New York: Oxford University Press.

Hawley, Thomas M. 2005. *The Remains of War: Bodies, Politics, and the Search for American Soldiers Unaccounted For in Southeast Asia*. Durham, N.C.: Duke University Press.

Hellmann, John. 1986. *American Myth and the Legacy of Vietnam*. New York: Columbia University Press.

Henderson, Joan C. 2000. "War as a Tourist Attraction: The Case of Vietnam." *International Journal of Tourism Research* 2: 269–280.

Herr, Michael. 1977. *Dispatches*. New York: Alfred A. Knopf.

Hirsch, Marianne. 1999. "Projected Memory: Holocaust Photographs in Personal and Public Fantasy" In *Acts of Memory: Cultural Recall in the Present*, edited by Mieke Bal, Jonathan Crewe, and Leo Spitzer, 3–24. Hanover, N.H.: Dartmouth College Press.

———. 2001. "Surviving Images: Holocaust Photographs and the Work of Postmemory." In *Yale Journal of Criticism* 14, no. 1: 5–37.

Hirschman, Charles, Samuel Preston, and Vu Manh Loi. 1995. "Vietnamese Casualties during the American War: A New Estimate." *Population and Development Review* 21, no. 4: 783–812.

Hồ Chí Minh. 2004. *Về báo chí* [On Journalism]. Hanoi: Chính Trị Quốc Gia.

Hồ Trung Tú. 1998. "Những nghĩa trang liệt sĩ đầu tiên ở nước ta" [The First Martyr Cemeteries in Our Country]. *Xưa và Nay* [Past and Present] 54: 29, 32.

Hoàng Đạo Kính. 1999. "Vài suy nghĩ về xây dựng tượng đài" [Thoughts about the Construction of Monuments]. *Kiến Trúc Việt Nam* [Vietnamese Architecture] 5: 26–27.

Hoàng Kim Đáng. 2007. *Đường Hồ Chí Minh trong chiến tranh* [The Hồ Chí Minh Trail in Wartime]. Hanoi: Chính Trị Quốc Gia.

Hobsbawm, Eric. 1983. "Introduction: Inventing Traditions." In *The Invention of Tra-*

dition, edited by Eric Hobsbawm and Terence Ranger, 1–14. Cambridge: Cambridge University Press.

Hoffman, Joyce. 1998. "On Their Own: Female Correspondents in Vietnam." *Quest 2*, no. 1. http://www.odu.edu/ao/instadv/quest/femalecorrespondents.html.

Hội Nghệ Sĩ Nhiếp Ảnh Việt Nam [Vietnam Association of Photographic Artists]. 1993. *Lịch sử nhiếp ảnh Việt Nam* [History of Vietnamese Photography]. Hanoi: Văn Hóa—Thông Tin.

Hoskins, Andrew. 2004. *Televising War: From Vietnam to Iraq*. New York: Continuum.

Hoskins, Janet. 1988. *Biographical Objects: How Things Tell the Stories of People's Lives*. New York: Routledge.

Huyssen, Andreas. 1995. *Twilight Memories: Marking Time in a Culture of Amnesia*. New York: Routledge.

———. 2003. *Present Pasts: Urban Palimpsests and the Politics of Memory*. Stanford, Calif.: Stanford University Press.

Ignatieff, Michael. 2005. "Introduction: American Exceptionalism and Human Rights." In *American Exceptionalism and Human Rights*, edited by Michael Ignatieff, 1–27. Princeton, N.J.: Princeton University Press.

Jay, Martin. 1988. "The Scopic Regimes of Modernity." In *Vision and Visuality*, edited by Hal Foster, 3–28. Seattle, Wash.: Bay Press.

Jeffords, Susan. 1989. *The Remasculinization of America: Gender and the Vietnam War*. Bloomington: Indiana University Press.

Jellema, Kate. 2007. "Everywhere Incense Burning: Remembering Ancestors in Doi Moi Vietnam." *Journal of Southeast Asian Studies* 38, no. 3: 467–492.

Jennings, Eric T. 2003. "Remembering 'Other' Losses: The Temple du Souvenir Indo-chinois of Nogent-sur Marne." *History and Memory* 15, no. 1: 5–48.

Johnson, Reed. 2002. "Through a Lens Darkly: A Bitter Conflict Is Seen Anew in Rare Images Captured by North Vietnamese Photographers." *Los Angeles Times*, April 24, E1, 3.

Jones, Brennon. 2005. "Tet and Remembrance of the Dead; Vietnam II." *International Herald Tribune*, February 28, 8.

Kaplan, E. Ann. 2005. *Trauma Culture: The Politics of Terror and Loss in Media and Literature*. New Brunswick, N.J.: Rutgers University Press.

Kelly, David. 1998. "Freedom—a Eurasian Mosaic." In *Asian Freedoms: The Idea of Freedom in East and Southeast Asia*, edited by David Kelly and Anthony Reid, 1–17. Cambridge: Cambridge University Press.

Kennedy, Laurel B., and Mary Rose Williams. 2001. "The Past without the Pain: The Manufacture of Nostalgia in Vietnam's Tourism Industry," In *The Country of Memory: Remaking the Past in Late Socialist Vietnam*, edited by Hue-Tam Ho Tai, 135–163. Berkeley: University of California Press.

Kerkvliet, Benedict J. Tria. 2005. *The Power of Everyday Politics: How Vietnamese Peasants Transformed National Policy*. Ithaca, N.Y.: Cornell University Press.

"Khởi công xây dựng đài tưởng niệm các liệt sĩ." [Construction Begins on Martyr Memorial]. 1989. Nghệ Tĩnh, August 6, 1.

Kidd, William. 2002. "Representation or Recuperation? The French Colonies and 1914–1918 War Memorials." In *Promoting the Colonial Idea: Propaganda and Visions of Empire in France*, edited by Tony Chafer and Amanda Sackur, 184–194. New York: Palgrave.

Kim, Hyun Sook. 2001. "Korea's 'Vietnam Question': War Atrocities, National Identity, and Reconciliation in Asia." *Positions* 9, no. 3: 621–635.

Kinney, Katherine. 2000. *Friendly Fire: American Images of the Vietnam War*. New York: Oxford University Press.

Kirshenblatt-Gimblett, Barbara. 1998. *Destination Culture: Tourism, Museum and Heritage*. Berkeley: University of California Press.

Klein, Kerwin Lee. 2000. "On the Emergence of *Memory* in Historical Discourse." *Representations* 69: 127–150.

Kleinen, John. 1999. *Facing the Future, Reviving the Past: A Study of Social Change in a Northern Vietnamese Village*. Singapore: Institute of Southeast Asian Studies.

Kleinman, Arthur, and Joan Kleinman. 1997. "The Appeal of Experience; The Dismay of Images: Cultural Appropriations of Suffering in Our Times." In *Social Suffering*, edited by Arthur Kleinman, Veena Das, and Margaret Lock, 1–23. Los Angeles and Berkeley: University of California Press.

Klima, Alan. 2002. *The Funeral Casino: Meditation, Massacre, and Exchange with the Dead in Thailand*. Princeton, N.J.: Princeton University Press.

Knightley, Phillip. 2004 [1975]. *The First Casualty*. New York: Harcourt Brace Jovanovich.

Kopytoff, Igor. 1986. "The Cultural Biography of Things: Commoditization as Process." In *The Social Life of Things: Commodities in Cultural Perspective*, edited by Arjun Appadurai, 64–91. Cambridge: Cambridge University Press.

Kugelmass, Jack. 1996. "Missions to the Past: Poland in Contemporary Jewish Thought and Deed." In *Tense Past: Cultural Essays in Trauma and Memory*, edited by Paul Antze and Michael Lambek, 199–214. New York: Routledge.

Kuhn, Annette, and Kirsten Emiko McAllister. 2006. "Locating Memory: Photographic Acts—an Introduction." In *Locating Memory: Photographic Acts*, edited by Annette Kuhn and Kirsten Emiko McAllister, 1–17. New York: Berghahn Books.

Kwon, Hoenik. 2006. *After the Massacre: Commemoration and consolation in Ha My and My Lai*. Berkeley: University of California Press.

Laderman, Scott. 2002. "Shaping Memory of the Past: Discourse in Travel Guidebooks for Vietnam." *Mass Communication & Society* 5, no. 1: 87–110.

———. 2007. "'The Other Side of War': Memory and Meaning at the War Remnants Museum of Vietnam." In *Decentering America*, edited by Jessica C. E. Gienow-Hecht, 171–209. New York: Berghahn Books.

Lahusen, Thomas, and Evgeny Dobrenko, eds. 1997. *Socialist Realism without Shores*. Durham, N.C.: Duke University Press.

Lamb, David. 1998. "His Life Is Linked to the Pilot He Saved." *Los Angeles Times*, July 21, A1.

———. 1999. "Landmark Trade Pact at Hand for US and Vietnam." *Los Angeles Times*, June 6, A2.

Landsberg, Alison. 2004. *Prosthetic Memory: The Transformation of American Remembrance in the Age of Mass Culture*, New York: Columbia University Press.

Laqueur, Thomas W. 1994. "Memory and Naming in the Great War." In *Commemorations: The Politics of National Identity*, edited by John R. Gillis, 150–167. Princeton, N.J.: Princeton University Press.

Latour, Bruno and Steve Woolgar. 1986. *Laboratory Life: The Construction of Scientific Facts*. Princeton, N.J.: Princeton University Press.

Laub, Dori, M.D. 1992. "An Event without a Witness: Truth, Testimony and Survival." In *Testimony: Crises of Witnessing in Literature, Psychoanalysis, and History*, edited by Shoshana Felman and Dori Laub, M.D., 75–92. New York: Routledge.

Lavine, Steven D., and Ivan Karp. 1991. "Introduction: Museums and Multiculturalism." In *Exhibiting Cultures: The Poetics and Politics of Museum Display*, edited by Ivan Karp and Steven D. Lavine, 1–9. Washington D.C.: Smithsonian Institution Press.

Lê Duẩn. 1977. *Xây dựng nền văn hóa mới con người mới xã hội chủ nghĩa* [On Building a New Socialist Culture and a New Socialist Man]. Hanoi: Văn Hóa, 1977.

Lê Thị Quý. 1995. "Social Policies on Preventing and Curbing Prostitution." *Vietnam Social Sciences*, no. 45: 97–100.

Lederer, Edith. 2002. "My First War." In *War Torn: Stories of War from the Women Reporters Who Covered Vietnam*, edited by Tad Bartimus, et al. 155–185. New York: Random House.

Ledgerwood, Judy. 1997. "The Cambodian Tuol Sleng Museum of Genocidal Crimes: National Narrative." *Museum Anthropology* 21, no. 1: 82–98.

Lenin, V. I. 1952. *Socialism and War*. Moscow: Foreign Languages Publishing House.

Lennon, John, and Malcolm Foley. 2000. *Dark Tourism: The Attraction of Death and Disaster*. New York: Continuum.

Leshkowich, Ann Marie. 2003. "The Ao Dai Goes Global: How International Influences and Female Entrepreneurs Have Shaped Vietnam's 'National Costume.'" In *Re-Orienting Fashion: The Globalization of Asian Dress*, edited by Sandra Niessen, Ann Marie Leshkowich, and Carla Jones, 79–115. New York: Berg.

———. 2008. "Wandering Ghosts of Late Socialism: Conflict, Metaphor, and Memory in a Southern Vietnamese Market Place." *Journal of Asian Studies* 67, no. 1: 5–41.

Lewinski, Jorge. 1978. *The Camera at War: A History of War Photography from 1848 to the Present Day*. London: W. H. Allen.

Linenthal, Edward T. 1995. *Preserving Memory: The Struggle to Create America's Holocaust Museum*. New York: Columbia University Press..

Linenthal, Edward T., and Tom Engelhardt, eds. 1996. *History Wars: The Enola Gay and Other Battles for the American Past*. New York: Henry Holt.

Lippard, Lucy R. 1999. *On the Beaten Track: Tourism, Art, and Place*. New York: New Press.

Lisle, Debbie. 2000. "Consuming Danger: Reimagining the War/Tourism Divide." *Alternatives* 25: 91–116.

Liss, Andrea. 1998. *Trespassing through Shadows: Memory, Photography, and the Holocaust*. Minneapolis: University of Minnesota Press.

Löfgren, Orvar. 1993. "Materializing the Nation in Sweden and America." *Ethnos* 58, nos. 3–4: 161–196.

Logan, William S. 2000. *Hanoi: Biography of a City*. Seattle: University of Washington Press.

Louvre, Alf, and Jeffrey Walsh, eds. 1988. *Tell Me Lies about Vietnam: Cultural Battles for the Meaning of the War*. Philadelphia: Open University Press.

Luong, Hy Van. 1993. "Economic Reform and the Intensification of Rituals in Two North Vietnamese Villages, 1980–90." In *The Challenge of Reform in Indochina*, edited by Börje Ljunggren, 259–291. Cambridge, Mass.: Harvard University Press.

Lutz, Catherine. 2006. "Empire Is in the Details." *American Ethnologist* 33, no. 4: 593–611.

Ly, Boreth. 2003. "Devastated Vision(s): The Khmer Rouge Scopic Regime in Cambodia." *Art Journal* 62, no. 1: 66–81.

MacCannell, Dean. 1999 [1976]. *The Tourist: A New Theory of the Leisure Class*. Berkeley: University of California Press.

MacLean, Ken. 2008. "The Rehabilitation of an Uncomfortable Past: Everyday Life in Vietnam during the Subsidy Period (1975–1986)." *History and Anthropology* 19, no. 3: 281–303.

Maclear, Kyo. 2003. "The Limits of Vision: *Hiroshima Mon Amour* and the Subversion of Representation." In *Witness and Memory: Discourse of Trauma*, edited by Ana Douglass and Thomas V. Vogler, 233–249. New York: Routledge.

Mai Nam. 2001. *Một thời hào hùng* [Once a Glorious Time]. Ho Chi Minh City: Thanh Niên.

Maier, Charles S. 1988. *The Unmasterable Past: History, Holocaust, and German National Identity*. Cambridge, Mass.: Harvard University Press.

Malarney, Shaun Kingsley. 1996. "The Limits of 'State Functionalism' and the Reconstruction of Funerary Ritual in Contemporary Northern Vietnam." *American Ethnologist* 23, no. 3: 540–560.

———. 2001. "'The Fatherland Remembers Your Sacrifice': Commemorating War Dead in North Vietnam." In *The Country of Memory: Remaking the Past in Late Socialist Vietnam*, edited by Hue-Tam Ho Tai, 46–76. Berkeley: University of California Press.

———. 2002. *Culture, Ritual and Revolution in Vietnam*. Honolulu: University of Hawaii Press.

Maleuvre, Didier. 1999. *Museum Memories: History, Technology, Art*. Stanford, Calif.: Stanford University Press.

Malkki, Liisa H. 1992. "National Geographic: The Rooting of Peoples and the Territorialization of National Identity among Scholars and Refugees." *Cultural Anthropology* 7, no. 1: 24–44.

————. 1994. "Citizens of Humanity: Internationalism and the Imagined Community of Nations." *Diaspora* 3, no. 1: 41–68.

————. 1995. *Purity and Exile: Violence, Memory and National Cosmology among Hutu Refugees in Tanzania*. Chicago: University of Chicago Press.

————. 1996. "Speechless Emissaries: Refugees, Humanitarianism, and Dehistoriciza-tion." *Cultural Anthropology* 11, no. 3: 377–404.

Mangold, Tom, and John Pennycate. 1985. *The Tunnels of Cu Chi*. London: Pan Books.

Marcus, George E. 1995. "Ethnography in/of the World System: The Emergence of Multi-Sited Ethnography." *Annual Review of Anthropology* 24: 95–117.

————. 1998. *Ethnography through Thick and Thin*. Princeton, N.J.: Princeton University Press.

Martini, Edwin A. 2007. *Invisible Enemies: The American War on Vietnam, 1975–2000*. Amherst: University of Massachusetts Press.

McCain, John, with Mark Salter. 1999. *Faith of My Fathers*. New York: Random House.

McNamara, Robert S., with Brian VanDeMark. 1995. *In Retrospect: The Tragedy and Lessons of Vietnam*. New York: Time Books.

Milton, Sybil. 1984. "The Camera as Weapon: Documentary Photography and the Holocaust." *Simon Wiesenthal Center Annual* 1: 45–68.

Mitchell, Timothy. 1988. *Colonizing Egypt*. Cambridge: Cambridge University Press.

Moeller, Susan D. 1999. *Compassion Fatigue: How the Media Sell Disease, Famine, War and Death*. New York: Routledge.

Morgan, David. 2005. *The Sacred Gaze: Religious Visual Culture in Theory and Practice*. Berkeley: University of California Press.

Morris, David B. 1997. "About Suffering: Voice, Genre, and Moral Community." In *Social Suffering*, edited by Arthur Kleinman, Veena Das, and Margaret Lock, 25–47. Berkeley: University of California Press.

Morrison-Welsh, Anne. 2006. *Fire of the Heart: Norman Morrison's Legacy in Vietnam and at Home*. Wallingford, Pa.: Pendle Hill.

Mosse, George L. 1990. *Fallen Soldiers: Reshaping the Memory of the World Wars*. New York: Oxford University Press.

Mueggler, Eric. 2001. *The Age of Wild Ghosts: Memory, Violence, and Place in Southwest China*. Berkeley: University of California Press.

Musil, Robert. 1987. *Posthumous Papers of a Living Author*. Hygiene, Colo.: Eridanos Press.

Mydans, Seth. 2000. "Clinton in Vietnam: The Overview; Clinton Basks in the Adula-tion of a City Once Called Saigon." *New York Times*, November 20, A:1.

Ngô Huy Quỳnh. 1986. *Tìm hiểu lịch sử kiến trúc Việt Nam* [Understanding the History of Vietnamese Architecture]. Hanoi: Xây Dựng.

Nguyễn Bá Đang, Nguyễn Vũ Phương, and Tạ Hoàng Vân. 2006. *Traditional Viet-namese Architecture*. Hanoi: Thế Giới.

Nguyễn Hồng Kiên. 1996. *Điêu khắc trên kiến trúc cổ truyền Việt* [Sculpture in Ancient Viet Architecture]. *Kiến Trúc Việt Nam* [Vietnamese Architecture] 2: 40–42.

Nguyễn Huy Thiệp. 1992. *The General Retires and Other Stories*. Translated by Greg Lockhart. Oxford: Oxford University Press.

Nguyễn Khắc Viện. 2007. *Vietnam: A Long History*. Hanoi: Thế Giới.

Nguyễn Quân. 1982. *Nghệ thuật tạo hình Việt Nam hiện đại* [Modern Vietnamese Plastic Arts]. Hanoi: Văn Hóa.

Nguyễn Tiến Mão. 2006. *Cơ sở lý luận ảnh báo chí* [Theoretical Foundation of Photojournalism]. Hanoi: Thông Tấn.

Nguyen, Viet Thanh. 2002. *Race and Resistance: Literature and Politics in Asian America*. New York: Oxford University Press.

Nguyễn Văn Thạc. 2005. *Mãi mãi tuổi hai mươi—nhật ký thời chiến tranh* [Forever Twenty: A War Diary]. Hanoi: Thanh Niên.

Nguyễn Vinh Phúc. 2000. "Vài suy nghĩ về công việc dựng tượng và đài ở Hà Nội hiện nay" [A few thoughts on the construction of statues and monuments in Hanoi today]. *Kiến Trúc Việt Nam* [Vietnamese Architecture] 4: 11–13.

Nguyễn-võ, Thu-hương. 2008. *The Ironies of Freedom: Sex, Culture, and Neoliberal Governance in Vietnam*. Seattle: University of Washington Press.

Ninh, Kim N. B. 2002. *A World Transformed: The Politics of Culture in Revolutionary Vietnam, 1945–1965*. Ann Arbor: University of Michigan Press.

Nora, Pierre. 1989. "Between Memory and History: Les Lieux de Mémoire." *Representations* 26: 7–25.

Norindr, Panivong. 1996. *Phantasmatic Indochina: French Colonial Ideology in Architecture, Film, and Literature*. Durham, N.C.: Duke University Press.

Oliver, Kendrick. 2006. *The My Lai Massacre in American History and Memory*. Manchester, U.K.: Manchester University Press.

Ong, Aihwa. 1999. *Flexible Citizenship: The Cultural Logics of Transnationality*. Durham, N.C.: Duke University Press.

———. 2006. *Neoliberalism as Exception: Mutations and Citizenship and Sovereignty*. Durham, N.C.: Duke University Press.

Page, Tim. 2002. *Another Vietnam: Pictures of the War from the Other Side*. Edited by Doug Niven and Chris Riley. Washington, D.C.: National Geographic Press.

Parameswaran, Radhika. 2006. "Military Metaphors, Masculine Modes, and Critical Commentary: Deconstructing Journalists' Inner Tales of September 11," *Journal of Communication Inquiry* 30, no. 1: 42–64.

Pedelty, Mark. 1995. *War Stories: The Culture of Foreign Correspondents*. New York: Routledge.

Pelley, Patricia M. 2002. *Postcolonial Vietnam: New Histories of the National Past*. Durham, N.C.: Duke University Press.

Peterson, Mark Allen. 2001. "Getting to the Story: Unwriteable Discourse and Interpretive Practice in American Journalism." *Anthropological Quarterly* 74, no. 4.: 201–211.

Phạm Hồng Phước. 2004. "Những liên hệ và đối chiếu đau lòng" [Connections and Heart-Wrenching Contrasts]. *Công An Thành Phố Hồ Chí Minh* [Ho Chi Minh City Police] May 11, 13.

Phạm Quốc Trung and Nguyễn Hoàng Hà. 2006. "Statutory Reform." *Việt Nam News,* July 30, 7.

Phạm Văn Đồng. 1975. *Xây dựng nền văn hóa văn nghệ ngang tầm vóc dân tộc ta thời đại ta* [Building an Artistic Culture to Match the Stature of Our Nation and Our Time]. Hanoi: Sự Thật.

Pratt, Mary Louise. 1992. *Imperial Eyes: Travel Writing and Transculturation*. New York: Routledge.

"Prisoners of War." 2004. Voice of America (Vietnamese), Washington D.C. May 29.

Quinn-Judge, Sophie. 2002. *Ho Chi Minh: The Missing Years*. Berkeley: University of California Press.

Rafael, Vicente L. 1995. "Introduction: Writing Outside; On the Question of Location." In *Discrepant Histories: Translocal Essays on Filipino Cultures*, edited by Vicente L. Rafael. Philadelphia: Temple University Press.

Rejali, Darius. 2007. *Torture and Democracy*. Princeton: Princeton University Press.

Renan, Ernest., 1990 [1882]. "What Is a Nation?" In *Nation and Narration*, edited by Homi K. Bhabha, 8–22. New York: Routledge.

Rival, Laura. 1998. "Trees, from Symbols of Life and Regeneration to Political Artefacts." In *The Social Life of Trees: Anthropological Perspectives on Tree Symbolism*, edited by Laura Rival, 1–39. Oxford, U.K.: Berg.

Roeder, George H., Jr. 1993. *The Censored War: American Visual Experience during World War Two*. New Haven, Conn.: Yale University Press.

Rofel, Lisa. 1999. *Other Modernities: Gendered Yearnings in China after Socialism*. Berkeley: University of California Press.

Rowe, John Carlos, and Rick Berg, eds. 1991. *The Vietnam War and American Culture*. New York: Columbia University Press.

Ryan, Chris, ed. 2007. *Battlefield Tourism: History, Place and Interpretation*. Oxford, U.K.: Linacre House.

Salemink, Oscar. 2003. *The Ethnography of Vietnam's Central Highlanders: A Historical Contextualization, 1850–1990*. Honolulu: University of Hawaii Press.

Sampson, Steven. 2003. "From Reconciliation to Coexistence." *Public Culture* 15, no. 1: 181–186.

Sanger, David E. 2000. "Clinton in Vietnam: The Overview; Huge Crowd in Hanoi for Clinton, Who Speaks of 'Shared Suffering.'" *New York Times*. November 18, A1.

Savage, Kirk. 1994. "The Politics of Memory: Black Emancipation and the Civil War Monument." In *Commemorations: The Politics of National Identity*, edited by John R. Gillis, 127–149. Princeton, N.J.: Princeton University Press.

Scarry, Elaine. 1985. *The Body in Pain: The Making and Unmaking of the World*. New York: Oxford University Press.

Schudson, Michael. 1978. *Discovering the News: A Social History of American Newspapers*. New York: Basic Books.

———. 1984. *Advertising, the Uneasy Persuasion: Its Dubious Impact on American Society*. New York: Basic Books.

Scott, James C. 1990. *Domination and the Arts of Resistance: Hidden Transcripts*. New Haven, Conn.: Yale University Press.

Scott, Joan. 1991. "The Evidence of Experience." *Critical Inquiry* 17: 773–797.

Seaton, A. V. 1996. "From Thanatopsis to Thanatourism: Guided by the Dark." *Journal of International Heritage Studies* 2, no. 2: 234–244.

Seremetakis, Nadia C. 1994. "The Memory of the Senses, Part 1: Marks of the Transitory." In *The Senses Still: Perception and Memory as Material Culture in Modernity*, edited by C. Nadia Seremetakis, 1–18. Chicago: University of Chicago Press.

Sherman, Daniel J. 1998. "Bodies and Names: The Emergence of Commemoration in Interwar France." *American Historical Review* 113, no. 2: 443–466.

———. 1999. *The Construction of Memory in Interwar France.* Chicago: University of Chicago Press.

Shipler, David K. 1997. "Robert McNamara and the Ghosts of Vietnam." *New York Times*, August 10, 30–35.

Simpson, Moira G. 2001. *Making Representations: Museums in the Post-Colonial Era.* New York: Routledge.

Smith, Valene L. 1996. "War and Its Tourist Attractions." In *Tourism, Crime and International Security Issues*, edited by Abraham Pizam and Yoel Mansfeld, 247–264. New York: John Wiley and Sons.

Sontag, Susan. 1968. *Trip to Hanoi.* New York: Farrar, Straus & Giroux.

———. 1990 [1977]. *On Photography.* New York: Anchor Books.

———. 2003. *Regarding the Pain of Others.* New York: Farrar, Straus & Giroux.

Spivak, Gayatri Chakravorty. 1988. "Subaltern Studies: Deconstructing Historiography." In *Selected Subaltern Studies*, edited by Ranajit Guha and Gayatri Chakravorty Spivak, 3–32. New York: Oxford University Press.

Spyer, Patricia. 2000. *The Memory of Trade: Modernity's Entanglements on an Eastern Indonesian Island.* Durham, N.C.: Duke University Press.

Stark, David. 1996. "Recombinant Property in East European Capitalism." *American Journal of Sociology* 101, no. 4: 993–1027.

Stark, David, and László Bruszt. 1998. *Postsocialist Pathways: Transforming Politics and Property in East Central Europe.* Cambridge: Cambridge University Press.

Starrett, Gregory. 2003. "Violence and the Rhetoric of Images." *Cultural Anthropology* 18, no. 3: 398–428.

Stern, Lewis M. 2005. *Defense Relations between the United States and Vietnam: The Process of Normalization, 1977–2003.* Jefferson, N.C.: McFarland and Company.

Stewart, Susan. 1993. *On Longing: Narratives of the Miniature, the Gigantic, the Souvenir, the Collection.* Durham, N.C.: Duke University Press.

Stoler, Ann Laura. 2006. "Intimidations of Empire: Predicaments of the Tactile and Unseen." In *Haunted by Empire: Geographies of Intimacy in North American History*, edited by Ann Laura Stoler, 1–22. Durham, N.C.: Duke University Press.

———. 2008. "Imperial Debris: Reflections on Ruins and Ruination." *Cultural Anthropology* 23, no. 2: 191–219.

Stoller, Paul. 1997. "Globalization Method: The Problems of Doing Ethnography in Transnational Spaces." *Anthropology and Humanism* 22, no. 1: 81–94.

Struk, Janina. 2004. *Photographing the Holocaust: Interpretations of the Evidence.* New York: I. B. Tauris and Co..

Sturken, Marita. 1997a. *Tangled Memories: The Vietnam War, the AIDS Epidemic, and the Politics of Remembering*. Berkeley: University of California Press.

——. 1997b. "Absent Images of Memory: Remembering and Reenacting the Japanese Internment." *Positions* 5, no. 3: 687–708.

——. 2007. *Tourists of History: Memory, Kitsch, and Consumerism from Oklahoma City to Ground Zero*. Durham, N.C.: Duke University Press.

Suarez-Orozco, Marcelo M., and Antonius C. G. M. Robben. 2000. "Interdisciplinary Perspectives on Violence and Trauma." In *Cultures under Siege: Collective Violence and Trauma*, edited by Antonius C. G. M. Robben and Marcel M. Suarez-Orozco, 1–41. Cambridge: Cambridge University Press.

Sutherland, Claire. 2005. "Repression and Resistance? French Colonialism as Seen through Vietnamese Museums." *Museum and Society* 3, no. 3: 153–166.

Ta Van Tai. 1988. *The Vietnamese Tradition of Human Rights*. Berkeley: Institute of East Asian Studies (University of California).

Tagg, John. 1988. *The Burden of Representation: Essays on Photographies and Histories*. Amherst: University of Massachusetts Press.

Tai, Hue-Tam Ho. 1994. "Hallowed Ground or Haunted House: The War in Vietnamese History and Tourism." Contemporary Issues 3. Cambridge, Mass.: Fairbank Center for East Asian Research, Harvard University.

——. 1995. "Monumental Ambiguity: The State Commemoration of Ho Chi Minh." In *Essays to Vietnamese Pasts*, edited by K. W. Taylor and John K. Whitmore, 272–288. Ithaca, N.Y.: Southeast Asia Program Publications.

——. 1998. "Representing the Past in Vietnamese Museums." *Curator: The Museum Journal* 41, no. 3: 187–199.

——, ed. 2001a. *The Country of Memory: Remaking the Past in Late Socialist Vietnam*. Berkeley and Los Angeles: University of California Press.

——. 2001b. "Introduction: Situating Memory." In *The Country of Memory: Remaking the Past in Late Socialist Vietnam*, edited by Hue-Tam Ho Tai, 1–17. Berkeley: University of California Press.

——. 2001c. "Faces of Remembrance and Forgetting." In *The Country of Memory: Remaking the Past in Late Socialist Vietnam*, edited by Hue-Tam Ho Tai, 167–195. Berkeley: University of California Press.

Tappe, Oliver. 2008. *Geschichte, Nationsbildung und Legitimationspolitik in Laos: Untersuchungen zur laotischen nationalen Historiographie und Ikonographie* [History, Nation Building, and Legitimation Politics in Laos: Examinations of Lao National Historiography and Iconography]. Muenster, Germany: Lit Verlag.

Taylor, John. 1998. *Body Horror: Photojournalism, Catastrophe and War*. New York: New York University Press.

Taylor, K. W., and John K. Whitmore, eds. 1995. *Essays into Vietnamese Pasts*. Ithaca, N.Y.: Southeast Asia Program Publications.

Taylor, Keith W. 1983. *The Birth of Vietnam*. Berkeley: University of California Press.

Taylor, Nora A. 1999. "'Pho' Phai and Faux Phais: Market for Fakes and the Appropriation of a Vietnamese National Symbol." *Ethnos* 64, no. 2: 232–248.

———. 2001. "Framing the National Spirit: Viewing and Reviewing Painting under the Revolution," In *The Country of Memory: Remaking the Past in Late Socialist Vietnam*, edited by Hue-Tam Ho Tai, 109–134. Berkeley: University of California Press.

———. 2004. *Painters in Hà Nội: An Ethnography of Vietnamese Art*. Honolulu: University of Hawaii Press.

Taylor, Philip. 2000. "'Music as a 'Neocolonial Poison' in Post-War Southern Vietnam," *Crossroads* 14, no. 1: 99–131.

———. 2001. *Fragments of the Present: Searching for Modernity in Vietnam's South*. Honolulu: University of Hawaii Press.

———. 2004. *Goddess on the Rise: Pilgrimage and Popular Religion in Vietnam*. Honolulu: University of Hawaii Press.

Thongchai Winichakul. 1994. *Siam Mapped: A History of the Geo-Body of a Nation*. Honolulu: University of Hawaii Press.

———. 2003. "Writing at the Interstices: Southeast Asian Historians and Postnational Histories in Southeast Asia." In *New Terrains in Southeast Asian History*, edited by Abu Talib Ahmad and Tan Liok Ee, 3–29. Athens: Ohio University Press.

Thu Hà and Uyên Ly. 2004. "Tượng đài hay . . . tượng vườn?" [Monument or Statue Garden?]. Tuổi Trẻ [The Youth], July 5, 12.

Tran, Mai. 2006. "Visit to Vietnam Sparks Optimism: Many in Little Saigon Believe President Bush's Trip to Hanoi for Trade Summit Can Help Speed Human Rights Reform." *Los Angeles Times*, November 16, B4.

Trần Thanh Giao. 1999. "Under the Bamboo Grove." *Vietnamese Literature Review* 1: 171–184.

Trinh T. Minh-ha. 1991. *When the Moon Waxes Red: Representation, Gender and Cultural Politics*. New York: Routledge.

Trouillot, Michel-Rolph. 1995. *Silencing the Past: Power and the Production of History*. Boston: Beacon Press.

Trường Chinh. 1997 [1948]. "Chủ nghĩa Mác và văn hóa Việt Nam." In *Tuyển Tập Văn Học: Tập 1* [Selected Writings, Volume 1], 82–175. Hanoi: Văn Học.

Trương Như Bá. 2000. "Tái hiện vùng giải phóng Củ Chi" [Restoration of the Cu Chi Liberation Zone]. *Xưa và Nay* [Past and Present] 75, no. 3: 38–39.

Truong Nhu Tang, with David Chanoff and Doan Van Toai. 1986. *A Vietcong Memoir*. New York: Vintage Books.

Tsing, Anna Lowenhaupt. 2005. *Friction: An Ethnography of Global Connection*. Princeton, N.J.: Princeton University Press.

Tuchman, Gaye. 1972. "Objectivity as Strategic Ritual: An Examination of Newsmen's Notions of Objectivity." *American Journal of Sociology* 77, no. 4: 660–679.

Turner, Fred. 1996. *Echoes of Combat: The Vietnam War in American Memory*. New York: Anchor Books.

Um, Khatharya. 2005. "The 'Vietnam War': What's in a Name?" *Amerasia Journal* 31, no. 2: 134–139.

Urry, John. 2002 [1990]. *The Tourist Gaze*. 2nd ed. London: Sage Publications.

U.S. House of Representatives. 1969. Hearings before the Subcommittee on National

Security Policy and Scientific Developments of the Committee on Foreign Affairs. Ninety-first Congress. First Session. November 13 and 14.

——. 1979. Hearing before the Subcommittee on Asian and Pacific Affairs. Ninety-sixth Congress. First Session. December 12.

——. 1982. Hearing before the Subcommittee on Asian and Pacific Affairs of the Committee on Foreign Affairs. Ninety-seventh Congress. Second Session. September 30.

——. 1995. Joint Hearing before the Subcommittees on Asia and the Pacific and International Operations and Human Rights of the Committee on International Relations. One Hundred Fourth Congress. First Session. November 8.

——. 1997. Hearing before the Subcommittee on Asian and Pacific Affairs of the Committee on International Relations." One Hundred Fifth Congress. First Session. June 18.

——. 2005. Hearing before the Subcommittee on Africa, Global Human Rights and International Operations of the Committee on International Relations. One Hundred Ninth Congress. First Session. June 20.

U.S. Senate. 1977. Hearing before the Committee on Foreign Relations. Ninety-fifth Congress. First Session. April 1.

——. 1992. Hearings before the Select Committee on POW/MIA Affairs. One Hundred Second Congress. Second Session on Analysis of Live Sightings. August 4 and 5.

Vasavakul, Thaveeporn. 1997. "Art and Politics: Nationalism in Vietnamese War Posters," *Asia-Pacific Magazine* 8: 3–6.

Verdery, Katherine. 1991. *National Ideology under Socialism: Identity and Cultural Politics in Ceausescu's Romania.* Berkeley: University of California Press.

——. 1996. *What Was Socialism and What Comes Next?* Princeton, N.J.: Princeton University Press.

Việt Hà. 2004. "Hồi ký—hồi ức về chiến tranh đang 'ăn khách'" [Memoirs and Recollections of the War Are Selling Well], *Sài Gòn Giải Phóng,* December 26.

"Vietnam Reforms 'Too Slow.'" 2003. BBC News. August 7. Available online at http://news.bbc.co.uk/1/hi/business/3130979.stm.

Visweswaran, Kamala. 1994. *Fictions of Feminist Ethnography.* Minneapolis: University of Minnesota Press.

Võ Nguyên Giáp. 1962. *People's War, People's Army: The Viet Cong Insurrection Manual for Underdeveloped Countries.* New York: Bantam Books.

VUFO (Vietnam Union of Friendship Organizations) and NGO Resource Center. 2000. *Vietnam INGO Directory, 2000–2001.* 9th ed. Hanoi: Chính Trị Quốc Giá.

Walters, Ian. 1999. "Where the Action Was: Tourism and War Memorabilia from Vietnam." In *Converging Interests: Traders, Travelers, and Tourists in Southeast Asia,* edited by Jill Forshee, Christina Fink, and Sandra Cate, 265–278. Berkeley, Calif.: Center for Southeast Asia Studies.

Watson, Rubie S., ed. 1994. *Memory, History and Opposition under State Socialism.* Santa Fe, N.M.: School of American Research Press.

Webb, Kate. 1972. *On the Other Side: 23 Days with the Viet Cong*. New York: Quadrangle Books.

Weissman, Gary. 2004. *Fantasies of Witnessing: Postwar Efforts to Experience the Holocaust*. Ithaca, N.Y.: Cornell University Press.

Werner, Jayne S. 2006. "Between Memory and Desire: Gender and the Remembrance of War in Doi Moi Vietnam." *Gender, Place and Culture* 13, no. 3: 303–315.

White, Geoffrey M. 1995. "Remembering Guadalcanal: National Identity and Transnational Memory-Making." *Public Culture* 7, no. 3: 529–555.

———. 1997. "Moving History: The Pearl Harbor Film(s)." *Positions* 5, no. 3: 709–744.

White, Hayden. 1973. *Metahistory: The Historical Imagination in Nineteenth Century Europe*. Baltimore: John Hopkins University Press.

———. 1978. *Tropics of Discourse: Essays in Cultural Criticism*. Baltimore: Johns Hopkins University Press.

Wilson, Ara. 2004. *The Intimate Economies of Bangkok: Tomboys, Tycoons, and Avon Ladies in the Global City*. Berkeley: University of California Press.

Wilson, Richard A. 2001. *The Politics of Truth and Reconciliation in South Africa: Legitimizing the Post-Apartheid State*. Cambridge: Cambridge University Press.

———. 2003. "Justice and Retribution in Postconflict Settings." *Public Culture* 15, no. 1: 187–190.

Winegar, Jessica. 2006. *Creative Reckonings: The Politics of Art and Culture in Contemporary Egypt*. Stanford, Calif.: Stanford University Press.

Winter, Jay. 1995. *Sites of Memory, Sites of Mourning: The Great War in European Cultural History*. Cambridge: Cambridge University Press.

Wittfogel, Karl A. 1957. *Oriental Despotism: A Comparative Study of Total Power*. New Haven, Conn.: Yale University Press.

Wolf, Eric. 1982. *Europe and the People without History*. Berkeley: University of California Press.

Wolfe, Thomas C. 2000. "Cultures and Communities in the Anthropology of Eastern Europe and the Former Soviet Union." *Annual Review of Anthropology* 29: 195–216.

Wright, Gwendolyn. 1991. *The Politics of Design in French Colonial Urbanism*. Chicago: University of Chicago Press.

Wyatt, Clarence R. 1993. *Paper Soldiers: The American Press and the Vietnam War*. Chicago: University of Chicago Press.

X. Trung. 2000. "Gặp lại người cứu sống McCain" [Reunion with Rescuer of McCain]. Tuổi Trẻ [The Youth], April 29, 16.

Yoneyama, Lisa. 1999. *Hiroshima Traces: Time, Space and the Dialectics of Memory*. Berkeley: University of California Press.

———. 2001. "For Transformative Knowledge and Postnationalist Public Spheres: The Smithsonian *Enola Gay* Controversy." In *Perilous Memories: The Asia-Pacific War(s)*, edited by T. Fujitani, Geoffrey M. White, and Lisa Yoneyama, 323–346. Durham, N.C.: Duke University Press.

———. 2003. "Traveling Memories, Contagious Justice: Americanization of Japanese

War Crimes at the End of the Post–Cold War." *Journal of Asian American Studies* 6, no. 1: 57–93.

———. 2005. "On the Unredressability of U.S. War Crimes: Vietnam and Japan." *Amerasia Journal* 31, no. 2: 140–144.

Young, Allan. 1995. *The Harmony of Illusions: Inventing Post-Traumatic Stress Disorder.* Princeton, N.J.: Princeton University Press.

Young, James E. 1993. *The Texture of Memory: Holocaust Memorials and Meaning.* New Haven, Conn.: Yale University Press.

———. 2000. *At Memory's Edge: After-Images of the Holocaust in Contemporary Art and Architecture.* New Haven, Conn.: Yale University Press.

Young, Marilyn B. 1991. *The Vietnam Wars: 1945–1990.* New York: Harper Perennial.

Yúdice, George. 2003. *The Expediency of Culture: Uses of Culture in the Global Era.* Durham, N.C.: Duke University Press.

Zelizer, Barbie. 1998. *Remembering to Forget: Holocaust Memory through the Camera's Eye.* Chicago: University of Chicago Press.

———. 2001. "Gender and Atrocity: Women in Holocaust Photographs." In *Visual Culture and the Holocaust,* edited by Barbie Zelizer, 247–271. New Brunswick, N.J.: Rutgers University Press.

Zemon-Davis, Natalie, and Randolph Starn. 1989. "Introduction: Memory and Counter-Memory." *Representations* 26: 1–7.

Zinoman, Peter. 2001. *The Colonial Bastille: A History of Imprisonment in Vietnam, 1862–1940.* Berkeley: University of California Press.

Italicized page numbers indicate illustrations.

communism: global capitalism versus privations due to, 28, 35–36, 38, 166; human rights violations, and connections with, 178–79, 185; U.S. historical memory, and containment of, 5–6, 28, 34, 38, 46, 81, 179, 202

Connerton, Paul, 95

Coutin, Susan Bibler, 99

Củ Chi district martyr cemetery, 140–41, *141*

Củ Chi Tunnels: Bến Đình area of, *90*, 91–93, *93*, 97; Bến Dược area of, 91–92, 95–97, *96*; commodified memories and, 19, 27, 88–97, *90*, *97*, 99, 225n17

Curtis, Paulette Gueno, 30, 58, 208n4

Đà Lạt, and "Chicken Village," 102, *103*

Đà Nẵng, 102–103, *104*, 149, 161, 163–64, 222n11

Daley, Matthew P., 196

Das, Veena, 29, 47, 51

Daston, Lorraine, 169, 202

Demilitarized Zone, 70, 83–84, 95, 100, 216n6

Democratic Republic of Vietnam, 111, 112, 153, 515

democratizaton practices, in museums, 20, 147, 174–75

Derrida, Jacques, 178–79

Desmond, Jane C., 85, 90, 216n9

Determined to Brave Death memorial, 111, *112*

Dickson-Gomez, Julia, 188

Điện Biên Phủvictory monument, 105, *106*, 225n20

Diller, Elizabeth, 84

directors of museums, and role as brokers of images and mediators of knowledge, 20, 169, 173–74

Dispatches (Herr), 57, 166

DMZ, 70, 83–84, 95, 100, 216n6

Do Lai Thuy, 220–21n19

Đoàn Công Tính, *60*, *61*

Doan Van Toai, 214n27

Dobrenko, Evgeny, 118

Đổi mới economic reforms: cultural practices and discourses of tradition after, 126–27, 135, 154; described, 4; effects of, 4, 8, 28, 126–27, 135, 154, 157, 203; free market economy after, 157; transnational spaces since, 8, 28, 203

Douglas, John Michael, 41

Douglas, Mary, 171, 173

Douglass, Ana, 99

Drummond, Lisa B. W., 87

DRV (Democratic Republic of Vietnam), 111, 112, 153, 515

Dương Trung Quốc, 108, 111, 114

Eastern values, and human rights, 185, 194, 224n14

Eco, Umberto, 89, 94

Ehrhart, W. D., 32–33

emasculated veterans, and human rights, 27, 28, 39, 190, *191*, 208n7

embodied experiences of war, and commodified memories, 84–86, 88–97, 91–94, 216nn9–10

emic terminology, 7

Endres, Kirsten W., 126

Engelhardt, Tom, 175

Enloe, Cynthia, 155

Erikson, Kai, 46

Errington, Shelly, 91, 94

ethnographic practices, 9–10, 13–18, 21

everyday life war experience, 10, 26, 47, 51, 58–62, *61*, *62*, 213nn21,23

Exhibition House for American War Crimes, in Đà Nẵng, 163–64, 222n11

Exhibition House for Crimes of War and Agression, 163, 164, 222n12

Exhibition House for French War Crimes, 163, 222n12

Exhibition House for U.S. and Puppet Crimes, 163, 164, 222n12

exoticization of sites, 94–95, 217n17

CHRISTINA SCHWENKEL is Assistant Professor of Anthropology at the University of California, Riverside.